內地判決
的
認可與執行

香港判例縱述

黃善端　著

商務印書館

內地判決的認可與執行——香港判例縱述

編　　著：黃善端

責任編輯：張宇程

出　　版：商務印書館 (香港) 有限公司

　　　　　香港筲箕灣耀興道 3 號東滙廣場 8 樓

　　　　　http://www.commercialpress.com.hk

發　　行：香港聯合書刊物流有限公司

　　　　　香港新界大埔汀麗路 36 號中華商務印刷大廈 3 字樓

印　　刷：美雅印刷製本有限公司

　　　　　九龍觀塘榮業街 6 號海濱工業大廈 4 樓 A 室

版　　次：2019 年 6 月第 1 版第 2 次印刷

　　　　　© 2019 商務印書館 (香港) 有限公司

　　　　　ISBN 978 962 07 6616 9

　　　　　Printed in Hong Kong

謹以此書
獻與
我的家人和摯友
北京大學和北京大學法學院
以及香港華仁書院的各位良師益友

總　序

　　國家「一帶一路」倡議的實施、粵港澳大灣區建設的啟動、深港現代服務業合作區建設的深化，對法律服務提出新的、更高的要求。在新形勢下，法律服務業的發展需要突破傳統模式，探索新的開放合作機制，以順應時代對提升中國涉外及國際法律服務能力的迫切要求。

　　因應上述需求，深圳前海合作區多家律師事務所發起創設了旨在推進創新法律服務業合作模式的專業性社團組織——前海一帶一路法律服務聯合會（簡稱「聯合會」）。在中央和地方的支持，深圳市司法局、前海管理局和深圳市貿促委的 指導，以及眾多法律服務界同仁的積極響應參與下，聯合會於 2018 年初完成組建，6 月 25 日正式登記成立。

　　聯合會以創設、推動法律服務混業合作、跨境合作、國際合作為目標，秉持共商共建共享理念，立足前海，面向港澳，輻射內地，聯動「一帶一路」，致力搭建跨業、跨境、跨法域法律服務交流合作平台。聯合會將充當橋樑紐帶，促進律師、公證、仲裁、調解、知識產權、會計服務、公司法務等專業服務行業探索混業合作，推動深港和粵港澳大灣區法律服務業實現深度合作和互補，拓展「一帶一路」沿線國家和地區華語律師聯動網絡與合作平台，共同打造開放包容、資源共享、優勢互補、互利共贏的合作模式，攜手為「一帶一路」建設、粵港澳大灣區建設提供優質、高效、跨境、配套的法律服務和法律保障。

　　為貫徹前述宗旨，聯合會將推出一系列的重點合作項目，包括推進深港及粵港澳大灣區法律服務業深度合作，搭建國際商事爭議調解平台，拓展「一帶一路」沿線國家地區華語律師合作網絡，促進法律服務業探索混業合作，等等。特別需要一提的是，聯合會倡議發起的共建「深港法律服務深度合作區」計劃已正式啟動。2018 年 12 月 4 日，深港兩地四十多家法律專業組織在前海共同簽署《關於共建「深港法律服務深度合作區」戰略框架協議》，並召開第一次共建單位聯席會議，一致通過《「深港法律服務深度合作區」建設 2019 年度合作計劃項目備忘錄》。深度合作區概

念和共建計劃的提出，旨在貫徹落實習近平總書記 2018 年 10 月 24 日視察深圳前海時提出「要深化深港合作，相互借助，相得益彰，在共建『一帶一路』、推進粵港澳大灣區建設、高水平參與國際合作方面發揮更大作用」的重要指示精神，貫徹落實粵港澳大灣區建設規劃關於「聯動香港打造國際法律服務中心和國際商事爭議解決中心」的部署，創新升級深港法律服務合作模式，拓寬法律服務合作領域，打造深度合作機制和平台，開創共建共享共贏的合作新天地。

聯合會宗旨的實現，「深港法律服務深度合作區」的建設，都離不開法學理論和法律實務的研究、交流與互鑑，這既是拓展合作的重要領域，也是深化合作的有效根基。如何應對「一帶一路」建設、粵港澳大灣區建設和中國企業「走出去」面臨的法律挑戰，協助政府、企業有效破解遇到的各種法律難題；如何借助港澳經驗，促進適應開放型經濟發展的法律體系建設，打造中國特色社會主義法治建設示範區高地；如何在「一國兩制三法域」格局下，有效解決區際法律衝突，促進區際司法交流和互助；如何突破現有框架模式，進一步在法律服務領域擴大深化相互之間的開放合作措施；如何在法律服務業之間加強常態化、互補型的專業對口交流互鑑，針對市場和客戶需求不斷改善法律服務供給模式、提升國際法律服務和爭議解決水平，等等，都是擺在深港和粵港澳三地法律人面前亟待破解的課題。聯合會甘做橋樑紐帶，願意匯集三地法律人的智慧和各方專業資源，以合作方式加強對上述問題的調查、比較、互鑑和研究，以各種方式支持三地法律人對上述問題研究作出探索和貢獻，創造有價值、有建樹的研究成果，為「一帶一路」和粵港澳大灣區建設，特別是法律制度及法治保障能力建設，提供有力的智力支持。

基於以上考慮，聯合會除了通過舉辦論壇、講座、研討、培訓等活動，積極搭建法律專業交流、互鑑、合作的平台外，更適時推出「前海一帶一路法律服務聯合會推薦——法學研究系列叢書」項目，以匯聚、推廣法律智慧成果。經聯合會推薦列入系列叢書的，均為與「一帶一路」和粵港澳大灣區建設特別是相關法治建設密切相關、並具有高度理論與實務價值的著作。法學研究系列叢書的推出，將為投身、關注「一帶一路」建設、粵港澳大灣區建設的法律專業人士從事專業研究、相互交流提供一個重要渠道和平台。我們更希望，推出的研究成果能為「一帶一路」和粵港澳大灣

區建設，為深化粵港澳三地法律和司法交流與合作，提供實實在在的智力支持。

杜春
前海一帶一路法律服務聯合會會長
2018 年 12 月

序 一

香港特別行政區（「香港特區」）於 1997 年 7 月 1 日設立。依據《香港特別行政區基本法》（「《基本法》」），香港特區保持普通法制度，並享有獨立的司法權和終審權。簡言之，在「一國兩制」的基本國策下，香港特區是中國不可分離的部分，但享有依據《基本法》賦予的獨特法律及司法制度。

雖然香港特區的法律和司法體制與內地的相關制度存在相當差異，但從「一國兩制」和兩地交往的角度而言，建立健全的司法協助機制尤為重要。兩地司法協助能維護兩地當事人的合法權益，亦能鞏固香港特區支援外資進入內地市場或內地企業經香港特區「走出去」的獨特角色。《基本法》第 95 條在這方面明確規定，「香港特別行政區可與全國其他地區的司法機關通過協商依法進行司法方面的聯繫和相互提供協助。」

司法聯繫和司法協助的範圍十分廣泛，而兩地法院判決的認可和執行是當中重要一環。自香港特區成立以來，兩地在人民、經貿等不同領域的交往越來越頻繁，但過程中少不免會產生爭端，最終需要透過法院裁決。從當事人的角度而言，其中一個關鍵問題是法院裁決能否獲得有效執行。由於香港特區與內地法律制度的迴異，而《外地判決（交互強制執行）條例》（香港法例第 319 章）亦不適用，在香港特區依據普通法原則執行內地判決一直面對法律、程序與證據等不同問題。

2006 年 7 月 14 日，內地與香港特區簽訂《關於內地與香港特別行政區法院相互認可和執行當事人協議管轄的民商事案件判決的安排》（下稱「《2006 年安排》」）。其後香港特區於 2008 年通過《內地判決（交互強制執行）條例》（香港法例第 597 章），從而落實《2006 年安排》。無論是從落實「一國兩制」或兩地司法協助的角度，《2006 年安排》的簽訂也是一個重要的里程碑。然而，《2006 年安排》存在客觀局限，不涉及當事人協議管轄的內地判決若要在香港特區執行，仍要依據普通法原則處理。

本書作者黃善端先生 1995 年入讀北京大學法學院，其後升讀北京大學法學院碩士研究生課程，從事中國民商事法律研究，更是首批取得中國大陸律師執業資格的香港居民之一。由於他的研究和執業背景，黃先生對內地法院判決在香港特區執行的情況有專業及深入的體會，在本書中解釋案例時如數家珍，有條有序地從不同角度分析和探討相關法律原則。我相信本書將成為研究兩地司法協助（特別是兩地法院判決的認可和執行）這課題的律師、學者和學生不容忽視的參考文獻。

兩地的司法協助日後仍有大量工作需要推展。2016 年 3 月，內地最高人民法院沈德詠常務副院長訪問香港特區，與香港特區政府律政司就兩地之間的民商事司法協助事宜簽訂會議紀要，為三項主要工作訂立目標。當中《民商事案件相互委託提取證據的安排》和《關於內地與香港特別行政區法院相互認可和執行婚姻家庭民事案件判決的安排》，已分別於 2016 年 12 月 29 日和 2017 年 6 月 20 日簽訂。這兩項安排的簽訂，將兩地司法協助的工作向前再推進一步。餘下第三項工作涉及非當事人協議管轄的民商事案件判決的認可和執行。本書在這時刻出版是非常合時，可引起法律界和社會大眾更關注兩地司法協助這重要課題，並對兩地司法協助的相關研究工作能產生正面和積極作用。

袁國強資深大律師

大紫荊勳賢、太平紳士
2018 年 6 月

序 二

我認識善端，已經 22 年。

1995 年，我從北大法學院碩士畢業後留校任教，擔任一年級本科生（95 級）的班主任，並在 1996 年春季為他們開設了民法課程。善端就是他們中間的一個。他的普通話很流利，但又不時流露出一點香港口音，有一種恰到好處的時尚感；白淨、斯文、洋氣，還是網球和足球健將，所以，他一時風頭十足，很有女生緣，當然也很有男生緣。

可是沒有想到的是，他還是個學霸。

這是我第一次講民法。那時年輕，只比學生大六、七歲，也沒有甚麼教學經驗。雖然儘量裝出老成持重的樣子，但還是常常 hold 不住。好在學生們不算很嫌棄我。而這個香港同胞，不僅沒有表現出對中文的陌生，而且展現了強大的學習能力，最後獲得了課程的最高分。

此後我們就成了朋友。切磋問難，一起成長。善端 1999 年開始繼續攻讀碩士學位後，我們的學術交往就更多了，其中包括，我們一起擬定了一個龐大的計劃，對於法院的重要民事案例的裁判要旨進行系統的整理，並且已經着手做了一些基礎工作。我們憧憬着它成為最好的工具書，順便也憧憬了它可以帶來的滾滾財源。可惜，由於案例體量巨大，我們的專業要求太高，執行力又不匹配，此事遂無疾而終。今天看着市面上流行的同類書籍，常會想起與善端一起工作的日子。

善端是一位極為優秀的法律學者。與我所遇到的最優秀的學者相比，善端可以無愧地列入其中，儘管，他不是一位職業學者。

善端 2002 年碩士畢業後，開始了律師生涯。雖然我不了解更多的細節，但是我毫不懷疑的是，善端是最優秀的律師。我所認識的律師中，沒有一個人有善端那樣雄厚扎實的理論基礎、對法律知識永不疲倦的飢渴以

及駕馭任何複雜法律問題的分析能力。十幾年來，我們還經常交流對法律問題的意見，討論之後我每每感嘆，他沒有成為一個專職教授，對於法學教育界是一件多麼遺憾的事情。這期間，我也得到了他許多的幫助，其中包括我 2010 年作為專家證人到香港高等法院出庭作證，善端幫助我熟悉法庭程序，受益頗多。

在繁忙的律師工作期間，善端從來沒有放棄對於法學研究的熱愛，並且，並非僅僅針對他執業過程中遇到的具體問題，而是對於一般理論保持着濃厚的興趣。他曾經基本完成了一部關於訴訟時效制度的書稿，不誇張地說，這是我見過的關於中國訴訟時效制度最好的專著，可惜沒有最終定稿、出版，並且，因為法律修訂、案例增加而必然導致修改工作量不斷增加，他近期也沒有修改、出版的計劃。

本書的主題，是我個人並不熟悉的。我拜讀了全書，深感受教，但同時也覺得，這遠遠不能代表善端最好的學術水平。這當然不是因為善端不認真。善端對學術作品的自我要求之苛刻，實在不多見。

本書的主要讀者，應該是在香港法院辦理申請認可與執行內地法院判決的案件的香港律師，其主要目的是徹底地梳理、分析香港法院的相關判決，為律師辦理此類案件（進而為法院判決案件）提供支持，而非對於「外國法院判決的承認與執行」問題進行全面的學術研究。善端使用的材料、方法與研究深度，都與此相適應。書中所表現出的對於香港法律與內地法律狀況的準確理解、對於法律論證方法的純熟、對於律師執業技巧的輕鬆駕馭，還有清晰練達的文字，都讓人印象深刻。尤為難得的是，作為一個主要在內地接受中國法（大陸法系）教育並從事內地法律業務的律師，善端常年學習、研究普通法，對於普通法系與大陸法系的法律方法都有精深的研究，因此，善端才能夠完成這個基於香港法（主要是普通法）的研究工作。我本人雖有在英國、美國學習的經歷，但是並無深入的研究以及執業經驗，沒有資格作出精當的評價，不過，根據我有限的相關知識，我覺得善端已經完美地完成了這一任務。我相信，它一定會成為處理此類案件的香港律師的必讀書，並且，或許香港法院有一天會在判決書中援引本書。

善端當初開始從事律師工作，主要是因為家庭的經濟壓力，因而不得不暫時放棄了成為專業學者的夢想。期待着他在律師生涯達到一個高度之後，能夠早日回歸校園，將他的滿腹經綸貢獻於講壇、學林。

葛雲松

2018 年 4 月 4 日

於北京大學法學院陳明樓

鳴　謝

　　本書終於出版，離不開眾多老師、學長和好友的支持。在此不僅要感謝前海一帶一路法律服務聯合會會長杜春學長對本書出版的支持，更要對杜學長一直以來對本人在專業業務及研究工作上的大力幫助和支持表示深深的謝意。感謝袁國強資深大律師在百忙中抽空閱讀本書初稿並慷慨賜序。要特別感謝北大法學院的兩位班主任，王新老師教導我如何成為北大人，葛雲松老師則教導我成為法律人，最終造就了我這個北大法律人。感謝我的研究生導師佟強老師，在畢業前後、在校內校外給予的各種指導和幫助。感謝學妹孫靜對本書寫作的支持，學妹為本書的寫作風格以及內容策劃均提供了大量寶貴意見。最後要感謝「區際衝突法研究」羣組的各位專家老師和法律同仁，能讓我這位業餘學術愛好者在遠離校園的狀態下，不至於與學術界脫節，而仍能持續了解學術界的各種動態和前沿問題。

目　錄

縮寫表

立法及司法互助安排	
《基本法》	《中華人民共和國香港特別行政區基本法》
《協議管轄判決安排》	《關於內地與香港特別行政區相互認可和執行當事人協議管轄的民商事案件判決的安排》
《家事判決互認安排》	《關於內地與香港特別行政區相互認可和執行婚姻家庭民事案件判決的安排》
《民事訴訟法》	《中華人民共和國民事訴訟法》
《釋義及通則條例》	《釋義及通則條例》（香港法例第 1 章）
《高等法院條例》	《高等法院條例》（香港法例第 4 章）
《判決條例》	《判決（強制執行措施）條例》（香港法例第 9 章）
《外地判決條例》	《外地判決（交互強制執行）條例》（香港法例第 319 章）
《內地判決條例》	《內地判決（交互強制執行）條例》（香港法例第 597 章）
《高等法院規則》	《高等法院規則》（香港法例第 4A 章）

判例	
Vanquelin 先例	Vanquelin v. Bouard 1863
Nouvion 先例	Gustave Nouvion v. Freeman and Another (1889) 15 App. Cas. 1
Chiyu 案	Chiyu Banking Corporation Limited v Chan Tin Kwun HCA 11186/1995

判例	
武漢中碩虹案	Wuhan Zhong Shuo Hong Real Estate Co. Ltd.（湖北省武漢中碩虹房地產開發有限公司） v. The Kwong Sang Hong International Ltd.（香港廣生行國際有限公司） HCA 14325/1998
Tan Tay Cuan 案	Tan Tay Cuan v Ng Chi Hung HCA5477/2000
Nintendo 案	Nintendo of America Inc v. Bung Enterprises Ltd HCA1189/2000
林哲民第一案	林哲民經營之日昌電業公司訴林志滔 CACV354/2001
林哲民第二案	林哲民日昌電業公司訴張順連 CACV1046/2001
New Link Consultants 案	New Link Consultants Ltd v. Air China and Others HCA515/2001
李祐榮案	李祐榮訴李瑞群 CACV159/2005
陳國柱案	陳國柱訴陳桂洲 HCA 663/2005
伍威禁制令案	Wu Wei（伍威） v. Liu Yi Ping（劉一萍） HCA1452/2004
伍威暫緩執行禁制令案	Wu Wei（伍威） v. Liu Yi Ping（劉一萍） CACV32/2009
Yick Tat 案	Yick Tat Development Company v. Yung Chung Yiu HCA1590/2007
中國銀行案	Bank of China Limited（中國銀行股份有限公司） v. Yang Fan（楊凡） HCMP1797/2015
北京橙天嘉禾案	北京橙天嘉禾影視製作有限公司 v. 張承勳 HCA2481/2013

第一部份

緒 論

一、寫作本書的緣由

作者在工作中所從事的主要法律業務為跨境民商事法律事務，其中更是以跨境債務執行為重點業務之一。因此，在工作中也經常需要處理在香港執行內地法院判決的個案，也清楚知道內地法院判決在香港執行所遇到的障礙。為了能更好地處理這類業務，作者一直希望可以全面、深入、體系化地理清香港法律中的有關問題，特別是其中的已經成為內地法院判決在香港執行重大障礙的「是否最終及不可推翻判決」問題。雖然無論在大學時因研究之需要，還是日後在從事跨境法律事務中因工作所要求，均已經常接觸、研習包括英國法、香港法在內的普通法，但作者畢竟作為內地律師，仍然感覺對於學習如此重大、專業的香港法律問題，最適當、直接的方法，仍然是求教於香港的同行。

目前在香港衝突法領域，最全面及權威的著作，應數 Graeme Johnston 的 *Conflict of Laws in Hong Kong*。作者畢業回港加入的律師事務所，正是 Johnston 律師當時所在的史密夫律師事務所，也因此而有幸與 Johnston 律師短暫共事。遺憾的是，在該書付梓之時，本書作者也早已離開該事務所，錯過了當面向 Johnston 律師請教的機會。但所幸的是，Johnston 律師當年也經常處理內地當事人在港的訴訟業務，相信也深知內地法院判決在香港執行的障礙以及是否最終及不可推翻問題的重要性，在書中設有專門篇幅討論此問題。然而，由於該書畢竟是關於衝突法所涉及各種問題的綜合性著作，而不是特定問題的專著，因此關於內地法院判決有關問題的討論，仍有欠深入，而且對部份判例的解讀似乎還存在偏差。加上相關案例發展迅速，Johnston 律師在書中的論述也難以及時更新。故此，仍有必要向其他富有經驗的香港同行討教。與作者在業務上長期合作的香港律師為數不少，可是在作者的討教中，始終無法獲得滿意的反饋。說到專題性的調研，許多香港同行的反應，不是認為無此必要，就是感嘆「難度很大」、「工程浩大」云云。後來，*Conflict of Laws in Hong Kong* 第三版出版，Johnston 律師自己並未參與修訂，而由資深大律師 Paul Harris 完成修訂工作。Harris 資深大律師在前言中強調，在新版中已經通過加入了自第二版以來的全部衝突法重要判例進行了全面更新。然而，頗感遺憾的是，作者發現在此新版中，有關內地法院判決最終及不可推翻問題的討論，實際上並未作任何改動，儘管期間也已經出現了諸如中國銀行訴楊凡案等重要判決。

求教而不得其果，作者亦對此情況有所反思。對於所求教的問題，即使是諸如 Johnston 律師、Harris 資深大律師等專家均未能更全面地予以剖析，作者不僅體會到求教於香港同行實非適途，更是發現這實際上是強人所難。之所以難，主要是因為香港同行多不以問題的全面及體系化研究作為工作重點。這不是水平高低或能力強弱之問題，而是「聞道有先後，術業有專攻」的問題而已。無顧別人之所長，恐怕其實是自己槐樹上要棗吃了。作者在長期與香港同行交流、合作的過程中，結合自己對普通法的研習，其實也了解到，香港法律人與內地法律人之間所存在的重大差異。香港律師行業，更注重辦案「技能」、「手藝」、「手勢」（對於沒學好技能的晚輩，老一輩香港律師形容為「學壞手勢」）和客戶服務方面的訓練，在工作中更注重細節的「精雕」，所體現的是一種工匠精神。至於法律問題的全面、深入及體系化研究，則非工作的重點所在。特別是在過去的體制下，這方面的工作更多是在英國完成，香港在這方面所需要的工作成果亦可直接從英國取得，香港法律界自可將學習、工作的重點放在辦理個案的技能上。而在思維習慣上，也形成了一種個案主導的實用經驗主義思維。即處理問題多以個案的實際所需為主導，在沒有具體個案的情況下，一般不會有在事前（發生真實個案前）對相關問題進行全面而體系化研究的習慣，也不認為有此需要。至於內地法律人，從在法學院接受法學教育階段開始，就更多將焦點放在問題的全面及體系化研究上（不僅是內地法律本身的問題，還包括不同法域法系的法律問題及其相互之間的比較），而相應地較為忽略對執業技能的培養。這固然會導致法科生一旦走上執業的前線時，會因欠缺技能性的知識和經驗而感覺吃力，但同時也使他們更習慣並擅長於對法律問題進行全面而體系化的研究。

由此可見，內地和香港兩地的法律人可謂各有所長，在專業能力的側重上具有強烈的互補性。對香港法律中的專項問題進行全面、深入及體系化的研究，要求對香港法律內容的認知有一定的積累，同時也需要具備相應的研究思維和方法。前者乃香港律師之所長，後者則為內地法律人的優勢。在實際上，讓掌握內容者改變思維和方法，顯然比具備思維和方法者掌握內容要困難得多。因此，由內地法律人在掌握研究的思維和方法的基礎上，再研習香港法律的內容，顯然更為可行且有效。特別是，在香港回歸以後，香港法律界不再享受英國所提供的直接支持（不僅是因為香港回歸而造成的制度原因，同時也因為英國法律在香港回歸以來急速歐洲化，

法律內容差異的擴大導致香港也難以再採用簡單的「拿來主義」）。近年內地法律界法律研究水平的急速提升及人才的充裕，足以填補英國人留下的空缺。

作者認識到，要對內地法院判決在香港執行的問題進行全面、深入及體系化的研究，必須親力親為。然而，對於是否開始本書的寫作，作者事前一度躊躇不前。原因在於，進行這項研究，雖不至像一些香港同行所誇言的「工程浩大」，但也需要投入相當的時間和精力。更嚴重的是，正如作者自己經常自我介紹時所言，「我是一個解釋論者，是一個徹頭徹尾的法教義學踐行者；解釋論者需要勇氣，敢於面對自己的任何著作和文字，均將因法律的修改而成為一堆廢紙的殘酷」，作者知道內地與香港的有關部門，正在密鑼緊鼓地就兩地判決互認的框架性安排進行協商，一旦兩地達成協議，本書所探討的問題將不再是問題，本書實用價值必然「跳崖」。

但是，基於以上的反思，作者發現了此項研究的價值，可以遠遠超出所研究的問題本身。本書的研究，實際上也是一次內地法律人在研究上為香港法律界提供支持的一次嘗試。若能獲得認同，這更能成兩地法律界的一次深度交流。作者長期從事跨境法律服務，在外國律師事務所工作時，以為外國客戶尋找、篩選、監督內地律師為工作之一，獨立執業後又經常為內地客戶物色、挑選、指引香港律師，因工作之需一直參與兩地法律界的各種交流。通過親身的參與，作者有感兩地法律界的各種交流往往流於表面和形式而有待推向縱深。因此，作者深感本書的研究在兩地法律界交流方面之潛在意義的重大。也正因如此，作者最後才能下定決心，懷著「我不下地獄誰下地獄」的心情開始了本書的寫作及相關問題的研究。

讓作者感到欣慰的是，本書的寫作及最終完稿給個人所帶來的提升超出預期。對內地法院判決在普通法上的最終及不可推翻問題相關判例進行縱向的深入、體系化研究，本身就是一次普通法思維和法學方法的歷練。經此歷練，讓作者對普通法的愛好不用停留於閱讀各種 leading texts 及諸如 Goodhart、Montrose、Cross、MacCormick、Bennion、Bingham 等普通法法學大家著作的自娛自樂，更是深入地接觸到普通法在實踐中的思維和應用。僅此意義，即足以讓作者無悔於本書最終因相關法律的發展和修改而成為廢紙。

二、背景知識：香港境外判決承認和執行制度簡介

為了準確了解香港承認和執行內地法院判決的相關法律，必須先對香港承認和執行境外判決制度及其歷史沿革有一個初步的認識。

（一）普通法之執行與成文法之執行

一直以來，在香港申請承認和執行境外判決，根據所適用的法律依據，可區分為根據普通法執行與根據成文法執行兩種途徑。前者顧名思義，是指所適用的法律依據為判例所確立的普通法規則，一般被稱為「根據普通法按照外地判決起訴（suing on foreign judgment at common law）」或簡稱為普通法之執行（enforcement at common law）。由於普通法之執行在程序上是採用訴訟方式，也可稱為訴訟執行（enforcement by action）。根據成文法執行，則是以成文立法為法律依據的承認和執行，一般被稱為成文法之執行（enforcement under statute），又因其在程序上是採用登記的方式，也可稱為登記執行（enforcement by registration）。原則上，基於相關立法明確規定屬成文法之執行適用範圍的境外判決，應根據相關立法的條件和程序申請承認和執行。只有不屬立法適用範圍的境外判決，才應通過普通法之執行申請承認和執行。

此外，原告人雖已取得境外法院的勝訴判決，但他也可以選擇不依賴該勝訴判決而在香港按照一般訴訟重新起訴，但這受限於香港法律中的不容反悔法原則（estoppel）。若香港法院認為已經取得的勝訴判決構成具有既判力（res judicata）的判決，原告人重新起訴則會被視為濫用訴訟程序而被駁回。但嚴格而言，重新起訴並不屬境外判決的承認和執行，在此不贅（關於此問題，可參見本書第四回、簡評案例五及總評第二部份中的相關討論）。

（二）《協議管轄判決安排》生效前的相關法律

2006年，內地與香港兩地簽署了《協議管轄判決安排》（即《關於內地與香港特別行政區法院相互認可和執行當事人協議管轄的民商事案件判決的安排》），隨後香港立法會根據《協議管轄判決安排》通過並頒佈了《內地判決條例》（即香港法例《內地判決（交互強制執行）條例》（第597章））。《協議管轄判決安排》與《內地判決條例》均於2008年8月1日生效。在此之前，作為成文法之執行的立法依據的，主要是《外地判

決條例》（即香港法例《外地判決（交互強制執行）條例（第 319 章）》）。而在香港回歸之前，同時並行適用的還有《判決條例》（即香港法例《判決（強制執行措施）條例（第 9 章）》）。《判決條例》與《外地判決條例》的區別，主要在於《判決條例》僅適用於英國（聯合王國）的判決，而《外地判決條例》則適用於主要是英聯邦國家或地區的判決，還有部份歐洲國家判決。

在香港回歸後，《判決條例》已經不再適用。根據香港法例《釋義及通則條例》（第 1 章）第 2A（2）（b）條的規定：「任何給予英國或英聯邦其他國家或地區特權待遇的規定，除實施香港與英國或英聯邦其他國家或地區的互惠性安排的規定者外，不再有效。」由於據以給予香港互惠性安排的英國立法 Administration of Justice Act 1920 在回歸時起不再適用於香港，根據《釋義及通則條例》的上述規定，《判決條例》亦不再生效。要注意的是，《判決條例》作為香港法例至今沒有被正式廢除，其中英文正式版本均列於香港法例之中（作為第 9 章），僅僅是通過上述香港立法與英國立法的適用而不再有效。總結而言，自香港回歸之後至《協議管轄判決安排》生效期間，成文法之執行只有根據《外地判決條例》執行一個類型。

根據《外地判決條例》第 8 條規定，凡可根據該條例執行的判決，不得通過其他方式執行該等判決。也就是說，普通法之執行僅適用於無法通過成文法之執行獲得執行的判決。

就內地法院判決而言，在《協議管轄判決安排》生效以前，內地法院判決在香港執行，由於不屬《外地判決條例》的適用範圍，只能採用普通法之執行。然而，在個案中，內地法院判決又往往難以滿足普通法所要求的條件及其他原因無法獲得認可與執行，其中比較突出的原因，是內地判決因內地的再審制度而不時被認定為不符合普通法之執行所要求的「最終及不可推翻（final and conclusive）」。此問題成為了內地法院判決在香港執行的重大障礙，這也是本書的焦點問題。

（三）《協議管轄判決安排》與《內地判決條例》

為了解決上述的內地法院判決「執行難」問題，兩地經過努力協商，於 2006 年達成了協議，根據《香港特別行政區基本法》第 95 條簽署了《協議管轄判決安排》。香港亦即制定了《內地判決條例》以落實《協議管轄

判決安排》。儘管由於《協議管轄判決安排》與《內地判決條例》的適用範圍較窄，適用條件亦頗為嚴格，仍然未能掃清兩地判決相互認可與執行的障礙，但其也不失為兩地在「一國兩制」框架下司法互助領域的一個重大里程碑，也在一定程度上（雖然有限）減少了內地判決在港執行的障礙。其中，比較有針對性的是放寬了對「最終及不可推翻」的認定標準，以及在程序上採用登記制以代替普通法之執行的直接訴訟方式。

可以說，在《協議管轄判決安排》及《內地判決條例》生效後，香港法律中的成文法之執行，又增加了根據《內地判決條例》執行的一個類別。但要注意的是，在《協議管轄判決安排》及《內地判決條例》生效前，儘管存在普通法上之執行與以《外地判決條例》為基礎的成文法之執行的區分，但在實際的承認和執行條件上，兩者並不存在根本上的不同，除了程序以外（普通法上之執行採用訴訟程序，《外地判決條例》執行採用登記程序），許多條件在實質上均高度一致。然而，由於《協議管轄判決安排》及《內地判決條例》是為內地法院判決「量身定制」，因此其中所規定的一些承認和執行條件，與普通法及《外地判決條例》所要求的條件，會有較大的出入。

至於不能適用《協議管轄判決安排》的內地法院判決，仍然只能通過普通法之執行的途徑獲得承認和執行，也因此仍然面對是否屬於最終及不可推翻判決所造成的障礙。本書的目的，正是要對涉及內地法院判決是否最終及不可推翻判決問題的香港判例進行縱向研究並予以評析，以嘗試尋找掃清內地法院判決根據普通法獲得承認和執行所遇障礙的可能途徑。

第二部份

本 論

第一回

為內地判決在香港的曲折遭遇奠定基礎的 Chiyu 案

案件	：	Chiyu Banking Corporation Limited v. Chan Tin Kwun
法庭	：	最高法院原訟法庭
案號	：	HCA 11186/1995
判決日期：		1996 年 7 月 12 日

在本案審理及判決之時，香港尚未回歸，審理本案的法庭為香港最高法院的原訟法庭（在回歸後根據《基本法》改名為香港特別行政區高等法院原訟法庭）。這個判決對於內地法院判決日後在香港的命運影響相當深遠。即使是回歸至今，內地法院判決在香港的認可與執行一直遇到相當大的障礙，正是起源於這個判決。

一、案情簡介

原告人集友銀行在內地向其客戶某公司提供貸款，由被告人香港居民陳某提供擔保。（3 段）

1994 年 3 月，原告人在福建某中級人民法院（「原審中院」）起訴被告人，並於 1995 年 1 月取得了對被告人的一審勝訴判決（「內地判決」）。一審判決後被告人向福建省高級人民法院提出上訴，亦被該院駁回並維持原判。（2 段）

原告人隨後以上述內地判決為訴因向香港高等法院起訴，請求執行內地判決。（1 段）

被告人於 1995 年 10 月根據內地法律中的審判監督程序向福建省人民檢察院提出再審申請。1996 年 3 月，福建省人民檢察院向最高人民檢察院提交了請求抗訴的報告。（7 段）

根據上述情形，被告人以避免重複訴訟為由，向香港高等法院提出了擱置（stay）訴訟程序的申請。（12 段）

原告人以專家證人證言為依據主張原審中院對案件具有管轄權，並且該院作出的內地判決為最終及不可推翻的判決，因此香港法院應予以承認及執行；被告人則通過專家證人證言認為內地判決僅為「暫時的 (for the time being)」最終及不可推翻的判決。（15 段、19 段）

二、裁判觀點

香港高等法院張澤祐法官在判詞中的裁判觀點如下：

1. 張法官首先指出，本案的真正問題，是內地判決是否為最終及不可推翻的判決 (16 段)；並以 Dicey & Morris 的 *The Conflict of Laws* 為依據，指出香港法院執行境外法院判決，該判決必須為最終及不可推翻的判決 (17 段)。

2. 對於甚麼是最終及不可推翻的判決，張法官引用了英國上議院法庭於 1889 年作出的 Nouvion v. Freeman & Another 案判決作為判例依據，認為境外判決符合最終及不可推翻的要求，必須對作出該判決的法院而言，該判決是最終及不可被改變。即作出該判決的法院不能再改變該判決。(18 段、20 段)

3. 張法官同時又指出，如果具有管轄權的法院已經作出最終及不可推翻 (由其自己) 的判決，確立了債務的存在，則儘管該判決可被上訴，該判決仍被推定為有效，直至上級法院將其推翻。(21 段)

4. 根據對判例規則的上述闡釋，張法官認為內地《民事訴訟法》下的再審制度不是簡單的上訴程序，若最高人民檢察院提出抗訴，原審中院可以在再審中變更其判決。在此制度下，如果一個內地法院作出的判決被提起抗訴，該法院即必須進行再審，其顯然保留了變更其原判決的權力。(20 段)

5. 儘管在本案中抗訴尚未被提出，但有關程序已被啟動。這表明內地判決並非最終及不可推翻。如果向最高人民檢察院提出的申請被批准，內地判決就有可能被改變，內地判決被用於作為終局性證據以證明存在的債務，可能根本就不存在。(22 段)

6. 根據上述理由，張法官裁定擱置訴訟。(23 段)

三、評析

1. 從張法官判詞所採用的表述看，作為其作出裁判結果的理據，張法官對於內地判決是否為最終及不可推翻判決的問題，作出了相當明確的判斷，即認為其不是最終及不可推翻的判決（22 段）。從他所使用的標題看，即 "Not final and conclusive"，也能反映他的判斷之明確。（20 段前）

2. 在論證理由上，張法官更是從最高人民檢察院監督職能及抗訴制度性質的層面進行說明，認為這並不是簡單的上訴程序，並據此認為為了通過香港法院承認及執行的目的，內地判決並非最終及不可推翻。張法官同時使用了 Lord Watson 在 Nouvion 先例判詞中的表述，認為內地判決「對於作出判決的法院而言不是最終及不可推翻」。（22 段）

3. 張法官更明確指出，若最高人民檢察院根據內地《民事訴訟法》提出抗訴，原審中院就有可能變更內地判決。而無論抗訴被提出的情況再少見，內地法院判決必須對案件進行重審，因此內地法院明顯地保留了變更其自己裁定的權力（clearly it retains the power to alter its own decision）。（22 段）

4. 從上述的說明看，可發現張法官在判詞中的判斷，不僅是針對在本個案中原審中院作出的內地判決，從關於最高人民檢察院監督職能、抗訴制度以及內地原審法院（不限於本案的原審中院）所保留權力的角度看，更是一般性地針對內地的審判監督程序。這似乎是認為，內地法院判決（不僅是本案原審中院的內地判決）基於審判監督制度的存在，就不是最終及不可推翻的判決。

5. 不過，張法官在判詞中的一項表述，似乎又為內地法院判決可能被視為最終及不可推翻判決，保留了一點空間。在明確表示內地判決不是最終及不可推翻時，張法官如此表述：「儘管抗訴尚未被提出，但程序已經被實際啟動（筆者注：被告人已經申請再審）。這表明該判決不是最終及不可推翻。」在此，張法官加入了「程序已經被實際啟動」的情形，於是就為程序未被實際啟動（或被終止）的案件，留下了將其內地法院判決認定為屬於最終及不可推翻判決的可能性。

四、本案的影響

本案是一起原告根據香港法律中的「普通法執行」請求執行內地法院作出判決的案件，也是香港法院首次明確就內地法院判決是否符合普通法的「最終及不可推翻」要求作出認定的判決，更是香港法院首次比較明確地裁定：由於內地再審制度的原因，內地法院作出的判決並不符合「最終及不可推翻」的要求，從而不應被執行。在此判決後，香港法院在隨後的多個案件中對本案判決的判詞作出了不同的闡釋和演繹，但多數均或直接或間接地將本案判決作為不直接承認及執行內地法院判決的依據，從而導致內地判決在香港難以獲得承認及執行。

儘管從近年的一些判決看，香港一些法官似乎對內地判決的觀點有所鬆動，但至今為止，債權人根據普通法申請執行內地判決仍然遇到很大的障礙，幾乎只要債務人提出「最終及不可推翻」的抗辯，香港法院均會擱置有關訴訟程序，或作出其他相應的裁定。

第二回

武漢中碩虹案：內地判決再度不被執行

案件	：	Wuhan Zhong Shuo Hong Real Estate Co. Ltd.
		（湖北省武漢中碩虹房地產開發有限公司）
		v. The Kwong Sang Hong International Ltd.
		（香港廣生行國際有限公司案）
法庭	：	高等法院原訟法庭
案號	：	HCA 14325/1998
判決日期	：	2000 年 6 月 12 日

在 Chiyu 案後，來到世紀之交，再有一個香港案件涉及到內地判決是否最終及不可推翻的問題。這個案件的審理結果，並沒有受到幾年前香港回歸祖國的影響而給有關的內地判決「放行」，這應該也算 是在「一國兩制」下香港享有高度自治權及司法獨立的體現。

一、案情簡介

（一）基本事實

1995 年，原告人向河北省高級人民法院起訴，並在 1996 年取得對被告人的勝訴判決。1998 年，被告人向最高人民法院提出的上訴被判決駁回（「內地判決」）。經強制執行後，被告人尚有港幣 290 萬元及人民幣 830 萬元債務未履行。（1 段至 4 段）

1998 年 8 月被告人向最高人民法院申請再審，法官也認定有證據表示最高人民法院正在進行審查並在處理被告人的再審申請。但被告人並未申請中止內地判決的執行。（9 段）

1999 年 1 月被告人再向最高人民檢察院申訴，要求對內地判決提出抗訴。（9 段）

被告人主張 1999 年 11 月最高人民檢察院函告被告人其已決定對內地判決進行審查，但法官認為並不存在有關最高人民檢察院何時進行審查及何時審查完畢的結論性說明。（10 段）

（二）被告人的主張

原告人於 2000 年向香港法院起訴，要求執行內地判決中未履行債務的部份。針對原告人的起訴，被告人提出了擱置訴訟程序的申請，並在答辯中提出了幾項理據，其中一項為以 Chiyu 案的判決作為依據提出其主張，認為內地判決並非最終及不可推翻的判決，最高人民檢察院對最高人民法院的審判行使審判監督職能，若最高人民檢察院提出抗訴，內地判決會被法院改變。據此，被告人主張內地判決可能因最高人民法院對案件進行再審而被撤銷為由，主張應擱置本案的訴訟程序。

二、裁判觀點

處理本案的香港高等法院楊振權法官的觀點及裁定：

1. 關於張澤祐法官在 Chiyu 案中的見解，楊法官作出了進一步的闡釋，並就相關法律原則闡述了其自己的見解：

（1）根據內地的《民事訴訟法》，若最高人民檢察院提出抗訴，法院即可以在再審中改變其裁決。基於法院保留改變其裁決的可能，其判決並非最終及不可推翻；張法官的觀點是，當境外判決本身並非最終及不可推翻時，允許根據境外判決進行的訴訟繼續進行並不適當。（14 段）

（2）要在香港執行境外判決，其中一項基本條件是該判決是最終及不可推翻。有判例表明若作出判決的法庭有權在其後撤銷或改變該判決，該判決即並非最終及不可推翻。同時，亦有判例表明，一個判決不會僅僅因為可以被提請向上級法庭或已實際被提起上訴而不再屬最終判決，除非該判決在境外已經因等待上訴而被中止執行。（15-17 段）

（3）關於最高人民檢察院提起抗訴的準確性質及效力的問題，並未在香港的審訊中經過嚴格審查。楊法官更明確指出，就此問題，他在此階段不應解決其爭議，甚至不應發表太明確的觀點。此問題只能在正式審訊階段，經過對專家證人的詢問以了解問題的相關事實後解決。（18 段、19 段）

（4）但至少可以認為，若已經確立內地判決並非最終及不可推翻，所應作出的正確命令，應當是駁回訴訟，而不是擱置訴訟程序。楊法官也針對被告人的申請指出，若被告人主張內地判決並非最終及不可推翻，其理應申請駁回原告人的起訴，而不是申請擱置訴訟。（20 段）

2. 在認為香港法律並未就內地判決是否為最終及不可推翻作出明確判斷的情況下，楊法官表示，他同意在若干情況下，在問題未決時擱置訴訟可能更為合適，以避免重複訴訟及降低訴訟成本。而對此問題，法庭根據其審判權享有決定的自由裁量權。但該自由裁量權必須依法行使，法庭必須對案件背景進行全盤考慮，並衡量當事人的利益，特別是要衡量決定擱置或不擱置對當事人的影響。（21 段、22 段）

3. 在上述觀點的基礎上，楊法官對案件相關的許多因素進行了分析，首先指出了不利於決定擱置訴訟的因素（24 段 -32 段），包括但不限於：（1）儘管根據最新的信息，最高人民檢察院仍在審查案件，但並不存在關於最高人民檢察院何時會對案件進行審查及何時會完成審查的結論性說明（24 段）；（2）有信息表明最高人民法院正在對再審申請進行審查及處理（25 段）；（3）被告人未在內地申請中止執行內地判決（26 段）；（4）若作出不利於原告人的裁決，原告人仍可重新提起實質訴訟（不是訴請執行內地判決）（28 段）；（5）若在最終及不可推翻的問題上作出有利於原告人的裁決，法庭仍需就內地判決是否基於欺詐而取得，以及執行內地判決是否違反自然正義及 / 或違反公共政策進行審理（29 段）（筆者注：被告人同時提出了執行內地判決違反自然正義及 / 或公共政策的理據）等等。

4. 楊法官緊接又分析了支持擱置訴訟的因素（33 段 -37 段），其中包括：（1）無疑若最高人民法院會改變先前的裁決，原告人將不具有成功執行內地判決的法律基礎（33 段）；（2）若訴訟不被擱置，被告人將需要作出重大的投入及很大的費用以準備案件的正式審理（由於案件涉及的問題非常困難及複雜）（33 段）；（3）若最高人民法院在香港法院作出了不利於被告人的裁決後作出有利於被告人的裁決，這將會為被告人帶來重大的損害及不公正（34 段）；（4）從所提供的信息看最高人民法院及最高人民檢察院已經根據被告人的申訴採取步驟（36 段）；（5）擱置訴訟對原告人的唯一損害是案件的進一步遲延（37 段）。

5. 經衡量上述的各項因素，楊官最終作出了將訴訟擱置 6 個月的裁決，同時表示在 6 個月期限屆滿後，必須允許案件進入正式審訊。（40 段、41 段）

三、評析

楊法官在本案的論證中引用了 Chiyu 案的判決及張澤祐法官在該案判詞中的陳述。若仔細分析楊法官的論證，可以發現他儘管引用了張法官的陳述，但他實際上在一定程度上否定了，或更準確地說是「軟化」了張法官的見解（認為內地法院判決是否最終及不可推翻尚無定論）。但無論如何，無論再「軟化」，其仍然得出了不能直接承認內地判決的結論，並作出了擱置訴訟程序的裁定。關於楊官的論證，詳析如下：

1. 在 Chiyu 案中，張法官將 Nouvion 先例的法律原則闡釋為：若作出判決的法院保留改變其自己裁決的可能性，該判決即不屬最終及不可推翻。張法官並且相當明確地認為，最高人民檢察院的抗訴的審判監督職能及抗訴制度並非簡單的上訴制度，若最高人民檢察院提出抗訴，無論其情形如何不常見，有關法院即須對案件進行再審，因此該法院明顯保留了改變其先前裁決的權力（該判決 20 段）。可見，張法官在 Chiyu 案判決中的論斷非常明確，並且直接針對最高人民檢察院提出抗訴的情形，認為法院因此而保留改變裁決的權力，有關判決因此不屬最終及不可推翻的判決（關於張法官在 Chiyu 案判詞中觀點的評析，見本書第一回。）。

2. 在引用 Chiyu 案的判決時，楊法官重述了該案所確立的原則，即：若作出判決的法院有權撤銷或改變其判決，該判決即並非最終及不可推翻（15 段）。

3. 但是，楊法官只是一般性地重述了上述原則，並未將該原則明確適用於最高人民檢察院提出抗訴的情形，同時認為最高人民檢察院抗訴的確切性質及效力，並未在香港的正式審訊中經過嚴格的審查（18 段）。相對於張法官在 Chiyu 案中明確對審判監督及抗訴制度進行評判，楊法官的立場明顯較為「軟化」，並明確表示自己不適合在本案中就此問題提出任何有力的觀點（19 段）。

4. 楊法官更進一步的指出，若內地判決並非最終及不可推翻，原告人

的起訴理應被駁回,而不是僅僅擱置訴訟(20 段)。實際上是認為,以內地判決並非最終及不可推翻為由擱置訴訟並不正確。楊法官雖未明確表示,但這實際上是張法官在 Chiyu 案中的處理。

5. 在上述觀點的基礎上,楊法官實際上並不是以內地判決並非最終及不可推翻為理據裁定擱置訴訟,而是根據香港法院司法審判權所賦予的自由裁量權,在衡量各種因素後所作出的裁決(21 段)。

四、本案的意義

根據本案判詞中的論證,楊法官的見解實際上導致境外判決在是否最終及不可推翻的問題上被分為三種情形,即:

	類型	效力(是否執行)
1	確定為最終及不可推翻的判決	直接執行,被告人無從主張駁回訴訟或擱置訴訟
2	確定為並非最終及不可推翻的判決	直接駁回原告人要求直接執行的起訴
3	暫未確定是否最終及不可推翻的判決	擱置訴訟,等待擱置期限屆滿後,再於正式審訊中進行裁決

針對本案的內地判決,楊法官即認定為屬第 3 種類型,並據以作出中止訴訟的裁決。儘管楊法官並未斬釘截鐵地認為內地判決並非最終及不可推翻,而是仍然留有餘地的以自由裁量權為基礎作出擱置訴訟的裁決。但在結果上,這仍然導致內地判決無法如同其他法域的判決般被直接執行。儘管在程序上,內地判決的原告人仍可在擱置期限屆滿後通過正式審訊爭取直接執行該判決,然而,結合香港訴訟所需的時間及費用等成本的現實因素的考慮,這已經使內地判決的原告人處於十分不利的位置,並且帶來極大的不便。

也要強調的是,楊法官在本案判決中,仍然重述了張法官就 Nouvion 先例法律觀點所作的闡述,即認為只要原審法院有權撤銷或改變原審判決,該判決即並非最終及不可推翻。從 Nouvion 先例的內容看,此法律觀點的闡述究竟是否準確,非無進一步探討的空間。關於此問題,將於本書

第十回中深入討論。

　　無論如何，所幸的是，楊法官的留有餘地，在一定程度否定或軟化了張法官的見解，至少使內地法院的判決未至被一概斷定為並非最終及不可推翻，為日後在此問題上的爭論亦仍然留有空間。

第三回

略有所退的 Tan Tay Cuan 案

案件	：	Tan Tay Cuan v. Ng Chi Hung
法庭	：	高等法院原訟法庭
案號	：	HCA5477/2000
判決日期：		2001 年 2 月 5 日

在武漢中碩虹案後不到一年，香港高等法院原訟法庭再次作出了一個涉及執行內地法院判決的裁決。儘管本案在武漢中碩虹案之後，然而本案在內地法院判決是否最終及不可推翻的問題上的裁判觀點，並未能在該案的基礎上更進一步。雖然本案同樣像武漢中碩虹案般「軟化」了張澤祐法官在 Chiyu 案中的觀點，但相比於武漢中碩虹案的觀點（關於該案的評論，見本書第二回），充其量只是原地踏步，甚至略有所退。

一、案情簡介

2000 年 3 月，福建省高級人民法院就原告人與被告人之間的股權轉讓合同糾紛作出了二審判決（「內地判決」），駁回了被告人針對廈門市中級人民法院支持原告人的一審判決所提出的上訴。根據內地判決，被告人應向原告人支付大約人民幣 500 萬元。

原告人隨後向香港法院提起訴訟，訴請香港法院根據簡易判決執行內地判決。聆案官（Master）作出了支持原告人的簡易判決。被告人遂提起上訴，要求撤銷該簡易判決。

同時，被告人在福建省高級人民法院作出內地判決後，已向最高人民法院提出再審申請。

二、裁判觀點

如同武漢中碩虹案，處理本案的香港高等法院王式英 William Waung

法官（王法官）引用了 Chiyu 案作為裁判依據。王法官的觀點及裁定分述如下：

1. 王法官並未對張澤佑法官在 Chiyu 案中的見解展開闡述，僅僅將其簡單總結並指出：張法官在該案中處理了涉及最高人民檢察院參與的內地判決是否為最終及不可推翻的問題，並拒絕作出簡易判決，同時認為具有一定的可爭辯理由（arguable case）認定案中判決並非最終及不可推翻，裁定擱置訴訟。（6 段）

2. 根據雙方專家證人提交的材料，所爭論的問題（內地判決是否最終及不可推翻）屬顯然可爭辯（plainly arguable）的問題。即在內地法律所規定的審判監督制度中，由於內地判決根據其程序可經審查而被修改，因此內地判決具有一定的可爭辯理由被視為並非最終及不可推翻。（7 段）

3. 據此，王法官認為簡易判決不應被頒發，而且有關爭議足夠複雜而應在正式審訊中處理。（8 段）

4. 王法官最後還補充指出，在本案中，被告人向最高人民法院申請再審後，最高人民法院已指示福建省高級人民法院對再審申請進行考慮。最高人民法院並未駁回再審申請，似乎表明本案再審具有一定的理據。就現階段而言，再審非必會被提起，但是有可能會被提起。（9 段）

5. 根據上述的考慮，王官裁定被告人上訴得直（撤銷簡易判決）。

三、評析

與武漢中碩虹案的判決相比，王法官在本案判決的判詞相對簡單，篇幅亦較短。篇幅雖短，但其中的若干內容亦值得注意，分析如下：

1. 本案雖是在武漢中碩虹案後不久的時間審理，但並未引用該案的判決，而是直接引用了 Chiyu 案的判決。

2. 與武漢中碩虹案不同，王法官在本案中並未以自由裁量權作為論證依據，而是直接以內地判決具有一定的可爭辯理由被認定為非最終及不可推翻來裁定撤銷簡易判決。

3. 在性質上，兩種論證有較大差異。武漢中碩虹案只是將內地法院判決的最終及不可推翻問題作為考慮因素之一，若其他考量因素的「分量」

超過最終及不可推翻問題，即使該問題尚未解決，法庭仍然可能允許執行內地判決。也就是說，該案判詞實際上為內地法院判決在香港法院根據普通法執行尚留下了較大的可能空間。但本案的判詞在實質上是直接以內地判決本身的制度性問題作為拒絕執行的理據，所留下的爭論空間要小很多。

4. 在判詞中，王法官並未明確引用張法官在 Chiyu 案的判詞作為依據，但提到內地判決因可以根據內地法律的程序在再審中被改變（7 段）。這似乎是認可有關的法律原則為：只要境外判決可按照法律程序在再審中被改變，即並非最終及不可推翻的判決。

5. 王法官雖未明確引用 Chiyu 案的判詞作為依據，但他將張法官在 Chiyu 中的觀點闡述為「存在具有一定可爭辯理由認定該判決不是最終及不可推翻」。若仔細閱讀張官的判詞，他實際上並未認為「具有一定的可爭辯理由」，而是十分明確地認為「最高人民檢察院的審判監督職能及抗訴制度不是簡單的上訴程序」（該判決 20 段），以及「程序（筆者注：審判監督程序）已被實際啟動，這表明該判決不是最終及不可推翻」（該判決 22 段）。可見，王法官的判詞實際上也是在「軟化」張官的見解。從非普通法律師的角度看，這似乎更像是一種「曲解」「誤讀」甚至是「歪曲」，但這可以說是英美法系判例法的一個特點，或可美其名為特有的「法系文化」。特別是在法官之間相互尊重（comity）的傳統下，這種情況十分常見。在一些案件中，甚至略為「誤讀」，就導致了後來法律的變化和發展。

四、對本案的評價

如上所述，本案與武漢中碩虹案雖然同樣否定了內地法院判決在香港法院的直接執行，但兩案論證並不相同，在實質上具有重大差異。武漢中碩虹案是以自由裁量權為基礎，並以案件的各種背景情形為考慮因素作為裁定擱置訴訟的依據，內地法院判決是否為最終及不可推翻該如何認定，僅僅是作為其中的一項考量因素（同時明確表示該問題在香港法院中從未經正式審訊處理），並未直接以關於內地法院判決在該問題上的認定為裁決理由。而在本案中，王法官不僅認為內地判決具有一定的可爭辯理由被認定為並非最終及不可推翻（而不僅是該問題有待在正式審訊處理），而是更明確地直接以此為理據作出推翻簡易判決的裁決。正是基於這種差異，本文認為本案在結果上雖與武漢中碩虹案基本相同，但實際上略有所

退。準確地說，本案判詞的觀點，實際上是在內地法院判決是否為最終及不可推翻判決的問題上，採取了更為苛刻的態度。

第四回

峰迴路轉的林哲民第一案

案件	：	林哲民經營之日昌電業公司 訴 林志滔案
法庭	：	高等法院原訟法庭
案號	：	CACV354/2001
判決日期：		2001 年 12 月 18 日

Tan Tay Cuan 案宣判的同一年，香港高等法院上訴法庭在林哲民經營之日昌電業公司訴林志滔案（「本案」）再次處理了內地判決是否最終及不可推翻的問題。

一、案情簡介

被告人及其擔任法定代表人的東莞榮豐錶業有限公司（「榮豐」）與原告人及其擔任法定代表人的恒昌電子（深圳）有限公司（「恒昌」）就位於東莞的廠房相關的租賃問題發生爭議。（2 段、3 段）

1999 年 6 月，原告人向香港高等法院原訟法庭起訴被告人；同年 7 月，被告人擔任法定代表人的榮豐（作為原告）於東莞市人民法院（「東莞法院」）對原告人擔任法定代表人的恒昌（作為被告）提起訴訟，恒昌（作為反訴原告）再對榮豐（作為反訴被告）提出反訴。兩地的訴訟同時進行。（3 段、4 段）

2000 年 11 月，東莞法院作出判決（「內地判決」）。簡單而言，榮豐勝訴而恒昌敗訴。從判決內容上看，雙方在東莞訴訟中的訴因及爭議點，與本案的並無差別。（4 段、5 段）

本案在原訟法庭中由鍾安德法官審理。在審訊開審的第一天，被告人向鍾法官申請撤銷原告人的各項請求。（1 段、21 段）

鍾法官根據被告人的申請作出了撤銷或擱置原告人相關請求的命令。

（1 段、9 段）

　　原告人向高等法院上訴法庭提起上訴，以內地判決並非最終及不可推翻的判決為其理據之一，要求推翻鍾法官的命令，並要求重新排期審訊本案。上訴法庭遂由高等法院首席法官梁紹中、上訴法庭法官胡國興及張澤佑共同審理本案，並由胡國興法官宣讀判案書。（1 段）

二、原訟法庭命令的依據和理由、原告人的上訴理由及上訴法庭裁判觀點

（一）原訟法庭命令的依據和理由

　　鍾法官根據被告人的申請作出了撤銷或擱置原告人請求的命令，其依據和理由為：

　　1. 鍾法官是「根據《高等法院規則》第 18 號命令第 19 條規則及 / 或法庭的固有司法權而撤銷本案的。」該規則所適用的情形，為「如原告的訴訟是沒有成功的機會，則容許他繼續進行訴訟，就會構成他濫用法庭程序，或案件所涉的是瑣碎無聊的訴訟」（15 段）。

　　2. 在適用上述規定時，鍾法官的其中一項主要理由，是認為東莞法院的判決，「相對於本案的與訟雙方而言，具有約束力，（或應被視為具約束力）。」（9 段）

（二）原告人的上訴理由

　　原告人提出了多項的上訴理由（10 段）。但其中最主要的理由，亦即本案判決提到的理由主要有：

　　1.《外地判決（交互強制執行）條例》（香港法例第 319 章）（「《外地判決條例》」）只適用於英聯邦國家的外地判決而不適用與內地法院判決（筆者注：按照其規定，《外地判決條例》所規定的可登記的外地判決，因具有既判力而阻卻當事人就相同訴因及爭議再次起訴）。（11 段）

　　2. 內地判決並非最終及不可推翻的判決（筆者注：若並不是最終及不可推翻的判決，內地判決即不具有既判力，原告人可就相同訴因及爭議再次起訴）。（13 段）

（三）上訴法庭的觀點

上訴法庭首先對鍾法官的觀點進行了修正：

1. 對於鍾法官根據《高等法院規則》第 18 號命令第 19 條規則及／或法庭的固有司法權撤銷本案，上訴法庭指出：「但是，只是在申索是清楚及明顯地會敗訴或法庭不應審理案件的情況下，法庭才可以運用該規則的權力，這是確定已久的法律（見 2001 年香港民事程序第 289 頁第 18/19/6 段）」。（15 段）

2. 上訴法庭進一步認為，鍾法官實際上只能根據不容反悔法（estoppel）作為撤銷本案的依據，即：「如東莞法院的判決對本案的與訟雙方具約束力，雙方都不能就該案的訴因及爭議再在香港法庭訴訟，因而法庭不審理本案」。（16 段）

在將鍾法官所應適用的法律修正為不容反悔法後，上訴法庭以 Dicey & Morris 的相關內容為依據（該書第 14 版 14R-018 段、第 14R-012 段、第 14R-109 段）作出了進一步闡釋（17 段）：

1. 不容反悔法的適用，要求所涉判決是最終及不可推翻的判決。

2. 就本案而言，內地判決為外地判決。對於外地判決，必須就該案件的爭議點作出是非曲直的判決，而判決是最終及不可推翻判決，則對與訟雙方來說，判決是已有了最終的結論，雙方都不能對判決就事實或法律方面進行任何質疑，或在另外一案中就同樣的訴因或爭議再次訴訟。

對於最終及不可推翻的問題，上訴法庭引用了張澤祐法官在 Chiyu 案中的判詞：

1. 指出在 Chiyu 案中，「因為該抗訴程序已展開，可能招致福建中級人民法院要重審該案，故張法官認為該法院的判決並不是最終及不可推翻的判決」。同時也明確認為「張法官在該案的裁決是正確及合法合理的」。（18 段）

2. 同時也強調了，在 Chiyu 案中，張法官是基於以下情況將香港案件的程序擱置：與訟雙方均提交了中國法律專家意見，指出檢察院基於監督職能可以對判決提出抗訴，導致作出該案內地判決的福建某中級人民法院須重審該案，加上抗訴程序已經展開。（18 段、20 段）

3. 在肯定張法官在 Chiyu 案中的裁決「正確及合法合理」的同時（19段），上訴法庭又指出本案與 Chiyu 案不同，因為該案有專家證據，而本案雙方則未就內地法律提交專家證據，因此法庭並不知道內地法律在相關問題上是否未發生變化，還是已經有所變更（20段）；在本案中原告人也未採取任何步驟向人民檢察院要求抗訴（21條）。

4. 然而，儘管本案與 Chiyu 案有所不同，但鍾法官撤銷本案，必須「無疑地證明本案受不容反悔法的約束，被告就有舉證責任，證明東莞的判決是最終及不可推翻的判決」。基於被告人並未作出此舉證，因此鍾法官「作出撤銷本案的命令，在這方面是錯誤的，是沒有所需的證據支持的」。（21段）

5. 此外，被告人延遲至審訊開審第一天才申請撤銷本案，根據香港相關法律，鍾法官本不應接納該申請。（21段）

6. 據上，上訴法庭命令原告人上訴得直，撤銷鍾法官的命令，並把案件發回原訟法庭由另一位法官審理。（21段）

三、評析

閱讀本案判詞關於內地判決是否屬最終及不可推翻判決問題的論證時，頗有峰迴路轉之感。在判詞中諸如「但是該案（筆者注：Chiyu案）的情況與本案的不同」、「該案有專家證據」、「法庭不知道現時國內的法律……是否如前一樣」、本案原告人未「向人民檢察院要求抗訴」等陳述，初看會以為上訴法庭要將本案區別於 Chiyu 案而作出不同認定。但可是最後還是以大轉折的方式，認為被告人未完成舉證而作出了支持原告人的裁決。對於本案判決的判詞及其論證，有以下數項可加以說明：

1. 上訴法庭闡釋不容反悔法所要求的最終及不可推翻的條件時，引用了張官在 Chiyu 案中的判詞，明確表示張官「在該案的裁決是正確及合法合理的」（19段）；同時，也明確重審了張法官的觀點，認為「因為國內法制的結構，檢察院對民事訴訟可以提出抗訴而使原審法庭把案件重審，故國內法院的判決不是最終及不可推翻的判決」（20段）。

2. 然而，在實際上，上訴法庭在本案中並未適用 Chiyu 案中的法律原

則以得出其裁判結論,而是直接認為被告人並未舉證而裁決原告人上訴得直。也就是說,由於被告人未就內地判決的相關內地法律完成舉證,法庭根本無需也無從根據 Chiyu 案的法律原則作出判斷。

3. 注意的是,在闡述 Chiyu 案的法律原則時,上訴法庭似乎是強調了在 Chiyu 案中抗訴程序已經開展的事實(19 段),並作為該案與本案的區別所在(21 段)。這或許能為未啟動審判監督程序的內地判決被認定屬最終及不可推翻的判決留下了空間。

四、本案的意義

在涉及內地判決是否最終及不可推翻問題的系列案件中,本案本身並未產生重大影響。如果一定要挖掘其意義,也只能說是前文所提到的,由於上訴法庭似乎強調了在 Chiyu 案中抗訴程序已經開展,因此本案判決有可能會為主張未啟動審判監督程序的內地判決,被認定為屬最終及不可推翻判決留下了空間。儘管如此,但也要同時注意到,本案一方面並未引用武漢中碩虹案和 Tan Tay Cuan 案(關於該兩案對的評論,見本書第二及第三回),另一方面則僅引用了 Chiyu 案,並由作為上級法院的上訴法庭對其裁判觀點給予了肯定,實際上又同時強化了 Chiyu 案所確立的「審判監督制度非最終及不可推翻」的立場。

值得一提的是,內地判決在香港的曲折遭遇經歷至此,張澤祐法官及鍾安德法官均已登場。在隨後的判決中,我們將會看到,兩位法官在涉及內地判決是否最終及不可推翻問題的系列判決中,扮演着頗為重要的角色。

第五回

對內地法院判決更為不利的林哲民第二案

案件	：	林哲民日昌電業公司 訴 張順連案
法庭	：	高等法院上訴法庭
案號	：	CACV1046/2001
判決日期	：	2002 年 7 月 12 日

　　本案的原告人林哲民與第四回案件的原告人為同一人，此人先後在香港提起了若干訴訟，並為內地法院判決最終及不可推翻問題貢獻了兩個案件，即本書第四回評論的林哲民第一案及本案。

一、案情簡介

　　原告人於 2000 年 11 月就與被告人在內地發生的租務相關爭議向香港法院提起訴訟，此前，原告人就相關爭議在深圳市龍崗區人民法院起訴，並取得了勝訴判決（「內地判決」）。（1 段）

　　被告人隨後則根據《高等法院規則》第 18 號命令第 19 條規則請求剔除本訴訟的申索陳述書（筆者注：相當於駁回訴訟請求，該規則適用於「如原告的訴訟是沒有成功的機會，則容許他繼續進行訴訟，就會構成他濫用法庭程序，或案件所涉的是瑣碎無聊的訴訟」的情形）。（3 段）

　　2001 年 1 月，聆案官經聆訊作出命令（「聆案官命令」）：除非原告人在 28 日內將廣東省深圳市龍崗區人民法院的判決作廢，否則剔除索償聲請書第 1 至 4 項（筆者注：原告人共提出 8 項索償，即聆案官命令剔除其中一半的索償；換成內地習慣表述，即原告提出 8 項訴訟請求，法庭對其中 4 項予以駁回）。（3 段）

　　原告人不服，向高等法院原訟法庭提出上訴。被告人亦提起上訴，請求剔除原告人的全部申索及撤銷本起訴（筆者注：換成內地習慣表述，即被告人要求駁回全部訴訟請求）。（3 段、4 段）

2001 年 5 月，原訟法庭任懿君法官（「原訟法官」）主要是以案件不宜由香港法院管轄為由，作出了支持被告人的判決，命令剔除原告人的申索陳述書及撤銷本訴訟。（1 段）

原告人向高等法院上訴法庭提起上訴，上訴法庭遂由胡國興法官及鍾安德法官（注意鍾法官是林哲民第一案原訟法庭原審的主審法官，其作出的原訟判決後來被上訴法庭撤銷）擔任主審法官審理本上訴，並由鍾法官頒佈判案書。（1 段）

二、上訴法庭裁判觀點

（一）裁判結果

1. 針對被告人上訴部份，上訴法庭以違反程序為由，裁定原訟法庭先前撤銷本訴訟及剔除申索陳述書第 5 至 8 項是錯誤的，因此撤銷該裁定。（9 段、10 段）

2. 針對原告人上訴部份（上訴請求撤銷聆案官命令及原訟法庭上述命令的相應部份），上訴法庭認為主要問題在於聆案官在作出該命令時，是否正確地行使了酌情權（筆者注：聆案官應該是根據《高等法院規則》第 18 號命令第 19 條規則作出該命令）；並最終以 Chiyu 案為主要依據，最終裁決聆案官命令及原訟法庭上述命令並無充分依據，並據以裁定原告上訴得直（即可繼續在香港進行訴訟）。（14 段、29 段、30 段）

（二）裁判理據

1. 針對原訟法官關於香港法院不宜對本案進行管轄的觀點，上訴法庭以林哲民第一案為依據認為香港法院對本案有管轄權。（23 段）

2. 對於聆案官是否正確行使酌情權，上訴法庭從兩個方面引用了 Chiyu 案作為依據，即：（1）以 Chiyu 案中關於內地法律的認定作為有關內地再審制度的證明；及（2）根據 Chiyu 案關於內地法院判決不是最終及不可推翻判決的司法觀點，認為聆案官命令沒有充分的理據支持。（21 段、27 段、29 段、30（b）段）

3. 由於當事人未就內地法律提交專家證人意見等證據，上訴法庭根據香港法例第 8 章《證據條例》第 59 條的規定，採用了 Chiyu 案判決中有關內地再審制度的認定，作為認定本案當時內地相關法律現狀的依據（21

段），即認定：「由於國內的法律容許有關方面提出『抗訴』，而『抗訴』經提出後，有可能引致裁決原訟的法院須對有關訴訟重行審理」（27 段）。

4. 同時，上訴法庭也基於上述有關內地再審制度的認定，指出「根據香港法律而言，該法院的判決，並非一最終及不可推翻的判決」（27 段）；上訴法庭還進一步認為，「國內的法律亦沒有對提出『抗訴』的期限作出任何規定」。基於這些原因，上訴法庭認為聆案官命令及任法官的命令並無充分理據，並據以裁定原告上訴得直（即可繼續在香港進行訴訟）（29 段、30 段）。

三、評析

驟眼一看，本案判決內容與前幾回的案件相似，均引用了 Chiyu 案作為裁定的依據。但若仔細分析，在幾個判決中，法官根據 Chiyu 案判決所進行的論證及其理據，並不完全相同。就本案的裁判理由而言，有以下數項需加以注意：

1. 嚴格而言，本判決在論證上並不嚴謹。上訴法庭將焦點問題界定為聆案官是否正確地行使酌情權，這似乎是採用了本系列第二回武漢中碩虹案的論證思路。然而，若分析其論證過程，可發現上訴法庭實際上又將內地判決是否為最終及不可推翻作為論證的重點以及作出裁定的核心甚至是唯一的依據。但是，從香港法律的角度看，內地判決是否最終及不可推翻的判決並不是判斷是否允許原告人在香港法院進行訴訟的直接依據。從張哲民第一案的判決看，是否適用「不容反悔法」才是真正的判斷依據，而是否為最終及不可推翻的判決，只是判斷是否適用「不容反悔法」的主要標準。然而，上訴法庭在本案中並未明確地以「不容反悔法」為處理依據，儘管從論證的內容看，似乎可以推斷上訴法庭的法官實際上是依此論證。

2. 上訴法庭相當明確地確認了 Chiyu 案的司法見解為內地法院判決基於內地的抗訴制度「並非一最終及不可推翻的判決」（27 段）。這是屬相對「強硬」的表述。

3. 在本案判決的最後，上訴法庭還以特別提示的方式，針對被告代表大律師的主張明確表示：「代表被告的劉大律師指 Chiyu Banking Corporation 一案中的被告，在該案聆訊時，已提出『抗訴』（筆者注：實際上是當事人已經提出抗訴申請），但本訴訟的原告，從未提出『抗訴』。

雖然如此，由於並無證據顯示，國內法律規定提出『抗訴』的期限，本庭認為但憑此點，不足以令本庭裁斷 Chiyu Banking Corporation 一案的裁決，不適用於本上訴」（31（b）段）。言下之意，就是認為無論是否已經提出抗訴申請，只要在法律上存在進入審判監督程序的可能，均屬 Chiyu 案司法見解（內地判決並非最終及不可推翻）的適用範圍。

四、本案的意義

從上述的評析看，本案對於內地法院判決的意義恐怕主要是負面的。主要體現在兩個方面：

其一，在引用 Chiyu 案時，上訴法庭在本案中對該案司法見解的闡釋比早前的 Tan Tay Cuan 案（見第三回）更為明確及「強硬」。在 Tan Tay Cuan 案中，王式英法官對 Chiyu 案的司法見解作出了相對「軟化」的闡釋，並不那麼斬釘截鐵地地認為內地判決「就是」非最終及不可推翻，而是表述為「存在具有一定可爭辯理由認定該判決不是最終及不可推翻」。相反，本案的闡釋為內地法院判決「並非一最終及不可推翻的判決」（27 段），表述上更為「強硬」。

其二，如前所述，上訴法庭在本案判決中實際上是認為，就算當事人未就內地判決提出抗訴申請，Chiyu 案仍有適用的餘地。也就是將 Chiyu 案司法見解的適用範圍，擴大到當事人未提出抗訴申請的案件，實際上是認為只要在法律上存在提起抗訴的可能，均屬並非最終及不可推翻的判決。這與上訴法庭在張哲民第一案判詞中的立場不太一樣。在該案中，上訴法庭在論證過程中反覆強調了在 Chiyu 案中審判監督程序已經被啟動的事實，似乎認為這是 Chiyu 案司法見解的重要事實（material fact）。然而，在本案中，上訴法庭又明確認為是否已經提起再審申請，實際上並非重要。

第六回（上）

李祐榮訴李瑞群案：Chiyu 案主審法官澄清立場

案件	：李祐榮 訴 李瑞群案
法庭	：高等法院上訴法庭
案號	：CACV159/2005
判決日期	：2005 年 12 月 9 日

　　從本案的陣容來看，就可知本案之精彩。本案的審理法官，為張澤祐法官、袁家寧法官及鍾安德法官。張法官正是將近十年前獨任審理 Chiyu 案的法官，鍾安德法官則為張哲民第一案原訟法庭原審的主審法官（其原訟判決被推翻）以及審理張哲民第二案上訴法庭上訴的兩位法官之一。在本案判決中，三位法官分別作出了判詞，其中張法官和袁法官的為多數判詞，鍾法官的則為異議判詞（dissenting judgment）。此外，法庭還邀請了後來成為律政司司長（現已卸任）的袁國強資深大律師擔任法庭之友，為法庭就內地相關法律問題提供協助。同時，清華大學法學院教授王亞新博士則擔任內地法律專家證人，就內地相關法律問題發表意見。

一、案情簡介

　　原告人向被告人出售位於廣東省清遠市的工廠業務，被告人未依約支付價款，原告人遂向清遠市清城區人民法院起訴，並於 2002 年 5 月取得勝訴判決。（1 段）

　　被告人不服判決，向清遠市中級人民法院提出上訴，該院於 2002 年 9 月駁回該上訴。（2 段）

　　被告人再向廣東省高級人民法院提出再審申請，該院於 2002 年 12 月駁回該再審申請。（3 段）

　　2002 年 10 月（即被告人申請再審前），原告人以清城區人民法院判決（「內地判決」）為訴因，向香港區域法院提交傳票，要求區域法院以

簡易程序判決確認其債權。（4 段）

　　區域法院將案件轉交高等法院原訟法庭審理，原訟法庭聆案官於 2003年 12 月駁回原告人申請。原告人遂向原訟法庭提出上訴，原訟法庭暫委法官陳江耀於 2004 年 5 月判決原告人上訴得直，確認了原告人基於內地判決所享有的債權。被告人就陳法官的命令向上訴法庭提出上訴。（5 段、6 段）

　　原告人在上訴中才提出內地判決是最終及不可推翻判決的主張，並提交了王亞新教授的法律意見書作為依據。（8 段）

　　被告人在再審申請被駁回後，並未進一步在內地根據審判監督程序採取其他行動。（21 段）

　　在香港程序中，被告人並未聘請律師代表。（8 段）

二、張澤祐法官的判詞

（一）裁判結果

　　1. 張法官最終裁定原告人敗訴，裁定被告人上訴得直，即裁定原告人不能通過簡易程序直接以內地判決為訴因要求被告人履行債務。（32 段）

　　2. 另一位審理法官袁家寧法官支持了張法官的裁決，鍾法官則作出了反對判決。（39 段）

（二）裁判理據

　　1. 張法官指出，原告人是引用簡易程序要求法院給予判決，法律規定若這類申請存有爭議點或涉及艱難的法律議題，法庭就不應頒佈簡易判決，而需給予被告人答辯機會，讓案件進行正式審訊然後才作出判決。（23段）

　　2. 張法官說明了本案的最大爭議（內地法院判決是否純是因為審判監督制度的存在而不能成為最終及不可推翻的判決）是具有較大爭議的問題，因此不能通過簡易程序處理。（24 段、26 段）

　　3. 張法官還表示本案涉及的議題明顯是一項具有公眾重要性的議題，作為不宜通過簡易程序處理的另一項依據。（27 段）

4. 針對原告人大律師關於內地判決類似於「因欠缺行動而作出的判決（default judgment）」（即缺席判決）的主張（即根據有關判例，「因欠缺行動而作出的判決」仍被視為最終及不可推翻判決，因此對內地判決亦應作相同對待），張法官也認為這也是本案的爭議點，應經過正式審訊處理。（28 段）

5. 此外，張法官也同時考慮了被告人未聘請律師及內地法律專家證人等因素，作為認為不宜在簡易程序中作出判決的理由（27 段、29 段）。袁家寧法官也表明了類似觀點（34 段、38 段）。

三、對張法官判詞的評析

僅就結果而言，張法官在本案中的裁判與十年前他在 Chiyu 案判決中所作的判決基本相同，即否定了原告人要求直接執行內地法院判決的主張。然而，儘管如此，就論證而言，張法官在判詞中所採用的理據實際上又與 Chiyu 案的截然不同。

（一）與 Chiyu 案判詞的比較

焦點問題

Chiyu 案：在該案中，張法官所處理的，是原告人是否能以內地法院判決為訴因起訴要求被告人履行債務的問題。

本案：張法官在判詞中強調，「本上訴只是一項有關簡易判決的上訴」（26 段），實際上是將所處理的問題界定為原告人能否**通過簡易程序**以內地判決為訴因請求香港法院判決被告人支付欠款，而不是 Chiyu 案所處理的原告人在香港法院是否能以內地判決為訴因起訴要求被告人履行債務的問題。基於所處理的問題有所不同，張法官在兩案中的論證實質上亦有不同。

對 Nouvion 先例的引用及闡釋

Chiyu 案：張法官在該案引用了英國 Nouvion v. Freeman 先例中，Lord Herschell 和 Lord Watson 兩位法官的判詞，並將該先例所確立的原則闡釋為：若作出判決的法院保留改變其自己裁決的可能性，該判決即不屬最終及不可推翻。同時，張法官在該判決中更相當明確地認為，法院因審判監督程序而明顯保留了改變其先前裁決的權力（該判決 20 段），繼而

認為內地法院判決不屬最終及不可推翻的判決。

本案：在本案判詞中，張法官以更大的篇幅引用了在 Nouvion 案中 Lord Herschell 的判詞（Lord Watson 的則未引用），並且翻譯成中文（10段）。但是，張法官在論證中實際上並沒有將所引用的 Nouvion 案判詞直接作為依據，而只是相對客觀地說明了所引用判詞所處理的問題（針對該案所處理的西班牙法院 remate judgment）（11 段、12 段），隨後更明確指出，在 Nouvion 案中，「法庭沒有清楚說明到底是不是只要存在着一個可以推翻『remate 判決』的制度，法庭就已具備穩固的基礎去裁定這類判決不是最終及不可被推翻的判決」。實際上是認為 Nouvion 並未明確確立「原審法院可推翻判決＝非最終及不可推翻」的原則，張法官的這一觀點與他在 Chiyu 案中的觀點甚至可以說是截然相反的。張法官主要是借助了 Nouvion 案來指出內地判決是否為最終及不可推翻問題是一個有爭議空間的問題，因此不適宜通過簡易程序處理，從而應撤銷原告人的原訟勝訴判決，並命令進行正式審訊。

（二）評析

據上可見，張法官在本案中，儘管並未明確表明，但他實際上已經調整了自己在 Chiyu 案中的立場。或可美其名為澄清，但實質上就是改變了其針對內地法院判決所持的觀點。一方面，改變了其在對 Nouvion 先例的解讀上的觀點；另一方面，則改變了在內地法院判決是否因再審制度而不是最終及不可推翻問題上的立場。

由於實際上張法官在本案中所處理的問題與 Chiyu 案中的問題並非相同的問題，他在判詞中也有效地「規避」了內地判決是否為最終及不可推翻判決的問題。但無論如何，他實際上也在無需明確就內地判決是否為最終及不可推翻判決發表意見的情況下，達到不直接承認和執行內地判決的結果。

四、張法官判詞及本案的意義

張法官的判詞，最終亦因屬多數意見而成為本案的判決內容。其意義主要體現在三個方面：

其一，本案作為一個重要判例，明確確認了對於是否承認內地法院判

決為最終及不可推翻的判決，必須在正式審訊的程序中處理，而不能像許多其他法域判決般直接通過簡易程序處理，並獲得承認。

其二，儘管在表述上，可以將內地法院判決在香港法律中的地位表述為「並未明確拒絕承認」，但實際上，原告人如希望以內地法院判決為訴因起訴要求被告人履行債務，原則上必須通過需時更久、成本更高的訴訟程序，才有可能達到目的。這實際上已確認了在香港法律程序中，內地法院判決在目前的地位不如多數其他法域判決的地位。

其三，也要注意到，在本案中，被告人已經停止了繼續推進審判監督程序，也明確表明不在內地繼續該程序。張法官未據此而認為內地判決因此而屬最終及不可推翻，實際上是認為，審判監督程序不在進行中的事實，也不足據以認為內地法院為最終及不可推翻（林哲民第一案的判決則強調了審判監督程序是否已啟動的事實）。

第六回（下）

李祐榮訴李瑞群案：具有突破意義的異議判詞

案件	：李祐榮 訴 李瑞群案
法庭	：高等法院上訴法庭
案號	：CACV159/2005
判決日期	：2005 年 12 月 9 日

張澤祐法官作為本案的法官及獨任審理 Chiyu 案的法官，通過本案的判詞對其在十年前 Chiyu 案中所陳述的立場作出了「澄清」。對此，本回上集已經作出了比較詳細的說明和評析。而本案的精彩，不僅在於張法官以今日的我否定了昨日的我，而是更在於本案的另一位法官——鍾安德法官的異議判詞（dissenting judgment）。在其異議判詞中，鍾法官明確認為並詳細論證了儘管內地存在審判監督制度，但本案所處理的內地判決並不因此而不屬最終及不可推翻。儘管鍾法官的判詞因屬少數異議判詞而未能成為先例原則，但其論證仍具有高度的參考意義。只要熟悉普通法，就能知道今日某案件的異議判詞，往往有機會成為明日案件所確立的先例原則。因此，對於鍾法官異議判詞的意義，不容忽視。

一、案情簡介

為了便於讀者閱讀，已載於本回上篇的案情簡介在此重複：

原告人向被告人出售位於廣東省清遠市的工廠業務，被告人未依約支付價款，原告人遂向清遠市清城區人民法院起訴，並於 2002 年 5 月取得勝訴判決。（1 段）

被告人不服判決，向清遠市中級人民法院提出上訴，該院於 2002 年 9 月駁回該上訴。（2 段）

被告人再向廣東省高級人民法院提出再審申請，該院於 2002 年 12 月駁回該再審申請。（3 段）

2002 年 10 月（即被告人申請再審前），原告人以清城區人民法院判決（「內地判決」）為訴因，向香港區域法院提交傳票，要求區域法院以簡易程序判決確認其債權。（4 段）

區域法院將案件轉交高等法院原訟法庭審理，原訟法庭聆案官於 2003 年 12 月駁回原告人申請。原告人遂向原訟法庭提出上訴，原訟法庭暫委法官陳江耀於 2004 年 5 月判決原告人上訴得直，確認了原告人基於內地判決所享有的債權。被告人就陳法官的命令向上訴法庭提出上訴。（5 段、6 段）

原告人在上訴中才提出內地判決是最終及不可推翻判決的主張，並提交了王亞新教授的法律意見書作為依據。（8 段）

被告人在再審申請被駁回後，並未進一步在內地根據審判監督程序採取其他行動。（21 段）

在香港程序中，被告人並未聘請律師代表。（8 段）

二、鍾安德法官的異議判詞

（一）判詞結論

鍾法官裁定駁回被告人的上訴，即認為原告人可以通過簡易程序直接以內地判決為訴因要求被告人履行債務。（81 段）

（二）裁判理據

1. 在本案的上訴中，被告人提出了上訴理由若干，但並未以內地判決不是最終及不可推翻為上訴理由。鍾法官在論證了被告人所提出的各項上訴理由均不成立後（因不涉及最終及不可推翻的問題，在此不予詳述），再就內地判決是否最終及不可推翻的問題進行詳細論證。（43 段至 50 段）

2. 鍾法官指出內地法院判決因審判監督制度而引起的問題起源於 Chiyu 案，並指出在該案中，原審法院根據當時所查明的內地審判監督制度的有關內容，以及英國上議院法庭 Nouvion 先例，裁定該案中的福建某中級人民法院判決，並非香港普通法中的「最終及不可推翻」的判決。（51 段）

3. 根據當時所查明的關於內地審判監督制度的法律規定，鍾法官首先

指出，審判監督程序的啟動理由涉及四種情形，即：（1）原判決、裁定認定事實的主要證據不足的；（2）原判決、裁定適用法律確有錯誤的；（3）人民法院違反法定程序，可能影響案件正確判決、裁定的；（4）審判人員在審理該案件時有貪污受賄，徇私舞弊，枉法裁判行為的。他繼而認為，這「四種情況，與香港法律已確立的上訴理由，實質上並無不同」。（52段、54段、55段）

4. 此外，香港法律亦「賦予法院在裁定上訴得直時，頒令訴訟應重新審訊的權力」，以及「原訟法庭在其自身頒佈的命令未完備及登錄前，亦具自行重新審訊訴訟的權力」。（56段、57段）

5. 鍾法官明確認為，即使香港法院的判決出現以上所述情況，「以香港的法律而言，香港法院的判決，仍屬『最終及不可推翻』的判決」（58段）。而對於內地法院判決而言，僅因審判監督制度所涉及的四種情況（提起理由），「並不足以令內地的判決，被裁定為不屬『最終及不可推翻』的判決」（59段）。

6. 針對當時擔任法庭之友的袁國強資深大律師（「法庭之友」）的陳詞（其觀點似乎較有利於被告人），鍾法官在論證中亦加以引用或反駁。法庭之友指出了內地審判監督制度與香港的法制有兩項實質性的不同：（1）除了當事人外，作為第三方的法院院長、上級法院及檢察院，均可提起再審；及（2）除了對當事人申請再審設定的時限外，對於法院或檢察院啟動的再審，並無時間限制。（62段）

7. 對於法庭之友的上述陳詞，鍾法官認為，即使再審是由第三方提出（法院或檢察院），也仍然限於前述的四項理由。根據前述理由，內地法院判決仍不因審判監督制度而不屬最終及不可推翻的判決。（63段、64段）

8. 針對關於時限的陳詞，鍾法官更認為，「實際上，香港法院亦具延展法律程序（包括上訴程序）的時限的權力。……因此，即使香港法院的判決，亦可能在規定時限屆滿後，被頒令撤銷及重審。」（65段）

9. 此外，針對法庭之友就最高人民檢察院司法解釋的評論（如效力為僅供各省級人民檢察院參考等），鍾法官明確表示也不足以影響其結論，並且認為這些評論「過分着重純理論性而未顧及本上訴所涉案情的合理可能性。」（69段）

10. 鍾法官更指出，被告人在上訴中並未證明在內地判決重審的問題上，「有應予審訊的爭論點……或為其他理由……應予審訊……」（筆者注：被告人提起上訴要求推翻簡易判決，須證明該案存在「有應予審訊的爭論點」或「其他理由應予審訊」）。（67段）

11. 在判例依據上，鍾法官通過引用 Biard Laboratoires SA v. Rosumi Ltd 及 Nintendo of America Inc. v. Bung Enterprise Ltd. 兩個案件（兩案分別裁定法國的中期判令及美國加州法院的缺席判決均與 Nouvion 先例中的 remate judgment 不同，而仍屬最終及不可推翻的判決），認為 Nouvion 先例中的 remate judgment，與可依審判監督而被命令重審的內地判決完全不同，而且「更沒有證據顯示，本上訴所涉的內地判決在內地被視為暫准判令」（70段至73段）。據此明確指出，「本席認為 Nouvion 一案的判決，不適用於本上訴」（74段）。

12. 此外，以 Nintendo 案為依據，並引用了法庭之友的陳詞，鍾法官指出了對於缺席判決可被作出該判決的法院撤銷，普通法仍視為最終及不可推翻的判決。（71段、72段）

13. 鍾法官繼續重申：「內地判決不應純因有可能被頒令重審而被視為不屬『最終及不可推翻』的判決。這是因為同一可能性，亦適用於至少部份採用普通法法律原則的國家或地區（包括香港）」。他同時引用法庭之友的陳詞：「法庭之友在本上訴聆訊時亦同意，在裁定內地判決是否屬『最終及不可推翻』的判決這一點時，香港法院不應只從純理論的角度考慮重審的可能性，而應兼顧涉案事實是否顯示有合理的可能性。」（75段）

14. 鍾法官更是明確表示更改自己在過去判例中的觀點：「基於以上個點，本席更改本席在林哲民日昌電業公司對張順連一案中（注：即本書的林哲民第二案），對內地『審判監督』制度是否導致內地判決不屬『最終及不可推翻』的判決的看法」。（77段）

三、對鍾法官判詞的評析

鍾法官在判詞中的觀點非常明確：即內地法院的判決不因審判監督制度而不屬最終及不可推翻。

其理由主要包括：（1）提起審判監督程序，僅適用於四種情況，而

這四種情況，與香港的上訴理由無異；（2）提起審判監督程序並無時間限制（就法院或檢察院提起的情況而言），香港法院也有權延長上訴時限；（3）作出判決的法院可撤銷其所作出的判決亦不表示判決就不是最終及不可推翻。

對於 Chiyu 案，鍾法官只是指出內地法院判決是否為最終及不可推翻的問題源自於該判例，而在論證過程中，他並未對 Chiyu 案的原則進行闡釋，而是直接通過內地審判監督制度與香港上訴制度的比較（認為基本相同），以及根據普通法原審法院有權力撤銷自己作出的判決必然導致該判決不屬最終及不可推翻（以 Nintendo 案為依據），以論證內地法院判決不同於 Nouvion 先例所處理的西班牙 remate judgment。實際上，通過此論證，鍾法官雖未明示，但實際上已經改變了 Chiyu 案所確立的見解（即認為根據 Nouvion 先例，最終及不可推翻的判決，是作出該判決的法院不能再改變的判決的見解）（見本書第一回的評論）。或者更準確地說，鍾法官實際上並不認為作出判決的法院有權改變所作出的判決，就等同於該判決不是最終及不可推翻，更不認為 Nouvion 先例確立了這樣的規則。

鍾法官的判詞，至少在內容上可以說在內地法院判決是否為最終及不可推翻的問題上具有重大突破，他以相當詳盡的論證為基礎，明確指出內地法院判決不因審判監督制度而不屬最終及不可推翻判決。但是，鍾法官在判詞中也作出了帶有保留性的陳述，即表示「香港以外國家或地區的法律，屬法院對涉案事實的裁斷⋯⋯因此香港法院對此點的裁斷，往往取決於在該訴訟中呈交的相關證據。亦基於此因，該等裁斷通常不具概括的適用性」（78 段）。也就是說，鍾法官自行對自己判詞的一般適用性作出了保留。

應該指出的是，本案的上訴請求為撤銷原訟法庭簡易判決，焦點問題為原告人的訴請是否應通過簡易判決獲得支持，因此鍾法官主要是認為被告人未能在內地判決是否為最終及不可推翻判例的問題上，證明其屬「應予以審訊的爭論點」。（67 段、76 段）

四、鍾法官判詞的意義

如前所述，鍾法官的判詞，至少就內容而言可以說是具有重大的突破意義。而且與先前認為內地法院判決因審判監督制度而不屬最終及不可推

翻判決的判詞相比，其論證應該是更為詳盡，更為充分及有力。遺憾的是，鍾法官的判詞並未獲得另外兩位法官的支持，只能成為少數異議判詞而未成為先例規則。

然而，從普通法的發展看，一些判決的少數異議判詞對日後判例發展的意義，往往不能輕視。今日的異議判詞，往往就是將來的先例原則。特別要注意的是，在本案中，張法官與袁法官實際上並未否定鍾法官的判詞，他們只是採用了「技術性」的理由（爭議不宜在簡易程序中處理），裁定被告人上訴得直，而且還明確表示內地法院判決是否為最終及不可推翻的問題，應有待在正式審訊中處理。實際上也為鍾法官的觀點日後被採納提供了更大的可能性。本案的重要性，在香港的立法文獻中亦有所體現。在本案的審理過程中，正值內地與香港協商《內地與香港特別行政區法院相互認可和執行當事人協議管轄的民商事案件判決的安排》之時，在當時香港立法會的討論文件中，也明確引述了本案，並指出鍾法官就最終及不可推翻的問題作出了異議判詞，以作為立法會議員在討論時的參考（見「立法會 CB（2）1202/05-06（02）號文件」）。

此外，從澄清最終及不可推翻判決問題的角度看，鍾法官的判詞仍有不足。鍾法官並未詳盡地對 Nouvion 的先例及其所確立的規則進行討論，也並未從正面指出 Chiyu 案對 Nouvion 先例的闡釋進行具體評論（如前所述）。Nouvion 先例作為最終及不可推翻判決的 leading case，對其進行全面而準確的闡釋，對於解決內地法院判決是否最終及不可推翻判決的問題，具有非常重要的作用（見本書第十回的評論）。

第七回

Nintendo 案：內地法院判決的「逆襲神器」？

案件	: Nintendo of America Inc v. Bung Enterprises Ltd.
法庭	: 高等法院上訴法庭
案號	: HCA1189/2000
判決日期	: 2000 年 3 月 21 日

　　這是一個並不涉及內地法院判決的案件，而是一個涉及美國加州 Central District 區域法院（「加州法院」）缺席判決（default judgment）的案件。這個案件的時間還要回溯到 2000 年的 3 月，判決頒佈時間比第二回的武漢中碩虹案還要早了三個月。然而，在隨後的第二回到第五回的判決中，此判決均未被引用。直到五年後，第六回的李祐榮訴李瑞群案（「李祐榮案」），鍾安德法官才在他的異議判詞中引用本案，作為他關於內地法院判決不因審判監督制度而不屬最終及不可推翻的觀點的判例依據之一。鍾法官何以以本案判決作為支持內地法院判決的依據？我們一起在本回中解剖一下。

一、案情簡介

（一）基本事實

　　1997 年，原告人以知識產權侵權為由向加州法院起訴。被告人應訴並提出反訴，並且在該訴訟中被告人具有一定的有力的抗辯理由（meritorious defence）。然而，後來加州法院對被告人作出了披露 / 發現程序（discovery）方面的命令，被告人認為此命令對其負擔過重及不公，決定不予遵循並停止參與訴訟。結果，加州法院在 1999 年作出了對被告人不利的缺席判決。（1 段）

　　隨後，被告人經諮詢其美國律師決定申請撤銷前述缺席判決。1999 年 10 月，被告人的撤銷申請獲得成功，但加州法院附加了若干條件：（1）

支付原告人先前發生的 5 萬多美元訟費（主要是律師費）；（2）按照先前的發現程序命令提交相關文件；（3）安排全部證人在 1999 年 12 月前可在加州作證。被告人再次認為這些條件不公平，特別是訟費的支付將導致它無力繼續在美國進行訴訟。結果，加州法院於 1999 年 12 月再度作出被告人敗訴的缺席判決，被告人須向原告人支付將近 750 萬美元的賠償加利息（「加州判決」）。（1 段、2 段）

原告人以加州判決為基礎，向香港法院申請作出簡易判決（summary judgment），要求被告人支付加州判決的判定賠款加利息。（3 段、4 段）

（二）被告人的主張

被告人以加州判決不是最終及不可推翻的判決為理據作為抗辯。被告人認為，在一方面，加州法院作出加州判決，並未對案件的是非曲直（merits）進行考慮，加州法院實際上未就案件的是非曲直作任何的調查；在另一方面，加州判決可根據重審動議（reconsideration motion）或在上訴後由作為原審法院的加州法院作廢（set aside）。（7 段）

被告人分別採用了 Nouvion v. Freeman 先例（「Nouvion 先例」）及 The Sennar（No.2）先例（「Sennar 先例」）作為其上述主張的判例依據。其中引用了 Lord Watson 在 Nouvion 先例中關於可在任何時間被撤回或修改的外國判決不是最終及不可推翻的判詞（8 段），以及 Lord Diplock 在 Sennar 先例中關於最終判決是不能由作出判決的法院變更、重審或廢除的判決的論述（9 段）。

此外，被告人亦同時提出了加州判決違反自然正義（natural justice）的抗辯，認為被告人未被給予提出其訴訟主張的機會（14 段），被告人被要求支付大額訟費作為提交訴訟主張的條件亦屬不公（15 段），案件的事實調查及損害數額的評估是由原告人的律師而不是法官來完成（16 段）。

二、裁判觀點

本案的主審法官 Edward Chan 特委法官（陳法官）最終判決原告人勝訴，並對被告人的抗辯主張逐一駁回。

（一）關於最終及不推翻問題的裁判觀點

1. 陳法官指出，Lord Watson 在 Nouvion 先例中的判詞，必須結合該

案所處理的外國判決來理解。該案所處理的是西班牙法院頒佈的 remate judgment，這種判決是在法院僅對有限的事項進行審理後即作出，並且於可在隨後被啟動的正式審訊（plenary proceedings）中，法院可對案件的全部是非曲直進行全面審理；而 Lord Watson 提到的不被承認的 Court of Session 命令，則屬法院保留了變更其內容的權力的判決。（8 段）

2. 針對 Lord Diplock 在 Sennar 先例中的論斷，陳法官作了更詳細的討論。他首先以 Dicey & Moris 的 The Conflict of Laws 為依據指出，法律早已確立，為在香港執行外國判決的目的，即使是一個可以被原審法院廢除的缺席判決，該外國判決也可以是最終及不可推翻。陳法官同時引用了 1863 年的 Vanquelin v. Bouard 先例（「Vanquelin 先例」）。該案審理法官 Erle C J 認為，被申請執行的法國判決，縱然為缺席判決，並且根據法國法律該判決可因被告人出現而當然成為無效（become void as of course），亦不構成不予執行該判決的抗辯。因此，一個原審法院可以有權廢除的缺席判決並不是該判決成為不是最終及不可推翻的理據。被告人也不可以通過拒絕遵循外國法院的程序要求，或拒絕抗辯以使其在法律上處於更有利的位置。（10 段）

3. 陳法官進一步處理了 Lord Diplock 在 Sennar 先例中的論斷與 Erle C J 在 Vanquelin 先例中的觀點之間的衝突。他認為，兩位法官在表面上互相衝突的觀點，實際上可以協調（reconciled）。陳法官表示他認為，Lord Diplock 在表示「關於該訴因的判決是一個不能由作出該判決的法院改變、重審或廢除的判決」時，他是指作出判決的法院意使該判決僅具有臨時效力的案件，比如法院保留了改變或廢除判決權力的案件。顯然他並不是指基於被告人缺席的判決，或一方並未能應訴而可被廢除的判決。（11 段）

4. 陳法官也認定，加州判決是這樣作出的，即：在被告人缺席後，法官指示原告人起草判決並指出調查結果以供加州法院審查，而加州法院在審查後予以頒佈。同時，被告人也可以在法定期限內申請變更或修改加州判決的內容，或申請延長該申請期限，但被告人並未採取任何相關行動。（12 段）

5. 據上，陳法官認為，加州判決作為加州法院基於審查是非曲直而作出並根據加州法律具有既判力（res judicata），並且已就雙方的爭議作出裁斷，從而為最終及不可推翻的判決，在此問題上並不存在可爭論之點。（13 段）

（二）關於違反自然正義的裁判觀點

陳法官認為，在被告人所主張的違反自然正義的問題上，同樣並不存在任何可爭論點：

1. 陳法官首先指出，被告人認為加州法院的命令不正確，並不會導致加州法院因被告人不遵循該命令而作出的加州判決成為不可執行。實際上，被告人是故意不遵循該命令，並且清楚知道不遵循的結果會導致加州法院作出加州判決。（14 條）

2. 此外，被告人認為被要求支付大額訟費作為進行訴訟的前提構成不公。陳法官認為，被告人的財務問題屬其個人問題，其因個人的財政困難而不能參與訴訟不等於它沒有機會提交其訴訟主張。（15 段）

3. 對於被告人認為賠償數額是由原告人律師所定，而不是由法官經審理而定，陳法官認為，並無證據顯示加州法院法官在裁斷賠償數額時並未行使其司法職權（18 段）。而關於被告人認為法官在裁斷賠償數額時十分武斷，陳法官認為這其實是在主張法官的關於賠償數額的裁斷有誤，但作為明確的法律，在執行外國判決的訴訟中，外國法院內容錯誤並不是有效的抗辯理由（19 段）。

三、評析

被告人提出了兩大理據，即：（1）加州判決不是最終及不可推翻判決；及（2）加州判決違反自然正義。陳法官分別對這兩大理據進行了論證並予以否定。其中，關於加州判決是否為最終及不可推翻判決的論證，與內地法院判決是否為最終及不可推翻判決的問題直接相關。至於加州判決是否違反自然正義的問題，儘管在申請執行內地法院判決的訴訟中也有可能遇到這個問題，但這暫時不是內地法院判決在香港遇到的最大問題，也不是本回及本書的焦點。

對於最終及不可推翻的問題，被告人在抗辯中引用了 Nouvion 先例及 Sennar 先例。其中 Nouvion 是張澤祐法官在 Chiyu 案中認為內地法院判決不是最終及不可推翻判決時所引用的判例依據，因此，陳法官在本案中對 Nouvion 先例的立場就具有一定的意義。同時也要指出，陳法官在本案中並未提到或引用 Chiyu 案。

對待 Nouvion 先例的判詞，陳法官強調了必須結合該案所處理外國判決的特點。他同時強調了該案所處理的 remate judgment 僅對爭議的部份事項作出了有限度的審理。

陳法官將更大的篇幅留給了 Sennar 先例的討論。值得注意的是，儘管陳法官在本案中並未涉及 Chiyu 案，但其所討論的 Sennar 先例判詞，與張澤祐法官對 Nouvion 先例所闡釋並理解的司法見解，基本上是一致的。在本案中被引用的這兩個先例的判詞，均表示最終及不可推翻的判決，應該是不可被作出該判決的法院改變、重審或廢除的判決。

與張澤祐法官在 Chiyu 案中以 Nouvion 先例的相關判詞為依據否定內地法院判決為最終及不可推翻判決不同，陳法官在本案中，對 Sennar 先例的相關判詞進行了論證及限縮，認為 Lord Diplock 在 Sennar 先例中的上述觀點，不可能是指因被告缺席而作出，並因此可被廢除的外國判決，而是指「作出判決的法院意使該判決僅具有臨時效力」的外國判決。

四、陳法官判詞的意義

如前所述，陳法官雖然是對 Sennar 先例而未對 Nouvion 先例（及 Chiyu 案）進行深入分析，但由於 Sennar 先例的相關判詞與 Chiyu 案所引用的 Nouvion 先例的相關判詞基本一致，因此，陳法官在論證中，以 Vanquelin 先例為依據，對 Lord Diplock 在 Sennar 先例中的判詞進行了限縮，該論證按理也可以被考慮用於 Nouvion 的相關判詞。於是就引起了一個疑問，即：Chiyu 案對 Nouvion 先例判詞的引用和闡釋（與 Sennar 先例的判詞基本相同），是否就應該如此理所當然地被視為正確？

從本案中可以發現一個具有重要意義的情況，就是關於最終及不可推翻的問題，原來存在兩組系列判例（lines of authorities）。其中一組以 Nouvion 先例為基礎，另一組以時間更早的 Vanquelin 先例為基礎。從本系列的前五回的案件看，在香港法院引用 Nouvion 先例及 Chiyu 案的案件中，Vanquelin 先例及以其為基礎的後續判例（如本案），均未被引用。在這種情況下，對於 Chiyu 案對 Nouvion 先例的引用和闡釋，就更值得進行檢討了。

直到李祐榮案，鍾安德法官才明確引用本案及 Vanquelin 先例，並據以認為 Nouvion 先例所處理的 remate judgment 不同於內地法院判決，繼

而認為內地法院判決也可以是最終及不可推翻的判決。這是香港法院首次在處理內地法院判決是否最終及不可推翻判決時引用以 Vanquelin 先例為基礎的系列判例。當然，很遺憾的是，鍾法官的判詞僅僅是該判決中的少數異議判詞（有關討論見第六回（下））。

但無論如何，本案的重要意義，在於陳法官的判詞已經為重新審視內地法院判決在普通法下是否最終及不可推翻判決的問題，在普通法的論證上提供了思路。

此外，張澤祐法官在李祐榮案中的新立場，即認為關於內地法院判決是否為最終及不可推翻判決的問題在判例中還沒有定論（實際上改變了其自己在 Chiyu 案中的觀點），並認為該問題應在正式審訊中處理（有關討論見第六回（上）），更是為重新審視內地法院判決是否最終及不可推翻判決的問題指出了在程序上的途徑。

第八回

中國銀行訴楊凡案：內地法院判決終局性問題的一次總結

案件	：Bank of China Limited（中國銀行股份有限公司）
	v. Yang Fan（楊凡）
法庭	：高等法院原訟法庭
案號	：HCMP1797/2015
判決日期	：2016 年 4 月 29 日

一、案情簡介

（一）基本事實

原告人在山東省高級人民法院及日照市中級人民法院以被告人及其他幾方為被告提起了訴訟（「內地訴訟」）。（1 段至 13 段）

原告人就內地訴訟向香港法院申請了凍結被告人在香港資產的資產凍結令（Mareva Injunction）（「該禁制令」），並在該禁制令屆滿時向香港法院申請延長其期限（「本案」）。（1 段、14 段）

被告人要求解除該禁制令，並提出了若干理由，其中包括：（1）內地訴訟所涉合同中的管轄協議（「管轄約定」）並未指明有關爭議由內地法院裁定「而其他司法管轄區的法院則無權處理該等爭議」，從而不屬《內地判決（交互強制執行）條例（第 597 章）》（「《內地判決條例》」）所規定的「選用內地法院協議」（「排他管轄協議」），致使內地訴訟的判決（「內地判決」）日後無法根據《內地判決條例》在香港執行；（2）由於內地判決不符合香港普通法中「最終及不可推翻」的要求，其最終亦不應被香港法院認可和執行。在內地判決不能根據《內地判決條例》或普通法在香港執行的情況下，該禁制令未能滿足其申請條件，從而應予解除。（25 段）

根據香港《高等法院條例（第 4 章）》第 21M 條及相關判例，該

禁制令作為協助外地訴訟程序的中期濟助（interim relief in aid of foreign proceedings），其申請條件之一為所涉及的外地訴訟可形成一個可以在香港執行的判決。也正是基於這項條件，被告人為了要求撤銷該禁制令，主張內地判決不符合在香港執行的條件。（18 段至 20 段）

（二）爭議的焦點

被告人同時主張內地判決不符合《內地判決條例》的條件（未約定排他管轄協議）及不符合普通法執行的條件（內地判決非最終及不可推翻），本回將先僅就後者進行討論，以說明香港判例發展至此（2016 年），內地法院判決在香港判例法中在是否最終及不可推翻問題上的狀態。在此問題上，本案的爭議焦點主要在於：

1. 被告人的專家證人認為，內地法院判決基於人民檢察院根據審判監督制度所享有的抗訴權而不屬最終及不可推翻；並認為一旦啟動抗訴，作出原判決或裁定的法院就可能需要重審該案件。（43 段）

2. 在法律依據上，被告人的大律師引用了若干香港法院判決，認為香港法院在判決中已經表明對內地法院判決終局性的保留態度（46 段）。所引用的判決包括：Chiyu 案（有關討論見本書第一回）、李祐榮案（有關討論見本書第六回（上））、吳威訴劉一萍案（有關討論見本書簡評部份案例三、四）。

3. 原告人的專家證人則認為，作出原判決的法院重審案件並不是抗訴的必然結果。（43 段）

二、裁判觀點

針對內地判決是否為最終及不可推翻的判決，本案的主審法官原訟法庭杜法官在判詞中陳述了如下觀點：

1. 境外判決是否最終及不可推翻，應根據執行地法律決定，依據為 Nouvion 先例（36 段）。

2. 同樣以 Nouvion 先例為依據，杜法官指出根據該案審理法官 Lord Watson 的表述，一個最終及不可推翻的判決，必須是在宣告該判決的法院為最終及不可改變（final and unalterable in the court which pronounced it），但無須為不可被上訴（36 段）。

3. 對於被告人的大律師所引用的判例，主審法官指出並反覆強調了這些判例均在內地 2012 年《民事訴訟法》施行之前作出（第 46 段、第 52 段）。

4. 對於 Chiyu 案，杜法官指出審理此案的張澤祐法官確實作出了明確的裁斷，認為儘管內地法院不能被提起上訴，但因為抗訴程序已經被啟動有可能被原來做出該判決的法院在再審中變更，從而不屬最終及不可推翻的判決。但同時，杜法官也指出，張法官未表示抗訴程序本身導致任何內地法院均不屬最終及不可推翻（48 段）。

5. 杜法官繼而引用了張澤祐法官後來在李祐榮案的判詞，指出張法官明確確認，抗訴程序本身是否導致內地法院判決不屬最終及不可推翻之判決的問題，並未經高等法院上訴法庭作出權威性的（authoritatively，即可作為具有約束力的先例規則）裁判（49 段）。

6. 杜法官同時指出，張澤祐法官在李祐榮案中明確表示，上述問題是一項涉及重大公共利益的問題，從而不能在非正審程序中，在未聽到內地法律專家的口述意見的情況下，對該問題作出決定。杜法官也指出此項原則亦在隨後的伍威訴劉一萍案中獲得確認（49 段、50 段）。

7. 根據以上觀點，杜法官表示對於本案的禁制令申請而言，他同樣無須回答內地判決是否確為最終及不可推翻的問題，他僅僅需要判斷，為《內地判決條例》之目的，該內地判決是否有一定的可能（likely）為最終及不可推翻。作為結論，他認為原告人已經證明了其主張（內地判決很可能為最終及不可推翻）具有「良好的可爭辯論點（good arguable case）」（54 段）。

三、評析

首先要指出的是，儘管筆者將杜法官在本案中對內地判決是否為最終及不可推翻判決的論證，評價為對內地法院判決在普通法中的地位到目前為止的最後總結，但實際上，杜法官在本案中是否有必要對此問題進行論證其實是有疑問的。

如前所述，本案的雙方就兩個主要問題進行了爭辯，第一個是關於案件所涉的管轄約定是否構成《內地判決條例》所規定的「排他管轄協議」，

第二個則是原告人內地判決是否為最終及不可推翻的判決。第二個問題的必要性是以對第一個問題作出否定回答為前提。即只有認為案中所涉的管轄約定不構成《內地判決條例》所規定的排他管轄協議，才需要進一步判定最終及不可推翻的問題。若管轄約定構成《內地判決條例》中的排他管轄協議，則該內地判決即可按照《內地判決條例》的規定被視為最終及不可推翻，從而無須根據普通法來進行判斷。由於杜法官在第一個問題上已認定管轄約定構成了《內地判決條例》中的排他管轄協議（關於該部份判詞的評論，見本書第一部份附文《再評中國銀行訴楊凡案：對管轄協議裁判觀點的商榷》），因此並無進一步討論最終及不可推翻問題的需要。換言之，杜法官實際上是在不需要對最終及不可推翻的問題進行評判的情況下，提出了其在該問題上的觀點（儘管杜法官也指出他認為為《內地判決條例》的目的該內地判決屬於最終及不可推翻（54 段），但他實際上是根據普通法上的最終及不可推翻標準來對該問題進行分析）。

　　由於被告人大律師在抗辯中引用了若干否認內地法院判決為最終及不可推翻判決的判例，因此杜法官也類似於對有關判決進行了一次「縱述」，其中包括了在內地法院判決地位問題上具有重大意義的 Nouvion 先例、Chiyu 案及李祐榮案，而對後兩個案件中張澤祐法官的判詞更進行了較為詳細的討論。杜法官就三個案件判詞的論述，分述如下：

　　（1）對於張澤祐法官在李祐榮案中的判詞，杜法官主要是依據在李祐榮案中張澤祐法官對自己在 Chiyu 案中觀點所作的「澄清」（即明確表示內地法院判決是否因審判監督制度的存在而不屬最終及不可推翻判決的問題，是一個未決問題），作出其裁判結論，即關於內地判決是否為最終及不可推翻判決的問題，應在正式審訊中處理，而不應在目前的非正審程序（interlocutory proceedings）中解決。對於張澤祐法官的自行「澄清」，杜法官更明確闡釋為「上訴法庭從未認定內地判決因抗訴制度而不屬最終及不可推翻」，更明確表示上訴法庭「明示地（expressly）將該問題保留開放（left open）」。（54 段）

　　（2）至於張澤祐法官在 Chiyu 案中的判詞，杜法官甚至表示，張澤祐法官當時在查明內地審判監督制度的內容時，有可能被嚴重誤導（seriously misled）。這在相當程度上表明了杜法官對 Chiyu 案裁判觀點的否定。（54 段）

（3）對於 Nouvion 先例，杜法官對其中 Lord Watson 關於最終及不可推翻判決應為不能被原審法庭改變之判決的觀點進行了闡釋，表示按照其理解，Lord Watson 是指最終及不可推翻判決應指不能被原審法院「自願地（voluntarily）」改變之判決。杜法官加入「自願地」的表述，並且在判詞原文中加入下劃線再以括號表明這是為強調而加入。這實際上也默示地不認可張澤祐法官在 Chiyu 案中對 Lord Watson 觀點的闡釋。（53 段）

對於內地判決是否為最終及不可推翻判決的問題本身，杜法官根據其對內地法律關於審判監督制度當時的最新規定進行分析，特別是認為抗訴程序的處理結果實質上與上訴程序相同（與鍾安德法官在李祐榮案中的判詞一致），並以其對 Lord Watson 在 Nouvion 先例中判詞的前述闡釋為依據，表明其不傾向於認定（slow to hold）內地法院判決因抗訴制度而成為不是最終及不可推翻的判決。（53 段、54 段）

最後，杜法官明確表示其必須受上訴法庭在張祐榮案中關於內地法院判決地位問題應在正式審訊中處理的見解約束，亦即明確確認了該見解已構成具有約束力的先例規則。（54 段）

四、本案的意義

本案是關於內地訴訟的原告人是否能夠根據《高等法院條例》第 21M 條申請針對被告人在港資產的資產凍結令的非正審案件。本案明確確認了在內地進行的訴訟，當事人亦可根據《高等法院條例》第 21M 條申請禁制令以保全其權益。這是本案的一項具體意義。但本案更重要的一項意義，在於本案是香港法院在內地法院判決在普通法中地位問題上，亦即在內地法院判決是否為最終及不可推翻的問題上，最為全面的總結：

（1）本案明確確認，關於內地法院判決是否為最終及不可推翻判決的問題必須在正式審訊中解決的見解，是一項有約束力的先例規則。

（2）本案判決在一定程度上接受了鍾安德法官在李祐榮案異議判詞中支持內地判決為最終及不可推翻判決的觀點（關於該異議判詞的討論，見第六回（下）），也同時在相當程度上否定了張澤祐法官在 Chiyu 案中的觀點。

從正面看，本案的上述總結，既確定了解決內地法院判決在普通法中地位的問題的具體程序和途徑（必須進入正式審訊），也為如何論證支持內地法院判決為最終及不可推翻判決提供了論證思路。但從反面看，杜法官明確表明內地法院判決在普通法中地位的問題必須在正式審訊中解決，構成具有約束力的先例規則，實際上也同時為內地法院判決在目前不應根據普通法通過簡易程序獲得執行提供了明確依據。也就是說，與其他可直接根據普通法承認和執行的境外判決相比，內地法院判決仍然受到「歧視」。

第九回

協議管轄案件互認安排下的「優待」

司法協助安排 ： 《關於內地與香港特別行政區法院相互認可和執行
當事人協議管轄的民商事案件判決的安排》

香港本地立法 ： 《內地判決（交互強制執行）條例》（香港法例第
597 章）

案件 ： Bank of China Limited（中國銀行股份有限公司）
v. Yang Fan（楊凡）

法庭 ： 高等法院原訟法庭

案號 ： HCMP1797/2015

判決日期 ： 2016 年 4 月 29 日

　　講述內地法院判決在香港的曲折遭遇，當然不能不提 2008 年 8 月生效的《協議管轄判決安排》（即《關於內地與香港特別行政區相互認可和執行當事人協議管轄的民商事案件判決的安排》）。《協議管轄判決安排》的生效在「一國兩制」下的兩地區際司法協助實踐上是一件重要事件，它是內地與香港之間第一個有關法院判決相互認可和執行的司法協助安排，是內地法院判決在香港曲折遭遇中一個重要的「轉折」（儘管也是有限度的）。

一、《協議管轄判決安排》簡介

　　關於《協議管轄判決安排》的介紹，完全可以寫成一本書。但本回及本書的重點，在於講述內地法院判決的曲折遭遇，因此對《協議管轄判決安排》的介紹，也僅側重於這一角度，即重點介紹《協議管轄判決安排》與內地法院判決曲折遭遇密切相關的內容。

（一）香港本地立法

《協議管轄判決安排》作為內地與香港特區之間的司法協助安排，在香港的法制下，香港還需要通過本地立法予以實施。為此，香港立法會通過了《內地判決條例》（即《內地判決（交互強制執行）條例》（香港法例第 597 章））。在法律適用上，香港法院在處理相關案件時，所直接適用的是《內地判決條例》，而不是《協議管轄判決安排》。

（二）認可內地法院判決的條件

根據《協議管轄判決安排》相互認可和執行的民商事案件判決，限於《協議管轄判決安排》所規定的「特定法律關係」案件的判決，即當事人之間的民商事合同，其中並不包括僱傭合同以及自然人因個人消費、家庭事宜或者其他非商業目的而作為協議一方的合同（《協議管轄判決安排》3 條 2 款）。在此範圍內，可被認可和執行的判決還須符合一系列的具體條件。《內地判決條例》所規定的認可內地法院判決的條件是以《協議管轄判決安排》所規定的相互認可判決條件為依據，因此兩者所規定的條件基本一致。在《內地判決條例》的規定下，香港法院認可內地法院判決所採用的是登記程序，因此認可內地法院判決的條件亦體現為登記條件，包括：

（1）內地法院判決在《內地判決條例》生效當日（即 2008 年 8 月 1 日）或之後由符合條件的法院作出（5 (2) (a) 條）；

（2）選用內地法院協議是在《內地判決條例》生效當日或之後訂立（5 (2) (b) 條）；

（3）內地法院判決是最終及不可推翻的判決（5 (2) (c) 條）；

（4）內地法院判決在內地可以執行（5 (2) (d) 條）；及

（5）判決內容為款項的支付（5 (2) (e) 條）。

同時，《內地判決條例》也從反面的角度規定了已辦理的內地法院判決登記須作廢的情形：

（1）內地法院判決不符合上述五項登記條件（18 (1) (a) 條）；

（2）內地法院判決在違反《內地判決條例》的情況下登記（18 (1) (b) 條）；

（3）根據內地法律選用內地法院協議屬無效（18（1）（c）條）；

（4）內地法院判決已經履行（18（1）（d）條）；

（5）香港法院對有關案件享有專屬管轄權（18（1）（e）條）；

（6）債務人未經合法傳召，或經合法傳召但未獲得充分時間進行答辯，經內地法院公告送達除外（18（1）（f）條、18（2）條）；

（7）內地法院判決以欺詐手段取得（18（1）（g）條）；

（8）香港法院或仲裁機構已就內地法院判決各方之間的同一訴因作出判決或仲裁裁決（18（1）（h）條）；

（9）香港以外地方的法院或仲裁機構已就內地法院判決各方之間的同一訴因作出判決或仲裁裁決，該判決或仲裁裁決已獲香港法院承認或強制執行（18（1）（i）條）；

（10）強制執行內地法院判決違反公共政策（18（1）（j）條）；或

（11）內地法院判決經內地上訴或再審被推翻或作廢（18（1）（k）條）。

二、《協議管轄判決安排》及《內地判決條例》下的「最終及不可推翻的判決」的問題

在普通法下，內地法院判決遇到最大的障礙，就是「最終及不可推翻的判決」的條件。《協議管轄判決安排》及《內地判決條例》即有針對性地將此問題徹底解決。《內地判決條例》儘管仍然在第5（2）（c）條明確規定了內地法院判決須為最終及不可推翻的判決作為認可和執行的條件，但同時又在第6（1）條中，規定了按照《協議管轄判決安排》香港一方所必須認可的內地法院判決，視為符合第5（2）（c）最終及不可推翻判決的要求，實質上是「虛化」（甚至是變相放棄）了最終及不可推翻的條件。

不過，要注意的是，基於 Chiyu 案判詞所帶來的潛在困難（即認為內地法院判決可因原審法院可重新審理爭議〔基於審判監督程序〕而不屬最終及不可推翻判決），最高人民法院與香港律政司雙方在協商過程中達成了一項特別安排的協議，即在《協議管轄判決安排》中加入一項規定，明確規定經對於香港法院認可和執行的內地法院判決，若內地法院按照審判

監督程序進行再審，則必須由作出生效判決的上一級人民法院提審（《協議管轄判決安排》3 款）。基於這一安排，基本有效避免了內地法院判決在獲得香港法院認可和執行後可由原審法院進行再審的情形。但也要注意，這其實並沒有把問題完全解決，因為當作出生效判決的法院為最高人民法院時，即不可能由上級法院進行再審。也就是說，倒是最高人民法院作出的生效判決在獲得香港法院認可和執行後，仍可能基於審判監督程序而由最高人民法院重審。但無論如何，即使如此，最高人民法院作出的生效判決，仍然基於《內地判決條例》6（1）條的規定而被視為最終及不可推翻的判決。

三、「具有唯一管轄權」約定的要求及內地法院判決目前享受的「優待」

在《協議管轄判決安排》《內地判決條例》的規定下，內地法院判決的「最終及不可推翻」障礙算是清除了，但這是否就意味着內地法院判決在香港的認可和執行就能一路暢通？恐怕還不能這樣定論。作為以協議管轄為基礎的判決互認安排，《協議管轄判決安排》對當事人管轄協議的要求作出了明確的規定。《協議管轄判決安排》3 條 1 款規定：「以書面形式**明確約定**內地人民法院或者香港特別行政區法院具有**唯一管轄權**的協議。」起碼就此規定的文義而言，內地法院判決在香港獲得承認和執行，理應以當事人通過書面形式「明確約定」了內地法院「具有唯一管轄權」為前提。此要求是相當嚴格的，即要求當事人約定了所選擇的內地法院「具有唯一管轄權」，而且其約定必須明確。若未表明內地法院的管轄具有唯一性（採用「排他性」的表述應有相同效力），或約定不明確，則不符合該規定。

不過，《內地判決條例》在定義管轄協議時，其表述與《協議管轄判決安排》的上述規定並不完全一致。《內地判決條例》將所要求的管轄協議稱為「選擇內地法院協議」，並定義為「**指明**由內地法院或某內地法院裁定在或可能在與該指明合約有關連的情況下產生的爭議，而**其他司法管轄區的法院則無權處理該等爭議**」的協議。與《協議管轄判決安排》的表述相比，《內地判決條例》的定義未採用「明確約定」而採用了「指明」的表述。在文義上，應該可以比較肯定的認為，「明確約定」要求其約定

是明確，而不是沒有約定或約定不明。如果僅約定「由內地法院／內地某法院管轄」，而未約定由內地法院／內地某法院「排他」管轄，或未表明所選擇的內地法院／內地某法院「具有唯一管轄權」，就很可能會被認定為不符合《協議管轄判決安排》「明確約定」的要求。然而，《內地判決條例》所採用的「指明」是否與「明確約定」等同，則可引起疑問。在文義上，固然可以將指明中的「明」解釋為「明確」，但若將「指明」與「明確約定」比較，似乎在感觀上「指明」的要求不如「明確約定」的要求強烈和嚴格。

在實際上，香港法院在根據《內地判決條例》處理認可和執行內地法院判決的申請時，確實對管轄協議的要求採取了較為寬鬆的立場，認為無需當事人「明確」採用「唯一」或「排他」等表述。這也就是本回標題所說的內地法院判決目前所享受的「優待」。在中國銀行案中，法官即認為儘管合同中的管轄條款並未採用「唯一」或「排他」等表述，亦可構成《內地判決條例》中的選擇內地法院協議，其論證主要是以合同解釋規則為理據，通過解釋認定當事人具有約定排他管轄的意思表示。關於該判決見解的分析，詳見本書第一部份附文《再評中國銀行訴楊凡案：對管轄協議裁判觀點的商榷》，在此不贅。

四、「優待」的意義

既然香港法院已經在判決中認為對選擇內地法院判決可從寬解釋，豈非香港判例法已確立了從寬解釋的先例原則？恐怕不能這麼認為。一方面，該案僅僅是原訟法庭的判例，並不具有當然的約束力；另一方面，在該案中，法官的論證是否已足夠充分，不無可商榷之處，而被告人似乎亦未進行充分的抗辯。如前所述，在該案中，法官主要是根據合同解釋的判例原則認定案中的管轄條款屬選擇內地法院協議，然而，似乎仍然有不少問題存在可爭議的空間。以下列舉若干：

1. 在將問題作為合同解釋問題來處理時，法官是否有考慮到，這可能不是一個純粹的合同解釋問題，而首先還可能是一個成文法解釋的問題，即關於《內地判決條例》中有關選擇內地法院判決的條文及術語的解釋問題。在邏輯上，是否應先解釋法律條文（作為第一步），然後再解釋合同條款（作為第二步），最後再判斷後者是否符合前者的要求（作為第三步）？

2. 如果確認此問題首先是一個成文解釋問題，那還可能引起一個在「一國兩制」法制下的特殊法律問題，即在解釋作為本地立法的《內地判決條例》時，法官是否須考慮及如何考慮《內地判決條例》與《協議管轄判決安排》相應規定的關係（特別是在兩者的表述不甚一致的情況下）。

3. 在該案中，法官直接適用了香港判例法上的合同解釋規則來解釋當事人之間的管轄約定，是否未注意合同解釋的準據法本身需要先根據衝突法規則予以確定？

4. 如果應先根據衝突法規則確定準據法，該案中的合同解釋問題的準據法，是否有可能是內地法律，而不是香港法律？

5. 如果準據法為內地法律，是否還能得出當事人所約定的管轄條款（根據內地法判斷），就是符合《內地判決條例》中選擇內地法院協議定義的結論？在程序上是否需要先調查內地相關法律的內容？

由此可見，認為香港判例已經確立了在選擇內地法院協議問題上應採用從寬解釋的先例原則，未免言之過早。至少從律師的角度看，目前還不宜給客戶提供這樣的法律建議：只要有選擇內地法院的管轄約定，那怕沒有明示「唯一」或「排他」，內地法院判決也符合在香港承認和執行的要求。

第十回

終局篇：溯源 Nouvion 先例，重新審視 Chiyu 案

案件	：	Nouvion v. Freeman and Another
法庭	：	英國上議院法庭 House of Lords
案號	：	（1889）15 App. Cas.1
判決日期	：	1889 年 11 月 22 日

　　1889 年，光緒十五年，光緒皇帝親政，第二國際成立，李大釗先生誕辰，梵高畫了 Starry Night……英國上議院法庭還作出了一個判決。這個判決，居然成為了在一百多年以後新中國法院所作出判決的桎梏。哪怕是已經進入了新時代，哪怕香港已經回歸祖國並成為特別行政區，這個判決仍然讓內地法院的判決在香港難以獲得承認和執行。這就是 Nouvion v. Freeman and Another 案的判決（「Nouvion 先例」或「本案」）。Nouvion 先例是內地法院判決在香港所遇到的曲折遭遇的源頭，因此，要對內地法院判決在香港獲得承認和執行所遇到障礙的問題追根溯源，就必須追溯至此先例。

一、案情簡介

　　1872 年，原告人（上訴人）與 Henderson 先生簽署兩份讓與契據，據以將位於西班牙的兩個礦場讓與於 Henderson 先生，Henderson 先生則須向原告人支付價款若干。該讓與契據在塞維利亞聖羅曼（San Roman, Seville）的登記部門辦理了登記。

　　根據西班牙法律，按照上述登記方式辦理了登記的讓與契據，其債權人可在債務人未履行債務時，直接根據特定的簡易程序（在本案判決中法官翻譯為 "summary proceedings" 或 "executive proceedings"，本文稱「特別簡易程序」）向法院提起訴訟。只要符合條件，法院即作出原告勝訴的簡易判決（按照西班牙語稱 "remate" 判決，本案法官表述為 "remate judgment" 或 "executive judgment"，本文稱「特別簡易判決」）。

1878 年，原告人按照特別簡易程序向西班牙法院起訴，要求 Henderson 先生支付讓與契據下尚未付清的價款。西班牙法院作出了支持原告人的特別簡易判決（「本案簡易判決」）。

1883 年，當時 Henderson 先生已經離世，被告人（被上訴人）成為了 Henderson 先生的遺囑執行人。原告人以簡易判決為依據，主張自己是 Henderson 先生的債權人，並據以在英國起訴，主張自己應成為 Henderson 先生在英國的遺產管理人。

經指示，訴訟中所涉及的其中一個法律問題，即「原告人在本訴訟中據以起訴的簡易判決，是否為一個可獲得支持（could be sustained）的判決」，須經由 Chancery Division 的法官通過正審（trial）審理。

Chancery Division 的法官 North J.，經審理作出了支持原告人的裁決，認為本案簡易判決是一個可獲得支持的判決。但此裁決隨後被上訴法庭推翻，原告人遂上訴至上議院法庭，並由 Lord Herschell、Lord Watson、Lord Bramwell 及 Lord Ashbourne 四位法官審理。四位法官分別發表了判詞。

四位法官均支持了上訴庭的裁判，認為本案簡易判決並不是可在英國直接執行的外國判決，駁回了原告人的上訴。

二、裁判觀點

如前所述，在本案中，經指示提交審訊處理的法律問題，是「原告人在本訴訟中據以起訴的簡易判決，是否為一個可獲得支持（could be sustained）的判決」的問題。這也是本案爭議的焦點。在訴訟中，原告人的代表大律師認為，能在英國執行的外國法院判決，必須是經過具有管轄權的法院審理，並且為最終及不可推翻的判決。四位法官中的三位法官均直接採用了原告人的此項觀點，並依照最終及不可推翻判決的標準展開論證。最終，四位法官雖作出了相同的裁判結果，但他們的論證各有側重，以下稍作展開，用儘量簡短的篇幅來對本判決及各法官的判詞加以概括說明。

（一）Lord Herschell

1. Lord Herschell 發表了本案的主要判詞（lead judgment），因此篇幅

相對較長。他首先比較具體地介紹了西班牙法律下的特別簡易判決及其據以作出的特別簡易程序所具有的特點：

（1）原告人通過特別簡易程序行使讓與契據下的權利，被告人在此程序中僅可以提出有限的抗辯，他只能在假設讓與契據為有效的基礎上，主張債權人已放棄債權，或其已經履行債務的抗辯。

（2）在作出特別簡易判決後，雙方當事人可完全任意（at perfect liberty）向相同的法院提起名為完全訴訟（plenary action）的訴訟程序（「完全程序」）。完全程序類似於普通程序，雙方當事人可就爭議進行全面的爭論，其中債務人可提出任何抗辯，法院亦須對案件的全部爭議事項進行審理。

（3）即使是在特別簡易程序中已經處理過的爭議事項，雙方均可再度爭論，法院亦須予以處理，並且不受特別簡易判決的影響。在完全程序中，特別簡易判決不被給予效力（no effect is given），更不具有既判力（res judicata）。

2. 在作出上述介紹後，Lord Herschell 引用了 William v. Jones 的先例，並以以下判詞為論證的基礎：「當一個具有管轄權的法院，經審理認定了某一人應向另一人支付一筆款項時，即產生了一項支付該款項的義務，據此一項以執行該判決的債務訴訟可獲得支持」。同時，Lord Herschell 也接受了原告人大律師所提出的以最終及不可推翻作為判斷標準的觀點。

3.Lord Herschell 進一步對上述判詞及標準進行闡釋，認為所謂最終及不可推翻是指作出判決的法院最終及不可推翻地作出了判決，從而永久地確立（for ever established）其成為債務存在的終局證據（conclusive evidence）。如果在作出判決的法院中，該判決不是終局，儘管存在該判決，但該判決可在該法院被異議，並經過適當的程序該異議會再經審理，並最終宣告當事人之間不存在任何債務，則不應被視為債務存在的最終及不可推翻的證據。

4. Lord Herschell 進一步解釋，可在英國法院執行的外國判決，應該是經過外國具有管轄權的法院根據其訴訟程序對案件的全部爭議進行了審理（whole merits of the case were open），並最後作出了認定債務存在的最終裁決，並且該判決不能在作出判決的法院中被爭議。但是，若當事人可

就該判決向上級法院上訴，則仍然屬最終及不可推翻的判決。

5. 據上，Lord Herschell 認為，本案簡易判決如同未確立債務的判決，並且相同的法院隨後可宣告不存在任何債務；同時，本案簡易判決也不同於可被上訴的判決，因此，並不屬可在英國執行的外國判決。

（二）Lord Watson

1. Lord Watson 引用了 Godard v. Gray 和 Schibsby v. Westenhloz 兩個案件作為判例依據。對於所引用判例所確立的法律原則，他闡釋如下：

（1）在論證中從反面表示，在被引用的判決中，並沒有任何判決裁定英國法院須承認可由原審法院廢止或改變的外國判決。

（2）從所引用的判例看，獲得英國法院承認的外國判決，均為基於「知悉原因（*causa cognita*）」（即經過調查）而作出的判決，從而英國法院無需對案件的爭議事項（merits of the controversies）進行審查。

（3）獲得承認和執行的外國判決，不必是不能被提起上訴，但必須是對於原審法院而言是最終及不可改變（final and inalterable）。

2. 關於本案簡易判決，Lord Watson 認為，據以作出本案簡易判決的特別簡易程序，並無需對案件的爭議事項作出全面的處理，被告人只能以已經履行、債權人已棄權為抗辯；更嚴重的是，作出特別簡易判決的同一個法院，隨後有權在完全程序中處理債務人所提出的任何及每一個爭議事項，在該程序中法院可重審特別簡易程序中已經處理過的爭議。若法院在完全程序中的裁判不同於特別簡易程序，實際上就是將特別簡易程序廢除（nullified）。

3. 據上，Lord Watson 認同 Lord Herschell 的裁判。

（三）Lord Bramwell

1. Lord Bramwell 同樣引用了 William v. Jones 作為其論證的判例依據，表示該案判詞認為：當有管轄權的法院所作出的判決表明存在一項債務，這就存在一項判定債務人支付該款項的法律義務。

2. 對於本案簡易判決，Lord Bramwell 以反問的方式來進行描述：當一個人有權表示「我不欠任何錢，並不存在一個要求我支付任何錢的判決」，該人怎麼可以被認為承擔了一項法律義務？

3. 據此，Lord Bramwell 認為本案簡易判決並不屬 William v. Jones 判決中的判決。

（四）Lord Ashbourne

1. Lord Ashbourne 並未明確引用判例，但直接採用了原告人大律師的觀點作為論證的大前提，表示：不存在任何爭議，外國判決在英國不會被支持並作為本案請求的基礎，除非該外國判決是最終及不可推翻。

2. 關於本案簡易判決，Lord Ashbourne 認為：據以作出本案簡易判決的訴求，只能以有限的事由予以抗辯。本案簡易判決，並不是一個其所處理的請求可被全面爭辯和抗辯的判決。因此，無論在任何意義上，這都不是一個就案件全部爭議進行審理的審訊。他並表示他不知道在英國存在任何一個承認這種判決的先例，在雙方的爭論中以及下級法院的審理中也沒有提到這樣的先例。

3. Lord Ashbourne 進一步認為，本案簡易判決是一個特殊（peculiar）判決，據他所知，在英國法律中不存在任何可類比的情形。他更強調，在英國法律和蘇格蘭法律中，均不存在類似特別簡易判決的、可以被一項可重新進行全面審理的程序完全廢除而成為一張絕對無用的廢紙的判決。

4. 他還指出，法庭實際上是在被要求承認一個判決在英國的法律下為最終及不可推翻，但實際上，據以作出該判決的西班牙法律本身，並不認為它是最終及不可推翻。

5. 據上，Lord Ashbourne 認同其他法院的裁定，駁回了上訴。

三、評析

本案四位法官的判詞，儘管篇幅長短不一，論證重點亦各有側重，但各人的論證均比較充分。綜合四位法官的判詞，有以下幾點值得注意：

1. 根據本案所引用的判例及幾位法官所作的說明，過去的判例承認外國判決的法理基礎，是外國判決已經確立了一項可執行的債務，但並未明確如何認定此項債務是否確已成立。在此案件中，以當事人的主張為基礎，本案法院明確確立了「最終及不可推翻」的判斷標準。即以外國判決是否為「最終及不可推翻」為標準，認定其是否應獲得英國法院的承認。

2. 四位法官的論證雖各有側重，但歸納他們的判詞，可發現在認定本案簡易判決是否為最終及不可推翻時，他們的主要考慮因素不外乎三個方面，即：其一，在特別簡易程序中，被告人只能提出有限及特定的抗辯，法院也只對這些相應的事項進行審理；其二，原審法院可因當事人的任意申請，而重新對案件進行全面的審理（不限於原先的有限事項）；其三，原審法院通過重新審理，可改變或廢除特定簡易判決。

3. 在判詞中，幾位法官在論證中均強調了「所引用的判例（cited authorities）」，說明他們的判詞及論證均以當事人提交的判例為依據，似乎說明了法官並未自行查明相關判例。

4. 最後，可能足以成為本案判例的重大瑕疵的是，在本案中，四位法官均未引用 1863 年的 Vanquelin v. Bouard 先例（「Vanquelin 先例」）。在 Vanquelin 先例中，審理法官 Erle C J 認為，被申請執行的法國判決，縱然為缺席判決，並且根據法國法律該判決可因被告人出現而被原審法院宣告為無效，亦不構成不予執行該判決的抗辯。在 Nintendo 案中，香港上訴法庭 Edward Chan 特委法官（陳法官）即引用了 Vanquelin 先例作為依據，認為該案中的美國加州法院缺席判決，並不因該法院可以宣告判決無效或重審案件而被認定為不是最終及不可推翻（關於該案的討論見本書第七回）。在 Vanquelin 先例下，外國法院判決是否僅僅因原審法院可廢除或改變該判決，即不屬最終及不可推翻，實際上尚有討論空間。也就是說，在未引用 Vanquelin 先例的情況下，本案四位法官的論證是否完全充分，甚至是否遺漏了應予適用的重要先例，均存在重新審視的空間。

四、Nouvion 先例引起的疑問：Chiyu 案及相關判例是否妥當？

在對 Nouvion 先例進行上述分析後，難以不對以 Nouvion 先例作為判例依據的 Chiyu 案（關於該案的討論見本書第一回）中的觀點產生疑問。筆者認為，至少有以下問題值得重新審視：

（一）對 Nouvion 先例判詞的引用斷章取義？

1. 如前所述，Nouvion 案一共有四位法官對案件進行審理，並且分別發表了判詞，對本案簡易判決是否可獲得英國法院承認的問題進行了論證。然而，Chiyu 案判詞僅引用了其中兩位法官（Lord Herschell 和 Lord Watson）的判詞，而且所引用的只是兩位法官判詞中的一小部份。

2. 也如前述，Nouvion 先例四位法官在論證中對本案簡易判決所考量的因素，並不限於作出特別簡易判決的法院是否能自行廢除或改變該判決，同時也考慮了在特定簡易程序中，案件的爭議事項不能獲得全面審理，以及考慮了在隨後的完全程序中法院可就爭議事項進行全面的審理。可見 Chiyu 案判決對 Nouvion 先例的引用，不僅在「量」上值得商榷，而且在「質」上也不無重新審視的空間。

（二）對 Nouvion 先例中規則的認定及解釋

1. Chiyu 案法官根據 Nouvion 先例所認定的法律原則，是境外判決必須是對於作出該判決的法院而言是最終的及不可改變的。如當事人在判決作出後可將相同的爭議提交給相同的法院重新審理，並可宣告債務根本不存在，則該判決並不是最終及不可推翻。

2. 這一法律原則的「提煉」，僅涉及 Nouvion 先例判詞所提到的三個考慮因素中的一個因素。對於 Nouvion 先例法官所考慮到的在特別簡易程序中法院僅審理有限而特定的爭議事項，以及在完全程序中可對案件進行全面審理，均未有涉及。

3. 不可否認，假若 Chiyu 案判決對 Nouvion 先例進行了更全面的引用，並對該先例中的其他考慮因素也進行了考慮，Chiyu 案法官仍然可以通過認為其他兩方面的因素不屬重要事實（not material facts）的相關因素，而將其排除在判例原則之外，從而仍然「提煉」出相同的法律原則。然而，Chiyu 案的判詞對其他兩個方面的因素不僅未加論證，而更是隻字未提，則上述的「提煉」是否屬對 Nouvion 先例所確立法律原則的準確闡述，恐怕是留下了極大的討論空間。

（三）未引用 Vanquelin 先例

1. 對於 Vanquelin 先例，Nouvion 先例本身亦未引用，對 Nouvion 先例也存在未全面引用之嫌的 Chiyu 案判決，自然也未引用 Vanquelin 先例。

2. Vanquelin 先例在境外判決的最終及不可推翻認定標準上具有非常重要的意義，其所確立的法律原則至少從表面上看，或與 Nouvion 先例法官的部份見解有所衝突，兩個先例的觀點有待調和。在這種情況下，Chiyu 案從 Nouvion 先例所「提煉」的法律原則，恐怕就難以認為是一項已確立的原則（established principle），而關於何謂最終及不可推翻的判決，法

律仍然處於懸而未決（unsettled）的狀態。

五、重新審視相關判例原則的意義

1. 從前文的分析可知，無論是如何對所引用先例進行引述和闡釋，抑或是否已經全面引用可適用的先例，Chiyu 案判決似乎均存在相當的不足。Chiyu 案判決不僅存在可重新審視的空間，而且對其進行重新審視意義亦非常重大。

2. Chiyu 案所確立的觀點，即作出境外判決的法院有權廢止或改變該判決，該判決即不屬最終及不可推翻；反言之，最終及不可推翻的判決，必須是對於作出判決的法院而言屬最終的及不可改變的判決。此觀點及其對後續判決的影響可謂根深蒂固，若干後來的案例均直接接受了此觀點作為判例原則，如 Tan Tay Cuan 案（見本系列第三回）、林哲民第一案（見第四回）、林哲民第二案（見第五回）等。

3. Chiyu 案的上述見解，不僅在後續判決中被採用，甚至，在有關兩地相互認可和執行協議管轄案件判決安排的香港立法會文獻中，亦被採用。在 2005 年 10 月，香港特區政府政務司司長辦公室行政處及律政司向立法會司法及法律事務委員會「香港特別行政區與內地相互執行商事判決」參考文件（立法會 CB（2）122/05-06（04）號文件）中，其中明確表示「特區及內地有不同方法決定一個判決是否可執行。**根據普通法，判決必須是最終及不可推翻的，才可執行。其意思是，一宗案件不可由原來的審判法院再審⋯⋯。**」

4. 誠然，在後來的李祐榮案中，作為 Chiyu 案主審法官的張澤祐法官（張法官）的立場有所改變，表示他並未認為內地法院判決因再審制度的存在而不屬最終及不可推翻，並認為此問題尚未有定論，應通過正式審訊而不是在非正審程序中處理。同時，張法官也重新解讀了 Nouvion 先例的判詞，表示 Nouvion 案先例的「法庭沒有清楚說明到底是不是只要存在着一個可以推翻『remate 判決』的制度，法庭就已具備穩固的基礎去裁定這類判決不是最終及不可被推翻的判決」（關於該案的討論見本書第六回（上））。然而，張法官判詞的重點，似乎主要還是在於作為事實部份的內地法院判決在再審制度下性質的問題，尚未明確地否定其在 Chiyu 案中所確立的「原審法院有權再審即不是最終及不可推翻」的原則。隨後在中

國銀行訴楊凡案中，該案判決仍然引用張法官在 Chiyu 案所確立的前述原則，似乎仍然是以該原則作為大前提，只是認為在再審制度下的內地法院判決，作為事實（小前提）是否應被認定為最終及不可推翻判決仍未有定論（關於該案的討論見本書第八回）。

5. 筆者認為，重新審視 Nouvion 先例及 Chiyu 案之所以重要，在於假若能通過重新審視，重新確立普通法中關於最終及不可推翻判例的認定標準，特別是若能按照 Vanquelin 先例及 Nintendo 案的見解完全改變「原審法院可以重審即非最終及不可推翻」的觀點，至少將內地法院判決按照類似於英美法國家的缺席判決處理，則將可徹底解決內地法院判決因審判監督制度的存在所引起的爭論，從而在最大程度上掃清內地法院判決根據普通法在香港執行所遇到的障礙。在審判監督制度下，內地法院的判決還可能存在各種不同的狀態。比如內地法院判決的狀態可因當事人、法院還是檢察院啟動審判監督程序而有所不同，亦可因是否為最高人民法院作出的終審判決（基本上只能由原審法院重審）而有不同。若「原審法院可以重審即非最終及不可推翻」的觀點維持不變，則內地法院判決恐怕仍有許多機會被認定為不屬最終及不可推翻。

6. 當然，目前內地與香港正在協商全面的相互認可和執行民商事案件判決的安排，日後一旦落實有關安排，也必然能更徹底地掃清內地法院判決在香港執行的障礙。但是，就目前而言，由於安排所設定的互認條件，要比一般認為的普通法承認條件嚴格許多，為兩地的協商亦帶來一些困難。若通過重新審視普通法原則，使普通法的承認條件與安排所設定的互認條件更為接近，則必能大大地降低兩地協商的難度。

7. 要強調的是，所謂重新審視，並不是指由哪個權力部門對問題進行檢討。既然是普通法的問題，就應通過普通法的方式來進行重新審視。簡言之，就是要在具體的案件中，由當事人（主要是原告人）的代表律師，對有關判例進行深入研究，發現其中的可爭論空間，據理力爭，以「重新發現」普通法的正確原則。

簡評：涉及內地法院判決是否最終及不可推翻問題的其他判例

案例一：New Link Consultants Ltd v. Air China and Others 案

案件	：New Link Consultants Ltd v. Air China and Others 案
法庭	：高等法院上訴法庭
案號	：HCA515/2001
判決日期	：2004 年 5 月 3 日

一、案情簡介

本案原告人同時起訴中國國航、南方航空及東方航空三家內地航空公司，主張三個被告人自己或其重組前主體未履行它們與原告之間的合資合同及相關協議。三個被告人則以非便利公堂（即不方便法院 forum non conveniens）為由申請擱置訴訟。

根據判例法的原則，在非便利公堂申請人（被告人）初步證明了香港並不是唯一的自然及合適的公堂，並存在一個更便利的替代公堂後，原告人即須證明在替代公堂進行訴訟會剝奪原告人依法擁有的任何個人或司法優勢（legitimate personal or juridical advantage），才可駁回被告人的申請。

在聆訊中，被告人成功完成了初步的證明責任，證明內地法院為合適的替代公堂。為了對抗被告人的申請，原告人提出以下理據以證明在內地進行訴訟會剝奪其依法擁有的個人或司法優勢：（1）內地判決缺乏終局性（lack of finality）（93-96 段）；（2）在內地進行訴訟會造成不公（bias）（97-100 段）；（3）內地法院缺乏經驗（103 段）。

二、簡評

儘管本案涉及到內地法院判決的終局性問題，但此項由原告人提出的

主張，與內地法院判決在香港的承認和執行並無關係。原告人只是將內地法院判決缺乏終局性作為其主張在內地進行訴訟將剝奪其依法所享有優勢的其中一項因素。因此，本書並未對本案進行重點評論。

但是，在本案中擔任被告人內地法律專家證人是知名法學家江平終身教授。江平教授在本案中所提供的法律意見堪稱典範，法官在判詞中亦高度稱讚，與原告人專家證人提供的法律意見形成鮮明對比（102 段）。

案例二：陳國柱訴陳桂洲案

案件	：陳國柱 訴 陳桂洲案
法庭	：高等法院原訟法庭
案號	：HCA663/2005
判決日期	：2008 年 7 月 29 日

一、案情簡介

原告人與被告人因雙方之間在內地投資設廠的協議發生爭議，原告人起訴要求被告人歸還其所投入的機器及／或賠償損害。被告人則反訴原告人要求償還貸款及賠償違約損害。（1 段至 3 段）

被告人則在香港訴訟之前已向汕頭市中級人民法院對原告人提起訴訟，並取得了勝訴判決（「內地判決」）。原告人上訴至廣東省高級人民法院被駁回。（4 段）

雙方大律師均同意內地判決並不構成事情已決（*res judicata*）（即既判力），因此內地判決對本案在香港的審理並無影響（4 段）；法官亦以張澤祐法官在李祐榮案中的判詞表示內地判決因再審制度的存在而可能不算是最終及不可推翻的判決（6 段）。

二、簡評

由於雙方代表律師並未就內地判決是否最終及不可推翻判決的問題發生爭議，反而同時認為內地判決不具有既判力，亦即認為內地判決不是最終及不可推翻判決；法官也未對此問題進行論證，只是簡單表示內地法院「可能不算」是最終及不可推翻判決；因此本案在內地判決是否構成最終及不可推翻判決問題上並不具有太大的判例價值。

但是，從這一判決的處理可知，在香港普通法的對抗式訴訟制度下，若當事人未就法律問題進行爭論，法官就未必會主動處理該法律問題。

案例三：伍威訴劉一萍申請禁制令案

案件	：Wu Wei （伍威） v. Liu Yi Ping （劉一萍） 申請禁制令案
法庭	：高等法院原訟法庭
案號	：HCA1452/2004
判決日期	：2009 年 1 月 30 日

一、案情簡介

本案的案情非常複雜，但為了本簡評的目的，以下僅對案情進行較簡單的說明。

本案所涉及的是夫妻在離婚後的財產歸屬糾紛，其中一項主要爭議是雙方曾經簽署的財產安排協議（「財產協議」）。

在本案之前，被告人以財產協議為依據在廣州法院起訴並取得勝訴判決（「內地判決」）。在本案的主程序中，原告人則主張財產協議無效，並要求確認在香港的若干存款屬其個人所有。

在本案的此項程序中，原告人根據《高等法院條例》第 21L 條申請禁制令，要求法庭判令被告人將若干款項存入法庭或被告人已被凍結的香港

銀行賬戶。

被告人在本案的主程序中對原告人提出反訴,要求承認和執行內地判決;在本案的此項禁制令申請程序中,則主張內地判決為最終及不可推翻判決,從而已不存在需要在正式審訊中審理的重大事項(serious issue to be tried)(即原告人無從勝訴),原告人的申請也不能獲得支持(存在需要正式審訊審理的重大事項是原告人成功申請禁制令的條件之一)。

法官引用李祐榮案的多數判詞,指出內地判決是否為最終及不可推翻的判決是一個複雜的問題,必須在正式審訊中處理。而內地判決是否為最終及不可推翻判決的問題,實際上本身就是更需在正式審訊中審理的重大事項(100段、101段),並據此支持了原告人的禁制令申請。

二、簡評

在這個判決中,法官只是以內地判決是否為最終及不可推翻判決必須在正式審訊中處理為由,認定此問題本身就是需要在正式審訊中審理的重大事項,並未對問題進行深入分析。因此,本書也未對本案進行深入的評論。

需要指出的是,被告人只是在反訴中主張內地判決為最終及不可推翻判決並應予以執行,並未主張原告人因內地判決構成具有既判力的判決而不應在香港重新起訴。但法官則主動提出此問題,說明香港法官對於當事人可主張但未主張的觀點,有時候也會主動提出(94段)。

案例四：伍威訴劉一萍申請暫緩執行禁制令案

案件	：Wu Wei（伍威）v. Liu Yi Ping（劉一萍）擱置執行申請 禁制令案
法庭	：高等法院上訴法庭
案號	：CACV32/2009
判決日期	：2009 年 3 月 27 日

一、案情簡介

本案是簡評案例三的延續。原告人在申請禁制令取得勝訴後，被告人即申請上訴。根據香港法律，一方提出上訴並不影響包括禁制令在內的法院判令的生效及執行，上訴人必須同時提出暫緩執行申請。只有成功申請暫緩執行，已經作出的判令方可暫停執行。本案所處理的，就是被告人申請暫緩執行的聆訊。

被告人在暫緩執行申請中，在多項理據中，再次主張內地判決為最終及不可推翻判決。但上訴法庭同樣以李祐榮案為判例依據重申此問題需要在正審中處理，最終亦駁回了被告人的申請。

二、簡評

本案判詞只是重複了李祐榮案多數判詞中關於內地法院判決必須在正式審訊中處理的觀點，本身並未對問題進行深入論證，因此本書亦未對本案進行詳細評論。

案例五：Yick Tat Development Co v. Yung Chung Yiu 案

案件	：	Yick Tat Development Co v. Yung Chung Yiu 案
法庭	：	高等法院原訟法庭
案號	：	HCA1590/2007
判決日期	：	2011 年 3 月 17 日

一、案情簡介

本案涉及的原告人與被告人之間因在東莞的房地產投資項目而發生的糾紛。在本案前，原告人在東莞對被告人提起訴訟，但被判敗訴（「內地判決」）。隨後就相同的爭議在香港提起本案的訴訟。

被告人以內地判決構成既判力（res judicata）的判決為由，申請剔除原告人的起訴。

原告人並未主張內地判決為不構成最終及不可推翻的判決作為抗辯，法官最終亦接受了被告人的主張，裁定內地判決為具有既判力的判決，剔除了原告人的起訴。

二、簡評

實際上，由於當事人未提出相關的主張，本案並未直接涉及內地判決是否為最終及不可推翻判決的問題。

但是，這個案件也說明了，在對抗式訴訟制度下，當事人的主張具有舉足輕重的地位。其實按照本案審理時相關判例的裁判觀點，只要原告人提出內地判決不構成最終及不可推翻的判決，被告人的申請即有極大的機會被駁回。但最終由於被告人未提出此主張，法官也未主動適用相關判例的裁判觀點，作出了認為內地判決具有既判力的裁判，甚有違反當時已被判例所確認的裁判觀點（內地判決是否最終及不可推翻判決須在正式審訊中處理）之嫌。

案例六：北京橙天嘉禾訴張承勷案

案件	：北京橙天嘉 訴 張承勷案
法庭	：高等法院原訟法庭
案號	：HCA2481/2013
判決日期	：2016 年 6 月 16 日

一、案情簡介

原告人在北京市朝陽法院對被告人就雙方之間借款合同項下的欠款提起訴訟，並取得勝訴判決（「內地判決」）。原告人隨後以內地判決為依據向香港法院起訴，以執行內地判決項下的欠款，並根據缺席判決的程序取得勝訴判決（「缺席判決」）。（3 段至 13 段）

本案聆訊程序所處理的，是被告人隨後向法院提出的兩項申請：（1）以不符合規定（irregularity）為由申請將缺席判決作廢；（2）許可提交證據，以證明相關的內地法律問題（筆者注：與內地判決是否最終及不可推翻問題相關的內地法律問題）。（1 段）

法官主要以原告人在取得缺席判決的程序中（送達）存在不符合規定的情形裁定將缺席判決作廢，同時也作出了允許被告人提交有關內地相關法律證據的許可。（103 段、107 段）

二、簡評

由於法官以送達存在不符合規定的情形將缺席判決作廢，因此被告人就提交關於內地法律證據的申請已不重要。但是，法官表示若案件進入正式審訊程序，將仍需證明相關的內地法律，因此仍然頒佈了允許被告人提交證據的許可（107 段）。

也由於法官已裁定將缺席判決作廢，法官並未對內地判決最終及不可推翻問題進行再進一步的論證，並且也重申了此問題並未經過任何案件的正式審訊處理。（106 段）

所要指出的是，從本案的緣由可知，儘管根據此前的判例內地判決是否符合最終及不可推翻判決的要求尚未明確，但在香港的對抗式訴訟制度下，由於法官並不一定對法律問題進行審查，原告人仍然有可能通過缺席判決程序取得執行內地判決的勝訴判決。可見，若被告人不提出抗辯，內地法院判決在實務中仍然有可能被執行。

附：再評中國銀行訴楊凡案：
對管轄協議裁判觀點的商榷

案件	：Bank of China Limited（中國銀行股份有限公司） 　v. Yang Fan（楊凡）（「中國銀行案」）
法庭	：高等法院原訟法庭
案號	：HCMP1797/2015
判決日期	：2016 年 4 月 29 日

　　本案涉及兩個主要問題，一個是內地法院判決是否為最終及不可推翻判決的問題，一個是如何認定《內地判決條例》所要求的管轄協議問題。對於前一個問題，已經在本書第八回進行了詳細評論，本文將對第二個問題進行探討。為了方便讀者閱讀，在此先重複已載於第八回的案情簡介。

一、案件簡介

　　原告人在山東省高級人民法院及日照市中級人民法院以被告人及其他幾方為被告提起了訴訟（「內地訴訟」）。（1 段至 13 段）

　　原告人就內地訴訟向香港法院申請了凍結被告人在香港資產的資產凍結令（Mareva Injunction）（「該禁制令」），並在該禁制令屆滿時向香港法院申請延長其期限（「本案」）。（1 段、14 段）

　　被告人要求解除該禁制令，並提出了若干理由，其中包括：（1）內地訴訟所涉合同中的管轄協議（「管轄約定」）並未指明有關爭議由內地法院裁定「而其他司法管轄區的法院則無權處理該等爭議」，從而不屬《內地判決條例》（即《內地判決（交互強制執行）條例（第 597 章）》）所規定的「選用內地法院協議」，致使內地訴訟的判決（「內地判決」）日後無法根據《內地判決條例》在香港執行；（2）由於內地判決不符合香港普通法中「最終及不可推翻」的要求，其最終亦不應被香港法院認可和執行。在內地判決不能根據《內地判決條例》或普通法在香港執行的情況下，該禁制令未能滿足其申請條件，從而應予解除。（25 段）

根據香港《高等法院條例（第4章）》第21M條及相關判例，該禁制令作為協助外地訴訟程序的中期濟助（interim relief in aid of foreign proceedings），其申請條件之一為所涉及的外地訴訟可形成一個可以在香港執行的判決。也正是基於這項要求，被告人為了要求撤銷該禁制令，主張內地判決不符合在香港執行的條件，其中的一項理據，為內地判決不符合《內地判決條例》所要求的條件，即當事人並未約定《內地判決條例》所要求的選用內地法院協議（18段至20段）

二、管轄約定的內容及裁判觀點

（一）管轄約定內容

基於被告人所提出的上述主張，法庭就有關合同中的管轄約定是否構成《內地判決條例》中的選用內地法院協議進行了分析及認定。本案涉及兩份合同中的管轄約定，分別如下：

「除當事人另有約定外，本協議、單項協議適用中華人民共和國法律。

除當事人另有約定外，在本協議、單項協議生效後，因訂立、履行本協議、單項協議所發生的或與本協議、單項協議有關的一切爭議，雙方可協商解決。協商不成的，任何一方可以採取下列第3種方式加以解決：

1. ……

2. ……

3. 依法向有管轄權的人民法院起訴。」

另一份合同的管轄約定條款則為：

「本合同適用中華人民共和國法律。

在本合同生效後，因訂立、履行本合同所發生的或與本合同有關的一切爭議，雙方可協商解決。協商不成的，任何一方可以採取下列第3種方式加以解決：

1. ……

2. ……

3. 依法向有管轄權的人民法院起訴。」

根據法庭在該判決中的說明,兩份合同的管轄約定條款中的第 1 及第 2 選項,均分別為提交仲裁機構仲裁(第 1 選項),及向原告所在地的人民法院提起訴訟(第 2 選項)(34 段)。

(二) 裁判觀點

對於上述管轄約定,被告人主張「任何一方可以採取下列……」中的「可以」是英文的 "may",是允許性的(permissive),而不是必要性的(imperative)(31 段)。法庭針對被告人的主張進行了分析及論證,其主要觀點如下:

1. 法庭同意在一般的使用中,"may" 或 "can"(即「可以」)是允許性的,而 "must" 或 "shall" 則是必要性的。一般而言,「可以」不會被解釋為必要性。但這僅僅是表面上的含義。不僅是在文件或合同中,甚至在立法中也有一些情況 "may" 被解釋為必要性的,而 "must" 或 "shall" 則被解釋為允許性的。具體的含義均取決於使用該表述的語境。這是關於文件起草者意向的問題(31 段)。

2. 法庭認為,所爭論的問題屬合同解釋問題,並引用了判例法中的合同解釋原則,認為應當根據合理人(reasonable person)在當事人簽署合同時所合理了解的背景事實情況(factual matrix)下所具有的理解,來確定有關合同中管轄約定的含義(33 段)。

3. 本案的背景事實情況包括:各方為內地當事人;原告人是在內地存續並運營的銀行;借款人在內地居住並經營業務;被告人是居住在山東日照的內地居民;各份協議均在內地簽署;合同履行地及違約地均在內地;合同約定的準據法為內地法律(33 段)。

4. 當事人從三項爭議解決選項中,選擇了第三個選項作為其爭議解決方式。從表面上看,當事人的意向必定是以第三種爭議解決方式作為他們

解決爭議的唯一方式。通過選擇第三個選項，當事人已經默示地排除第一及第二選項作為爭議解決方式。若認為當事人可選擇這三個選項以外的爭議解決方式（如在內地以外的地方進行訴訟），則會導致這個管轄協議條款變成多餘及沒有意義。從事實情況看，在境外進行訴訟不合常理（34段）。

5. 基於以上的分析，法庭作為結論，認為「可以」應被解釋為具有必要性的"shall（必須）"。從而，有關合同中的管轄約定構成《內地判決條例》所規定的選用內地法院協議（34 段）。

三、對裁判觀點的商榷

在本案判詞中，法庭實際上是在選用內地法院協議的問題上採用了一個較為寬鬆的立場。即使當事人在管轄約定中並未明確採用「排他管轄」「只能在內地法院提起訴訟」「唯一管轄」等表述，法庭通過判例所確立的合同解釋原則，論證並認定當事人在管轄約定過程中雖然採用了「可以」的表述，但其真實意思實為「必須」，從而符合《內地判決條例》對選用內地法院協議的排他性要求。若此觀點最終成為判例規則，這顯然更有利於內地法院判決在香港的認可與執行，無疑對兩地跨境爭議解決來說是個利好的司法見解。然而，若對判詞的論證進行更深入的分析，卻可發現其有重大的不足，存在很大的商榷空間。

（一）合同解釋問題還是成文法解釋問題？

在本案判詞中，法官直接認為當事人是否通過合同中管轄約定達成了「選用內地法院協議」是一個解釋的問題（a question of construction）（30段）。而從上下文看，這裏說的解釋，是指合同的解釋（不是成文法的解釋）。在此判斷的基礎上，法官引用了關於合同解釋的相關判例及法律原則對問題進行處理。然而，對問題性質的此項判斷，值得商榷。

既然所爭論的問題，是當事人合同中的管轄約定，是否符合《內地判決條例》所要求的「選用內地法院協議」，則首先就要解決：《內地判決條例》中的「選用內地法院協議」指的是甚麼？顯然，這是一個成文法解釋問題，而不是合同條款解釋的問題。這並不是說在處理這個問題時不涉及合同條款解釋問題，只是「首先」必須確定成文法（即《內地判決條例》）

的要求之後，才能通過合同解釋，判斷當事人的約定是否符合成文法的要求。否則，合同條款的解釋就會成為無的放矢的解釋。由此可見，本案判決越過成文解釋的問題而「直奔」合同條款解釋，對待決問題難以不存在誤判之嫌。

作為需要首先解決的成文法解釋問題，所要解決的是，《內地判決條例》中所規定的「選用內地法院協議」究竟是甚麼要求，即當事人達成的應該是甚麼樣的協議，其中包括在形式上的要求和在內容上的要求。在形式上的要求，《內地判決條例》的規定已比較清楚，選用內地法院協議必須採用書面形式，而何為書面，《內地判決條例》亦有所界定（3 條）。至於對內容的要求，在解釋上從嚴格到寬鬆大概可以分為三種可能的標準，即：（1）「表述法定」標準；（2）排他意思標準；（3）推定適格標準。

1.「表述法定」——成文法對合同表述或用語的要求

（1）「表述法定」的含義

「表述法定」標準是最嚴格的標準。這裏所說的「表述法定」，是指法律對當事人在訂立合同或達成協議時，要求必須採用特定的表述或用語。「表述法定」的要求，無論是在普通法系還是在大陸法系，均非十分常見，相信在普通法系更為少見（尤其是在商業領域），但在大陸法系雖少見但仍不乏其蹤影。起碼就內地法律而言，比較典型的「表述法定」規定，可見於定金合同。內地《擔保法》確立了專門的定金規則（或沒收或雙倍返還規則）（89 條以下），而根據《關於適用〈擔保法〉若干問題的解釋》的規定，當事人約定採用具有定金效力的定金，原則上必須採用「定金」的表述，若採用「留置金」「擔保金」「保證金」「訂約金」「押金」或者哪怕是同音不同字的「訂金」等其他表述，均被視為不構成定金合同（118 條）。這屬相當嚴格的「表述法定」要求。不過，對於普通法而言，在合同法以外領域的「表述法定」要求卻並不少見，特別是在程序法領域。普通法（特別是英國法系）往往對訴訟法律文書所採用的表述作出非常嚴格的要求，比如香港法律對當事人在遺產承辦申請文書中的稱謂有極為嚴格的要求（比如已婚者必須稱 "married man" 或 "married woman"，喪偶者必須稱 "widower" 或 "widow"，未成年人必須稱 "infant" 等）。

因此，當成文法對合同約定在內容上有所規定的時候，作為首要問題

的成文法解釋首先要回答兩個具體問題。其一，成文法的該項規定是否屬「表述法定」的規定，即是否對合同或協議中約定在陳述或用語上有所要求；其二，如屬「表述法定」的規定，該項規定對當事人所使用的陳述或用語有如何的或有多嚴格的要求。

(2) 在「表述法定」標準下成文法解釋與合同法解釋的關係

或有疑問，若經過解釋，確定《內地判決條例》的規定就是對選擇內地管轄協議作出嚴格的「表述法定」要求，比如要求當事人在協議中必須採用「具有唯一管轄權」的表述，豈非即沒有合同解釋的空間？誠然，「表述法定」無疑在客觀上會限縮可進行合同解釋的空間。在絕對嚴格的「表述法定」要求下，如要求必須採用「具有唯一管轄權」的表述，任何未採用這一表述的約定，均無法通過合同的解釋的方法而被認定為具有此表述的效力。然而，即使如此，這並不代表在這種情況之下合同解釋就全無用武之地。這主要體現在當事人已明確採用了所要求的表述後（如「由內地法院管轄並具有唯一管轄權」），同時存在其他約定可能推翻該表述的矛盾約定。比如，在採用了法定表述後，又約定若一方向其他法院起訴，另一方同意不提出抗辯（注：這是真實個案）。這就存在符合法定表述的約定卻不應具有法定表述效力的解釋空間。也就是說，在採用絕對「表述法定」的立法下，雖無法通過合同解釋「補正」不符合「表述法定」要求的約定，但卻可通過合同解釋推翻符合「表述法定」要求的約定。

若經成文法解釋認為成文法雖屬「表述法定」的規定，但並非絕對嚴格，則自然具有較大的合同解釋空間，以至有可能通過合同解釋將是否符合「表述法定」要求不完全明確的約定，「補正」為符合成文法內容要求的約定。比如，成文法要求當事人的約定必須具有明確的表示唯一管轄權表述，當事人雖未採用「具有唯一管轄權」的表述，但在約定內地法院有管轄權時，又同時存在合同各方同意「不通過其他方式處理爭議」的表述，即有可能通過解釋規則被認定為符合具有唯一管轄權約定的要求。

2. 排他意思標準

比「表述法定」標準較為寬鬆的，是排他意思標準。所謂排他意思，即當事人在管轄約定中所具有的由所選定法院對爭議進行排他管轄的意思。而排他意思標準，就選用內地法院協議而言，即是指只要當事人在管

轄約定中可被認為具有由選定內地法院對爭議進行排他管轄的意思，即符合《內地判決條例》的要求。在此標準下，法律對當事人在管轄約定中所採用的表述並無非常嚴格的要求。若當事人採用明確體現排他管轄意思的表述，比如「具有唯一管轄權」「排他管轄」等，固然符合排他意思標準的要求。即使當事人未採用明確的表述，只要可以一定方式確定當事人具有排他意思，亦足以認定管轄約定符合《內地判決條例》的要求。所謂「以一定方式確定」，實際上就是按照合同或意思表示解釋規則確定。由此可見，在排他意思標準下，相比在「表述法定」的標準下，合同解釋規則會具有更大的用武之地。

3. 推定適格標準

推定適格標準，就是指只要當事人在管轄約定中選擇了內地法院作為爭議解決的司法機關，在管轄約定中無論是否體現了排他意思，也無論是否採用了明確的諸如「具有唯一管轄權」的排他表述，均視為構成有效的選用內地法院協議。採用類似標準的可數仲裁條款。多數法域的法律實際上對仲裁條款均採用了這一標準，即只要當事人在爭議解決條款中提到「仲裁」，一般即足以構成有效的仲裁協議而排除其他爭議解決方式。在內地境內民事訴訟中，法律對協議管轄的管轄約定要求，同樣是採用了推定適格標準。只要當事人在管轄協議中選擇了特定人民法院作為審理爭議的法院，爭議即應由該法院管轄而排除其他法院對案件進行審理，無需認定當事人是否具有排他意思，更無需存在所選定人民法院具有唯一管轄權或排他管轄權的明確表述。

4.《內地判決條例》的標準？

如前所述，處理本案管轄約定是否構成《內地判決條例》所要求的選用內地法院協議，首先是一個成文法解釋問題，具體而言，就《內地判決條例》對選用內地法院協議的認定究竟採用哪一種標準。既然是成文法解釋問題，自然就應按照成文法解釋規則處理。香港法律繼承英國法律，本身有一套比較完善的主要以判例法為基礎的成文法解釋規則。本文的目的並非要全面闡述香港法律的成文法解釋規則，但擬就選用內地法院協議的認定標準問題，提出以下幾項觀點：

其一，在上述三種標準中，首先應可排除推定適格標準。推定適格實際上是對管轄約定的表述和當事人的排他意思均無所求，而從《內地判決條例》的規定看，特別是從「指明」的表述看，應難以認為《內地判決條例》對構成選擇內地法院協議的管轄約定毫無所求，至少其標準應不至於寬鬆如仲裁條款。

其二，再看《內地判決條例》第 3（2）條的規定，其對排他管轄協議的表述為：「指明由內地法院或某內地法院裁定在或可能在與該指明合約有關連的情況下產生的爭議，而其他司法管轄區的法院則無權處理該等爭議」的協議。至少從文義上看，上述規定是要求排他管轄協議應「指明」「其他司法管轄區的法院則無權處理該等爭議」，更像是一項對「明示」有所要求的規定。

其三，根據《協議管轄判決安排》的規定，作為其適用前提的管轄約定，必須是當事人之間「明確約定」的內地人民法院「具有唯一管轄權的協議」（《協議管轄判決安排》第 1 條第 5 款）。這項規定更接近於「表述法定」標準，應無疑問。當然，有待進一步討論的是，在解釋《內地判決條例》的規定時，是否可以以及在多大程度上可引用《協議管轄判決安排》的規定，有待進一步討論。此問題涉及在「一國兩制」的憲政體制下以及在《基本法》第 95 條的規定下，如何適用香港成文解釋規則的更深層次的問題。此問題超出本書的焦點問題，在此先不予探討。

如前所述，本案判詞在論證上的最大缺陷，在於在處理《內地判決條例》的成文法解釋問題，即「直奔」合同解釋問題。從上述的可能標準看，本案更像是理所當然地採用了排他意思標準。然而，基於上述討論，對於《內地判決條例》對選用內地法院協議所要求的標準，雖然尚不足以絕對排除排他意思標準，但解釋為「表述法定」標準顯然也具有相當的理據。若是未經論證上直接採用排他意思標準，恐怕在論證上有失嚴謹。

（二）衝突法及準據法問題

退一步說，即使假設可直接將問題作為合同解釋問題處理，本案判詞在論證上仍然存在另一個缺陷。即在確認管轄約定是否構成選用內地法院協議是關於合同解釋的問題後，直接引用了判例規則作為處理此問題的依據，忽略了應首先根據衝突法規則確定準據法。

根據普通法中的相關衝突法規則，管轄協議條款作為主合同的內容，其準據法應為主合同的準據法（*Dicey & Morris, The Conflict of Laws*（14th edition）第 12-103 段。）。既然主合同中已經明確約定以內地法律為準據法，則本案管轄約定的解釋，亦應適用內地法律。《合同法》第 125 條 1 款規定：「當事人對合同條款的理解有爭議的，應當按照合同所使用的詞句、合同的有關條款、合同的目的、交易習慣以及誠實信用原則，確定該條款的真實意思。」僅從此規定看，似乎也難以認為此合同解釋規則與香港判例法所確立的解釋原則有重大區別，也許就此個案而言，適用內地法律最終也可能得出相同的結論。但也要注意，無論是《協議管轄判決安排》還是《內地判決條例》，均明確規定了在香港認可和執行內地法院判決，應根據內地法律判斷管轄約定的效力。《協議管轄判決安排》第 9 條規定了「根據當事人協議選擇的原審法院地的法律，管轄協議屬無效」作為不予認可和執行的事由之一，《內地判決條例》第 18（1）條亦有對應及一致的規定。此規定是否可被理解為判斷管轄約定是否構成選用內地法院協議應以內地法律為準據法的規定？當然，這問題本身首先也是一個成文法解釋問題。但無論如何，也必須指出，本案判詞並未處理衝突法問題，未免成為了在論證上及法律適用上的重大瑕疵。基於《合同法》的上述規定，未處理衝突法問題雖然在本案中未必會產生不同的結果，但在其他個案中，是否適用內地法律則可能會對裁判結果產生重大差異，比如涉及管轄約定是否違反內地法律專屬管轄規定時，則可能引起管轄協議是否有效，從而是否構成有效的選用內地法院協議的問題。

（三）「無贅文推定」？

在本案判詞中，法庭特別指出，若認為當事人可以選擇第四種爭議解決方式（如在境外提起訴訟），則該條款即成為贅文，並以此為理由認為當事人第三個選項就只能是排他性約定。實際上是採用了「無贅文推定」的見解。也就是說，對於明示的合同條款，原則上應賦予其一定的含義，不應使其成為贅文。然而，此見解對於本案中的合同是否適用，亦存在疑問。只要對內地的法律實務有較多的接觸，就可以知道，這種無實質意義的「贅文約定」（有意識地作出無意義的約定）十分常見。比如關於在發生爭議時先「友好協商」在多數合同中也是一項無實質意義的約定（在理論上，也許可以認為在這種約定下，當事人在通過法律程序解決爭議前，有義務先進行協商，即認為協商是啟動法律程序的一項前提條件，但這一

解釋似乎在實踐中很少被採用）。而此案中的「依法向有管轄權的人民法院起訴」約定，也是一個典型的「贅文約定」。

首先，選擇「依法向有管轄權的人民法院起訴」，實際上等同於約定「根據法律有關管轄的規定提起訴訟」，也等同於將管轄協議條款刪除。只是在實踐中在使用標準合同時，為了方便使用，將此無意義的選項加入，可讓當事人更方便使用，也可以避免需要將標準合同中的整個條文刪除（如果選擇不約定管轄）。

其次，從另一個角度看，當事人約定選擇「依法……」的安排，實際上是約定在有關事項上選擇採用「法定機制」，而不通過自行約定選擇採用不同於「法定機制」的「意定規則」。在實務中，約定選擇法定規則，與不作任何關於約定的表示而適用法定規則，並沒有任何區別。若一定要將兩者作出不同的解釋並賦予不同的效力，未免有過度「人為化」的嫌疑。這種選擇「法定」情況的另一典型例子可見於保險領域：投保險對人壽保險受益人不作指定時，在習慣上經常會寫為「法定」。採用這樣的表述實際上與不寫明並無區別。

其三，還要注意的是，正如在本案判詞中所述，本案的法律關係的各項因素均在內地，從內地法律的角度看，是一個純粹的境內（非涉外）法律關係，就其所進行的訴訟也不可能是涉外民事訴訟。作為非涉外合同關係，很難認為當事人在訂立合同之時能夠設想境外訴訟為其爭議解決的一個選項。在法律上，非涉外法律關係的當事人實際上也不被允許通過協議管轄的方式選擇境外法院作為管轄法院（《民事訴訟法》第 34 條、《關於適用〈民事訴訟法〉的解釋》第 531 條）。境外訴訟實際上不是一個當事人在訂立合同之時所能預期的選項，因此當事人也不可能會對爭議是否只能由內地法院而不能由境外法院管轄的問題（即所約定的管轄是否排他地由內地法院管轄的問題）有所考慮。對於一項當事人實際上不可能存在的意向，通過事後解釋「強加」給當事人，是否符合合同解釋規則（無論內地法律還是香港法律），亦不無疑問。而假若當事人（特別是銀行）在訂立合同時預期到在香港執行的問題，甚至可以認為，其更可能不希望選擇非排他管轄約定，以為日後倘需執行債務時在訴訟地問題上提供更靈活的選擇。

其四，本案法律關係的非涉外性質似乎也能進一步説明此案中的管轄

約定實際上就是「贅文約定」。在非涉外民事訴訟管轄規則的框架下，所謂「依法向有管轄權的人民法院起訴」，實際上就是可以向「任何」根據《民事訴訟法》或其他法律享有管轄權的法院起訴，不存在任何「限定特定法院」的意思。可作為對比的是，若當事人約定「向原告住所地人民法院起訴」、「向合同簽訂地人民法院起訴」，才有可能具有「僅」向所約定法院起訴的排他性意思。這就是說，本案的管轄約定實際上僅有限定爭議解決方式的意思（訴訟），而並無限定特定法院的意思，更無限定地域的意思。當然，在理論上不能排除當事人約定「由任何內地法院」「排他地」管轄。是否如此解釋，同樣取決於個案事實，在本案中，恐怕必須考慮當事人在訂立合同之時很可能從未預期案件有可能在境外訴訟的因素。

據上所述，引起疑問的是，在採用判例法中的「合理人」合同解釋標準時（假設準據法為香港法律），在確定此「合理人」及「背景情況」時，是否應將上述因素考慮在內。

（四）「人民法院」等於內地法院？

在此案中的管轄約定中，如同許多內地機構製作的標準合同條款，採用了「人民法院」的表述。對此，本案判詞直接認為這所指的就是內地法院。儘管在文義上「人民法院」似乎只能是內地法院，但在解釋上是否必然只能被理解為內地法院，還是可以被理解為一般意義上的、相對於仲裁機構的司法機構（不限法域）？對此似乎仍有討論空間。如同「可以」被解釋為「必須」，「人民法院」似乎並非不能根據解釋規則被理解為境外法院。尤其要注意的是，在《民事訴訟法》中，在多數的條款中對於法院均採用了「人民法院」的表述，但在涉外民事訴訟也同時適用《民事訴訟法》全部規定的情況下（《民事訴訟法》第 259 條），《民事訴訟法》一些條款中的「人民法院」，本來就有可能被解釋為境外法院。

四、結論

綜上所述，儘管本案裁判觀點對內地法院判決根據《協議管轄判決安排》在香港獲得認可和執行更為有利，然而其論證在法律上存在不少可商權之處。因此，本案的裁判觀點最終是否能成為具有約束力的規則，也有待觀察。

第三部份

總評

一、各判例的要點及最終及不可推翻判決問題的案型

本書所評論判例的要點摘要：

案件	案型及程序
Chiyu Banking Corporation Limited v. Chan Tin Kwun 法庭：高等法院原訟法庭 日期：1996 年 7 月 12 日 本書評論：第一回	案型： 以內地判決債務為訴因起訴。 程序： 被告人申請擱置訴訟程序。
湖北省武漢中碩虹房地產開發有限公司 訴 香港廣生行國際有限公司案 法庭：原訟法庭 日期：2000 年 6 月 12 日 本書評論：第二回	案型： 以內地判決債務為訴因起訴。 程序： 被告人申請擱置訴訟程序。
Tan Tay Cuan v. Ng Chi Hung 法庭：原訟法庭 日期：2001 年 2 月 5 日 本書評論：第三回	案型： 以內地判決債務為訴因起訴。 程序： 被告人上訴訴請撤銷聆訊官作出的原告人勝訴簡易判決。

「最終及不可推翻」 主張的提出	主要裁判觀點 （對內地判決的立場）
原告人代表大律師主張內地判決為最終及不可推翻，被告人專家證人則主張僅為「暫時（for the time being）」為最終及不可推翻。	這是香港法院首次明確裁定，由於內地再審制度的原因，內地法院作出的判決並不符合「最終及不可推翻」的要求，從而不應被執行。 法庭將英國 Nouvion 的先例規則闡釋為：若作出判決的法院保留改變其自己裁決的可行性，該判決即不屬最終及不可推翻。 法庭明確地認為，最高人民檢察院的審判監督職能及抗訴制度並非簡單的上訴制度，若最高人民檢察院提出抗訴，無論其情形如何不常見，有關法院即須對案件進行再審，因此該法院明顯保留了改變其先前裁決的權力。 法庭並認為，儘管人民檢察院尚未提出抗訴，但當事人已經申請再審，有關程序已被啟動，即表明該判決並非最終及不可推翻。
被告人答辯中主張內地判決並非最終及不可推翻的判決，作為應擱置訴訟程序的理據。	法庭在一定程度上「軟化」了 Chiyu 案法庭所持的立場，認為最高人民檢察院抗訴的確切性質及效力，並未在香港的正式審訊中經過嚴格的審查。 法庭最終雖判決中止申請執行內地法院判決的訴訟，但並不是直接以內地法院不屬最終及不可推翻的判決為基礎作出該裁定，而是以香港法律所賦予法院的酌情權，在綜合多項因素後作出中止訴訟的裁定。
被告人主張內地法院不是最終及不可推翻判決，作為申請撤銷簡易判決的理據。	法庭認為具有一定的可爭辯理由將內地判決認定為並非最終及不可推翻，並據以撤銷原告要求執行內地法院判決的簡易判決申請。

案件	案型及程序
Nintendo of America v. Bung Enterprise Ltd. 案 法庭：上訴法庭 日期：2000 年 3 月 21 日 本書評論：第七回	案型： 以加州法院缺席判決債務為訴因起訴。 程序： 簡易程序聆訊
林哲民經營之日昌電業公司 訴 林志滔案 法庭：上訴法庭 日期：2001 年 12 月 18 日 本書評論：第四回	案型： 重新起訴（不容反悔法、濫用訴訟程序）。 程序： 原訟法庭法官根據被告人的申請撤銷了原告人的起訴，原告人隨後上訴，訴請撤銷原訟法庭撤銷其起訴的命令。
林哲民經營之日昌電業公司 訴 林志滔案 法庭：上訴法庭 日期：2001 年 12 月 18 日 本書評論：第四回	案型： 重新起訴（不容反悔法、濫用訴訟程序）。 程序： 原訟法庭法官根據被告人的申請撤銷了原告人的起訴，原告人隨後上訴，訴請撤銷原訟法庭撤銷其起訴的命令。

「最終及不可推翻」主張的提出	主要裁判觀點（對內地判決的立場）
被告以加州法院缺席判決不是最終及不可推翻判決作為抗辯理據之一。	法庭根據 Vanquelin 先例，裁定即使是缺席判決，仍然構成最終及不可推翻的判決，原告人可通過簡易程序取得勝訴判決。
原告人在上訴中主張內地判決並非最終及不可推翻的判決；上訴法庭則主動將爭議法律問題界定為不容反悔法問題，並認為被告人應舉證證明內地判決為最終及不可推翻的判決，從而具有既判力，方能適用不容反悔法的原則。	法庭以不容反悔法的原則為基礎，認為被告人未能舉證證明內地法院判決為最終及不可推翻，據以認為原告人不受不容反悔法約束而仍可在香港重新提起訴訟。 法庭在闡釋不容反悔法所要求的最終及不可推翻的條件時，引用了 Chiyu 案的相關判詞，並明確表示該案法庭「在該案的裁決是正確及合法合理的」，但是，本案法庭實際上是以被告人未能舉證為由駁回其主張，因此並未適用該案的法律原則。準確地說，是無需直接根據 Chiyu 案的法律原則作出裁決。 此外，在闡述 Chiyu 案的法律原則時，法庭似乎是強調了在 Chiyu 案中抗訴程序已經開展的事實，並作為該案與本案的區別所在，這似可為未啟動審判監督程序的內地判決被認定屬最終及不可推翻的判決留下了空間。
原告人在上訴中主張內地判決並非最終及不可推翻的判決；上訴法庭則主動將爭議法律問題界定為不容反悔法問題，並認為被告人應舉證證明內地判決為最終及不可推翻的判決，從而具有既判力，方能適用不容反悔法的原則。	法庭以不容反悔法的原則為基礎，認為被告人未能舉證證明內地法院判決為最終及不可推翻，據以認為原告人不受不容反悔法約束而仍可在香港重新提起訴訟。 法庭在闡釋不容反悔法所要求的最終及不可推翻的條件時，引用了 Chiyu 案的相關判詞，並明確表示該案法庭「在該案的裁決是正確及合法合理的」，但是，本案法庭實際上是以被告人未能舉證為由駁回其主張，因此並未適用該案的法律原則。準確地說，是無需直接根據 Chiyu 案的法律原則作出裁決。 此外，在闡述 Chiyu 案的法律原則時，法庭似乎是強調了在 Chiyu 案中抗訴程序已經開展的事實，並作為該案與本案的區別所在，這似可為未啟動審判監督程序的內地判決被認定屬最終及不可推翻的判決留下了空間。

案件	案型及程序
林哲民日昌電業公司 訴 張順連案 法庭：上訴法庭 日期：2002 年 7 月 12 日 本書評論：第五回	案型： 重新起訴（不容反悔法、濫用訴訟程序）。 程序： 原告人上訴，訴請撤銷原訟法庭案件不宜由香港法院審理的命令。
New Link Consultants Ltd v. Air China and Others 法庭：上訴法庭 日期：2004 年 5 月 3 日 本書評論：附一案件一	案型： 非便利公堂 程序： 被告人申請擱置訴訟程序。
李祐榮 訴 李瑞群案（多數判詞） 法庭：上訴法庭 日期：2005 年 12 月 9 日 本書評論：第六回（上）	案型： 以內地判決債務為訴因起訴。 案型： 原告人根據簡易程序起訴先被原訟法庭聆訊官（經區域法院轉交）駁回；在原訟法庭的上訴中則被裁定上訴得直，取得勝訴的簡易判決；被告人隨後再上訴至上訴法庭。
李祐榮 訴 李瑞群案（異議判詞） 法庭：上訴法庭 日期：2005 年 12 月 9 日 本書評論：第六回（下）	同上。

「最終及不可推翻」 主張的提出	主要裁判觀點 （對內地判決的立場）
被告人以濫用程序為理據申請剔除原告人的申索書及撤銷訴訟，實際上並未涉及內地判決是否最終及不可推翻的問題。上訴法庭則引用了 Chiyu 案的觀點以內地判決不是最終及不可推翻作為其裁判理據。	以較為明確而「強硬」的表述，根據 Chiyu 案認為內地法院判決基於內地的抗訴制度「並非一最終及不可推翻的判決」，從而認為原告人可以在香港重新起訴。 法庭所適用的香港法律理據並不明確，即究竟是以酌情權為基礎還是一不容反悔法為基礎並未清晰說明。
原告人以內地判決「缺乏終局性」作為不宜在內地法院進行訴訟的考慮因素。	法庭否定原告人包括缺乏終局性在內地的各項理據，裁定內地法院屬更便利公堂。
原告人在被告人上訴至上訴法庭之前的程序中並未提出關於內地判決為最終及不可推翻判決的主張，直至在上訴法庭的上訴中，方提出該主張。	內地判決是否為最終及不可推翻的判決，是一個具有重大爭議的問題，並且是一個具有公眾重要性的議題，加上被告人未聘請代表律師及內地法律專家證人，據以裁定不宜在簡易程序中作出判決。 張澤祐法官改變了自己在 Chiyu 案判詞中的立場，表示 Nouvion 先例並未明確確立「原審法院可推翻判決＝非最終及不可推翻」的法律原則。
同上。	內地法律中的審判監督制度，與香港的上訴制度相似，內地審判監督制度的存在，並不導致內地判決成並非最終及不可推翻的判決。 內地判決不同於 Nouvion 先例中的西班牙 remate judgment。 作出判決的法院可撤銷其判決，並不表示判決就不是最終及不可推翻。

案件	案型及程序
陳國柱 訴 陳桂洲案 法庭：原訟法庭 日期：2008 年 7 月 29 日 本書評論：簡評案例二	案型： 重新起訴（不容反悔法、濫用訴訟程序）。 程序： 正式審訊。
Wu Wei（伍威）v. Liu Yi Ping（劉一萍）申請禁制令案 法庭：原訟法庭 日期：2009 年 1 月 30 日 本書評論：簡評案例三	案型： 《高等法院條例》第 21L 條申請禁制令申請。 程序： 原訟法庭的禁制令申請程序。
Wu Wei（伍威）v. Liu Yi Ping（劉一萍）暫緩執行申請禁制令案 法庭：上訴法庭 日期：2009 年 3 月 27 日 本書評論：簡評案例四	案型： 同上 程序： 被告人申請暫緩執行禁制令。

「最終及不可推翻」 主張的提出	主要裁判觀點 （對內地判決的立場）
雙方代表律師同意內地判決不具有既判力，法院亦指出內地判決可能不是最終及不可推翻判決。	法庭在雙方代表律師同意的基礎上，對案件進行了正式審訊。
被告人在反訴中訴請執行內地判決，原告人提請就內地判決是否為最終及不可推翻的判決作出裁定。 針對原告人的禁制令申請，被告人則主張內地法院作出判決後，因內地判決為最終及不可推翻判決的判決而可在香港執行，從而已不存在需要審理的重大事項，禁制令申請不應被支持頒發。 法庭亦主動指出這同時是一個內地判決是否具有既判力的問題，這亦取決於內地判決是否為最終及不可推翻的判決。	指出承認和執行境外判決，與認定境外判決既判力，均須境外判決為最終及不可推翻的判決。 本案作為非正審程序，並未被要求對內地判決是否為最終及不可推翻的判決作出結論性的裁定，而僅需決定此問題是否構成需要審理的重大事項。 以李祐榮案為依據認定內地審判監督制度的內容，指出最高人民法院及最高人民檢察院可要求原審人民法院對案件進行再審，因此原告人向廣東省高級人民法院提出的再審申請被駁回，未能提供完整的答案（is not a complete answer）。 內地判決是否為最終及不可推翻，僅僅增加了在本案中需要審理的重大事項，從而禁制令應予頒發。
被告人以內地判決為最終及不可推翻判決作為申請暫緩執行禁止令的理據之一。	直接引用李祐榮案，裁定被告人關於內地判決為最終及不可推翻判決的主張不成立。

案件	案型及程序
Yick Tat Development Co v. Yung Chung Yiu 法庭：原訟法庭 日期：2011 年 3 月 17 日 本書評論：簡評案例五	案型： 重新起訴（不容反悔法、濫用訴訟程序） 程序： 被告人申請剔除原告人申索書。
Bank of China（中國銀行）v. Yang Fan（楊凡）案 法庭：原訟法庭 日期：2016 年 4 月 29 日 本書評論：第八回、第九回、附文	案型： 《高等法院條例》第 21M 條協助外地訴訟程序的資產凍結令申請。 程序： 原告人申請延長資產凍結令期限，被告人抗辯並訴請接觸該資產凍結令。
北京橙天嘉禾 v. 張承勳案 法庭：原訟法庭 日期：2016 年 6 月 16 日 本書評論：簡評案例六	案型： 以內地判決債務為訴因起訴。 程序： 被告人申請撤銷缺席判決。

「最終及不可推翻」 主張的提出	主要裁判觀點 （對內地判決的立場）
原告人未提出以內地判決並非最終及不可推翻判決抗辯，法庭裁定被告人勝訴。	法庭未主動提出內地判決的最終及不可推翻問題，直接接納被告人的陳詞裁定內地判決具有既判力而裁定剔除原告人的申索書。
被告人抗辯主張內地判決不是最終及不可推翻的判決，從而不符合根據《高等法院條例》第 21M 條申請資產凍結令的條件。	認為張澤祐法官在 Chiyu 案的判詞中遠未表示抗訴程序本身導致任何內地法院均不屬最終及不可推翻。 同時引用了張法官後來在李祐榮案的判詞，指出張法官明確確認，抗訴程序本身是否導致內地法院判決不屬最終及不可推翻之判決的問題，並未經高等法院上訴法庭作出權威性的，以及上述問題是一項涉及重大公共利益的問題，從而不能在非正審程序中對該問題作出決定。 認為對於本案的禁制令申請而言，無須回答內地判決是否確為最終及不可推翻的問題，而僅需要判斷，為《內地判決條例》之目的，該內地判決是否有一定的可能（likely）為最終及不可推翻。 作為結論，認為原告人已經證明了其主張（內地判決很可能為最終及不可推翻）具有「良好的可爭辯論點」。
被告人申請提交關於內地判決是否最終及不可推翻問題的證據。	法庭引用李祐榮案為依據指出內地判決是否最終及不可推翻判決需要在正式審訊中處理。

根據以上表格，縱觀相關香港判例，涉及內地法院判決是否最終及不可推翻判決問題的案件，可根據內地法院判決是（或不是）最終及不可推翻判決的主張方式和目的，分為四種案型即：（1）以內地法院判決債務作為訴因起訴的案型；（2）重新起訴（不容反悔法、濫用訴訟程序）的案型；（3）《高等法院條例》第 21M 條的案型；及（4）《高等法院條例》第 21L 條的案型。以下就此四種案型分別予以詳細說明。

（一）案型一：以內地法院判決債務作為訴因

1. 原告人主張內地法院判決為最終及不可推翻判決

根據普通法，原告人以境外判決債務（香港立法一般採用「判定債務」的表述）作為訴因起訴，並訴請承認和執行該債務，必須該境外法院判決為最終及不可推翻。因此，原告人必須證明其訴請承認和執行的判決根據普通法為最終及不可推翻的判決。在本書所評論的判例中，Chiyu 案、武漢中碩虹案、Tan Tay Cuan 案、李祐榮案、伍威案（被告人反訴）均屬這一案型。

在程序上，原告人以內地法院判決為訴因提起訴訟，固然可以在起訴時即在狀書中主張所依據的內地判決為最終及不可推翻的判決。但從本書所評論的案例來看，在多數原告人以內地法院判決為訴因起訴的案件中，原告人在程序開始之初均未提出內地法院判決為最終及不可推翻判決的主張，而更多是在後續被告人提起的程序中被提出。比如在 Chiyu 案、武漢中碩虹案中，該問題是被告人在擱置訴訟程序的聆訊中提出，在 Tan Tay Cuan 案、李祐榮案中，則是在撤銷簡易判決的上訴聆訊中提出。在伍威禁制令案中，該問題一方面是由被告人在反訴中提出（主張內地法院判決為最終及不可推翻判決，從而應予以承認和執行），另方面則是由原告人在申請《高等法院條例》第 21L 條禁制令的程序中（其基礎訴訟為原告人就內地訴訟的相同爭議所提起的訴訟（即在香港重新起訴）），以提請法庭對內地法院判決是否為最終及不可推翻的法律問題進行裁斷的方式提出，而被告人亦相應地主張由於內地法院判決是屬最終及不可推翻判決，原告人的訴請亦因此缺乏理據，從而其禁制令申請也應被相應駁回。

在上述案件中，之所以會出現原告人開始未提出內地法院判決為最終及不可推翻判決的主張，其原因很可能與對抗式訴訟制度的特點相關。在

對抗式訴訟制度下，法庭並不主動對原告人的訴訟請求作全面的審查（包括事實問題和法律問題），原告人在起訴中的主張即使並不全面，但若被告人未答辯或未作充分抗辯，原告人的訴訟主張仍有可能被視為充分，並通過缺席判決或簡易判決而獲得支持。此時被告人即必須進行更充分的抗辯（比如通過主張擱置訴訟程序或撤銷已經作出的缺席判決或簡易判決的上訴程序），才能對抗原告人的起訴。

2. 被告人主張內地法院判決不是最終及不可推翻判決的抗辯

在原告人以內地法院判決債務為訴因起訴的案型中，針對原告人的內地法院判決構成最終及不可推翻判決主張，被告人自然相應地需以內地法院判決不構成最終及不可推翻判決為抗辯。不過，對於被告人如何提出此項抗辯，則因訴訟程序所處的階段不同而有不同。

（1）申請擱置

如前所述，Chiyu 案及武漢中碩虹案均屬被告人以申請擱置訴訟作為抗辯方式的案例。就當時的法律而言，被告人申請擱置訴訟的法律依據，應為香港法院根據普通法所享有的固有司法管轄權（inherent jurisdiction）中的擱置任何訴訟程序的權力。據此作出的擱置裁定一般被稱為酌情決定的擱置（discretionary stay，簡稱「酌情擱置」）。根據普通法，當事人之間就相同爭議在境外法院存在訴訟即屬法院可行使酌情擱置的一種情形。在決定是否行使酌情擱置時，法庭須考慮以下原則：（i）法庭必須考慮如何才能在訴訟當事人之間實現正義並一般性地執行正義；（ii）擱置訴訟不會對原告人或被告人造成不正義；（iii）申請擱置的一方必須向法庭證明繼續進行訴訟程序會造成不公；及（iv）若原告人是基於固有權利而啟動訴訟程序時，他不應在缺乏非常有力的理由下被剝奪繼續進行訴訟程序的權利（參見 Annotated Ordinances of Hong Kong《高等法院條例》第 4 章 16.07 段）。

在武漢中碩虹案中，楊振權法官十分明確地表明了他是根據香港法院的固有管轄權（inherent jurisdiction）作為其裁判的法律基礎（該判決第 21 段），並基本上按照上述原則並根據案件事實進行了比較充分的論證（該判決第 22 段至第 40 段），而內地判決是否為最終及不可推翻判決則僅為考慮因素之一。至於在 Chiyu 案中，張澤祐法官則並未明確指出其裁判依據為酌情擱置的原則，但從判決關於被告人申請的表述看，被告人

應當是以內地訴訟仍然在進行作為理由之一（另一項理由為不方便法院原則）申請擱置香港訴訟程序（該判決第 1 段）。既然是以酌情擱置的原則為依據，則理應按照上述的幾項原則進行裁判。然而，從 Chiyu 案的判詞內容看，張法官並未全面適用上述的幾項原則。儘管張法官最終作出的是擱置訴訟的裁定，但從其論證過程看，更像是在處理「原告人的訴請是否因內地判決不構成最終及不可推翻判決而應被撤銷」的問題，而不是「訴訟程序是否因內地訴訟程序仍在進行而應被擱置」的問題，而且在論據上更像是以內地判決是否為最終及不可推翻作為唯一裁判標準。「內地判決是否仍在進行（因已啟動審判監督程序）」與「內地判決是否因存在或已啟動審判監督程序而不構成最終及不可推翻判決」的問題，固為一個問題的兩面，但是角度及法律效果應有所不同。前者的法律效果為擱置訴訟程序，後者的則為撤銷起訴。對此，楊振權法官在武漢中碩虹的判詞中亦有所說明（該判決第 20 段）。這似乎也是 Chiyu 案判詞另一個值得商權之處。正是這樣的論證方式，導致 Chiyu 案判詞更像是在宣告內地法院判決因審判監督程序制度的存在而不構成最終及不可推翻的判決。

順帶指出的是，在民事司法制度改革於 2009 年生效實施後，《高等法院規則》第 12 號命令第 8 條規則明確加入了酌情擱置的內容，從而將普通法上的酌情擱置納入成文法之中。對於前述規定中的酌情擱置與普通法上法院固有司法管轄權下酌情擱置之間的關係，在判例中亦有所討論，但這已經超出本書焦點問題的範圍，在此不作進一步的探討。

（2）申請撤銷簡易判決

若原告人以內地法院判決為訴因起訴，並已通過簡易程序取得勝訴的簡易判決，則被告人此時提出的抗辯在程序上即體現為申請將簡易判決作廢（set aside）。Tan Tay Cuan 案及李祐榮案均屬此類案型。根據《高等法院規則》第 14 號命令的相關規定，即「除非在聆訊根據第 1 條規則（筆者注：申請簡易判決的規則）提出的申請時，法庭駁回該申請或被告人使法庭信納，就該申請所關乎的申索或部份申索而言，有應予以審訊的爭論點或有爭議的問題，或為其他理由該申索或該部份申索應予以審訊，否則法庭在顧及所申索的補救或濟助的性質後，可就該申索或該部份申索，作出公正的原告人勝訴被告人敗訴的判決。」據此規定，作出簡易判決的條件應為申索不存在「應予以審訊的爭論點或有爭議的問題」或其他應予審

訊的理由。相應地，若被告人能證明申索存在「應予以審訊的爭論點或有爭議的問題」或其他應予審訊的理由，則不應作出簡易判決，若簡易判決已經作出，則應予以作廢。

就涉及內地法院判決是否為最終及不可推翻的案件而言，在申請將簡易判決作廢的程序中，法庭所要處理的是此項問題，即：內地法院判決在審判監督制度下是否最終及不可推翻，是否屬「應予以審訊的爭論點或有爭議的問題」，實際上亦即內地法院判決在審判監督制度下「是否可能」構成最終及不可推翻判決（或不構成最終及不可推翻判決）的問題。而不再是：內地法院判決在審判監督程序下「是否」構成最終及不可推翻判決的問題。

與簡易判決的情形類似，若原告人以內地法院判決債務為訴因起訴，並通過缺席判決程序取得勝訴判決（香港法例的正式表述為「因欠缺行動而作出的判決（default judgment）」，本書簡稱為「缺席判決」），在理論上被告人有權以內地法院判決不構成最終及不可推翻判決為理由（之一），提出撤銷缺席判決的申請（《高等法院規則》第13條第9條規則）。北京橙天嘉禾案即屬這種案型（見本書簡評案例六）。

（3）在簡易程序聆訊中抗辯

若原告人嘗試通過簡易判決程序取得勝訴判決，被告人也可以在簡易程序的聆訊中以內地判決不是最終及不可推翻判決為由進行抗辯。根據《高等法院規則》第14號命令，在被告人就原告人的申索發出擬抗辯通知書後，原告人可以被告人無法抗辯為理據，向法庭申請作出簡易判決。法庭會就簡易申請進行聆訊或書面審理。在此聆訊或書面審理中，被告人即可提出內地法院判決不構成最終及不可推翻判決的抗辯主張。在本書評論的涉及內地法院判決的判例中，並未涉及被告人在簡易程序聆訊中提出此項抗辯的案件。但是，在 Nintendo 案中，被告人即在簡易程序聆訊中，主張原告人據以起訴的加州法院判決不構成最終及不可推翻判決（見本書第七回）。

（二）案型二：重新起訴（不容反悔法、濫用訴訟程序）

在此類案型中，主張內地法院判決為最終及不可推翻判決的一方，是被告人而不是原告人。原告人是在存在內地法院判決的情況下，在香港法

院重新就相同或相關爭議（訴因）重新起訴，被告人則以內地法院判決屬最終及不可推翻判決為理由（或理由之一）作為抗辯。根據被告人抗辯的法律依據，此類案型可進一步分為不容反悔法（estoppel）與濫用訴訟程序兩種案型。就前者而言，被告人是以內地法院判決構成最終及不可推翻判決為由，主張內地法院判決構成「問題已決」或具有既判力（res judicata），從而原告人就已作出既判力判決的爭議重新起訴，違反不容反悔法的法律原則（林哲民第一案即屬這一案型）（見該案判決第 17 段）。就濫用訴訟程序的案型而言，被告人則是根據《高等法院規則》第 18 號命令第 19 條規則所規定的濫用法庭程序的原則提出抗辯，並以內地法院判決為最終及不可推翻判決作為原告人濫用法庭程序的考慮因素（林哲民第二案即屬這一案型）。但要注意的是，上訴法庭在林哲民的一案中，其實已經明確表示，涉及內地法院判決是否最終及不可推翻判決問題的案件，並不應適用《高等法院規則》第 18 號命令第 19 條規則處理，而只能根據不容反悔法處理（參見林哲民第一案判決第第 15 段、第 16 段），但在林哲民第二案中，上訴法庭似乎反過來又按照該規則處理。無論如何，在以上的兩個判例中，上訴法庭均在一定程度上採用了內地法院判決並非最終及不可推翻判決的觀點（從而或不適用不容反悔法原則，或不構成濫用訴訟程序），而認為原告人可在香港法院重新起訴。

可補充說明的是，在此類案型中，香港訴訟的原告人及被告人，既可以相應地同為內地訴訟的原告和被告，也可以互換角色，即香港訴訟原告人為內地訴訟被告，被告人則為內地訴訟的原告。比如，林哲民第一案的原告人為內地訴訟被告的法定代表人，被告人則為內地訴訟原告的法定代表人；林哲民第二案的原告人與被告人，則相應地同是內地訴訟的原告與被告。

（三）案型三：《高等法院條例》第 21M 條案型（在沒有實質法律程序進行的情況下的臨時濟助）

「在沒有實質法律程序進行的情況下的臨時濟助」一般更多被稱為「協助境外法律程序的臨時濟助」。在《高等法院條例》第 21M 條的規定下，原告人可就境外進行的法律程序申請支持該法律程序的臨時濟助（interim relief），其中較為常見的是臨時濟助為資產凍結令（Mareva injunction）。中國銀行案即屬這一案型。

按照《高等法院條例》第 21M 條的規定，原告人就境外法律程序申請臨時濟助的條件之一，即境外的法律程序能產生一個可在香港強制執行的判決。據此，原告人根據此項規定申請支持內地訴訟的臨時濟助，須證明日後取得的內地法院判決符合上述條件。按照中國銀行案的判詞，只要原告人關於內地法院判決構成最終及不可推翻判決的主張具有「良好的可爭辯論點（good arguable case）」即可。由此可見，在此類案型中，與申請將簡易判決作廢的案型類似，所處理的問題並不是內地法院判決「是否」構成最終及不可推翻判決的問題，而是內地法院判決「是否可能」構成最終及不可推翻判決的問題。

（四）案型四：《高等法院條例》第 21L 條案型（強制令及接管人）

在伍威禁制令案中，涉及內地法院判決是否構成最終及不可推翻判決問題的，是原告人的強制令申請。在此案中，主張內地法院判決構成最終能及不可推翻判決的是被告人，而不是原告人。實際上，本案的基礎申索，是原告人以內地法院判決不構成最終及不可推翻判決為前提所提起的重新起訴（即案型二）。被告人則主張內地法院判決構成最終及不可推翻判決，並以此為基礎，一方面對原告人提起反訴（訴請執行內地法院判決），另方面則作為原告人申請強制令的抗辯理由。根據《高等法院條例》第 21L 條的相關判例，原告人申請強制令的條件之一是存在一項需要審訊的重大問題。在伍威案中，內地法院判決是否構成最終及不可推翻判決的問題，實際上就是作為判斷是否存在一項需要審訊的重大問題時的一個主要考慮因素而被考慮。如同案型三及案型一中的申請將簡易判決作廢的情形，在此案型中，法庭所需要處理的問題，並不是內地法院判決「是否」構成最終及不可推翻判決的問題，而是內地法院判決「是否可能」構成或不構成最終及不可推翻判決的問題。

二、目前的法律狀態

（一）基本可確定的法律狀態

儘管對於內地法院判決在審判監督制度下是否為最終及不可推翻判決的問題本身，香港判例尚未形成明確的答案，但對於內地法院判決在普通法下的法律狀態，在李祐榮案後已經比較明確。張澤祐法官在李祐榮案判詞中所提出，並經隨後幾個判決所跟隨及確認的裁判觀點，基本上已經形成目前內地法院判決在普通法下的法律狀態，具體可分以下數項說明：

其一，香港法院並未確立內地法院判決因存在審判監督制度而不構成最終及不可推翻判決的判例規則（中國銀行案判決第 48 段、54 段），內地法院判決是否因存在審判監督制度而構成或不構成最終及不可推翻判決並未明確（李祐榮案判決第 34 段、第 37 段等）。

其二，內地法院判決在審判監督制度下是否構成最終及不可推翻的判決，是一個具有重大爭議的問題，也是一項具有公眾重要性的議題，不宜通過簡易程序處理（李祐榮案判決第 24 段、第 26 段、第 27 段、第 29 段，伍威第一案判決第 96 段，伍威第二案判決第 7 段）。

其三，內地法院判決在審判監督制度下是否構成最終及不可推翻判決的問題，必須通過正式審訊處理，據此：（1）原告人根據內地法院判決通過簡易判決程序取得的勝訴判決，經被告人申請應予撤銷（李祐榮案）；（2）原告人根據內地法院判決通過缺席判決程序取得的勝訴判決，有可能經被告人申請而撤銷（北京橙天嘉禾案，但該案首先是以送達不符合規定為依據而撤銷）；（3）被告人根據內地法院判決提起的反訴，不足以阻止原告人的禁制令申請，也不足以暫緩原告人禁制令的執行（伍威禁制令案、伍威暫緩禁制令執行案）；（4）內地法院判決足以作為申請協助境外訴訟程序禁制令的依據（中國銀行案）。

其四，處理內地法院判決在審判監督制度下是否構成最終及不可推翻判決的問題，必須經內地法律專家證人在正式審訊中出庭作證、接受盤問及全面解釋其意見後以查明相關內地法律的內容（李祐榮案第 27 段、第

29 段、第 36 段、第 37 段，中國銀行案第 54 段）。

（二）進一步引申的問題

在目前法律狀態可基本確定的上述四項內容下，還會引申出一些相關問題。以下分別加以說明：

1. 是否還能申請擱置？

在 Chiyu 案、武漢中碩虹案中，被告人是以申請擱置訴訟程序的方式對原告人的執行內地法院判決主張進行抗辯，其法律依據當時為法院固有司法管轄權中的酌情擱置原則（現在還包括《高等法院規則》第 12 號命令第 8 條規則）。根據該原則，擱置的原因理應是內地訴訟程序仍在進行（而不是內地法院判決不能在香港強制執行）。因此，在法庭裁定擱置訴訟程序後，應等待內地法院訴訟程序繼續進行的結果，再確定是否重啟香港的訴訟程序，亦即香港訴訟程序暫時停止進行。但是，在李祐榮案中，上訴法庭所作出的裁判結果，不再是擱置香港訴訟程序，而是撤銷簡易判決以及命令進行正式審訊（儘管實際上當事人後來並未進行正式審訊），亦即繼續進行香港訴訟程序。

那麼，是否可以依此認為，面對原告人以內地法院判決債務為訴因提起的訴訟，被告人不能再申請擱置訴訟，而必須進入正式審訊並在審訊中進行抗辯？恐怕尚不能如此認為。在對抗式的訴訟制度下，裁判結果在相當程度上受當事人的訴訟主張所影響。在李祐榮案中，被告人在沒有律師代表的情況下，只是針對原訟法庭作出的簡易判決表示上訴，並未進一步提出擱置訴訟程序的訴求，上訴法庭也並未考慮此問題。因此，被告人是否仍然可以主張擱置訴訟，還是只能繼續進行訴訟程序（進行正式審訊），是一項判例並未處理的問題，從而也不存在在此問題上的法律觀點。

2. 通過申請剔除（striking-out）狀書進行抗辯？

所謂剔除狀書，按照內地法律的習慣用語，即駁回全部或部份訴訟請求，其法律依據為《高等法院規則》第 18 號命令第 19 條規則。在本書評論的判例中，並未涉及被告人通過申請撤銷或剔除狀書的方式對原告人關於內地法院判決「構成」最終及不可推翻判決的主張進行抗辯的案件（只有通過此程序對原告人關於內地法院判決「不構成」最終及不可推翻判決

的主張進行抗辯的案件，見林哲民第二案）。

在理論上，若能證明內地法院判決確不構成最終及不可推翻的判決，被告人即可主張撤銷原告人的訴訟。在武漢中碩虹案中，楊振權法官亦表達了此觀點（見該判決第 20 段）。在程序上，被告人更可通過申請剔除狀書的程序進行其抗辯。然而，如同簡易判決程序，申請剔除狀書程序同樣屬非正式審訊程序中的簡易程序。不同之處只在於，簡易判決程序的目的在於不通過正式審訊作出原告人勝訴（被告人敗訴）的判決，剔除狀書程序的目的則經常在於（但不限於）不通過正式審訊作出被告人勝訴（原告人敗訴）的判決。既然在目前的法律狀態下，內地法院判決是否構成最終及不可推翻判決的問題，已被確定為必須通過正式審訊處理的事項，則按理也不存在被告人可通過剔除狀書程序進行抗辯的空間。

3. 通過就法律論點而處置案件程序進行抗辯？

在伍威禁制令案中，原告人提請了法庭處理內地法院判決是否不是最終及不可推翻判決的問題。儘管判詞中未明確說明，這應該是一項根據《高等法院規則》第 14A 號命令提出的申請，即「就法律論點而處置案件」的申請。此項申請，既可以由被告人提出，也可以由原告人提出。因此，似乎無論是原告人還是被告人，都可以提出此申請，要求法庭就內地法院判決是或不是最終及不可推翻判決作出裁定。然而，根據《高等法院規則》第 14A 條明確規定了此項申請的適用條件之一，是「該問題宜於不對該宗訴訟進行全面審訊而予以裁定」。既然判例已經明確指出內地法院判決是或不是最終及不可推翻判決的問題，必須經過正式審訊裁定，因此無論是原告人還是被告人均無從依此程序處理此問題。

（三）關於「法律狀態」的進一步說明——普通法的「多層次」觀念與內地法的「單一化」觀念

需要強調的是，上文所說的「法律狀態」，是指在普通法下的法律狀態，必須以普通法的觀念加以理解才能準確掌握。為避免內地法律界讀者因從內地法律的觀念理解而產生誤解，筆者在此嘗試根據個人對普通法觀念的一些體會來加以說明。

根據個人的經驗和體會，假設一位內地律師採用內地法律人的習慣思

維去理解這所謂的「法律狀態」，他很可能會得出類似這樣的判斷：「判例已經明確指出內地法院是否為最終及不可推翻判決的問題有待解決，而該問題必須在正式審訊中處理。據此，根據香港目前法律，原告人未經正式審訊，無從在香港直接執行內地法院判決。」然而，一位香港律師對於相同的法律狀態，很可能會有如下的不同解讀：「判例已經明確指出內地法院是否為最終及不可推翻判決的問題有待解決，而該問題必須在正式審訊中處理。據此，原告人未必能直接執行內地法院判決，但可以嘗試。」

香港律師之所以會認為只是「未必」能直接執行，並且「可以嘗試」，筆者個人認為主要是基於對抗式訴訟制度及其所產生的思維習慣的原因。在對抗式訴訟制度下，上文所指的「法律狀態」，是原訟法庭及上訴法庭法官所確立的法律觀點，而這些法律觀點，並不是在任何法律程序中都必然被引用，而是在相當程度上取決於對方是否在抗辯中提出，以及法官是否主動適用。如果對方未答辯或提出有力的答辯，法官又未能主動引用相關判例觀點，原告人以內地法院判決債務為訴因提起的訴訟，也有可能在缺席判決或簡易判決程序中勝訴。事實上，內地法院判決債務在被告人不予抗辯或抗辯不力的情況下通過缺席判決或簡易判決程序獲得執行的並不少見（只是缺席判決和簡易判決並不公開，也不構成有約束力的先例，其具體數量難以統計）。

由此可見，在香港的對抗式訴訟制度下，「原告人未經正式審訊，無從在香港直接執行內地法院判決」的判斷是不準確的；而對於一位內地律師而言，確實比較容易得出這樣的判斷。筆者根據個人觀察認為，對於特定法律規則的理解，一位普通法律師一般會認為該法律規則「可能是」或「很可能是」甚麼，而不是該法律規則「是」甚麼；而一位內地律師則更容易傾向於認為法律規則「是」甚麼，甚至「就是」甚麼，而不是「可能是」甚麼。因此，對於香港判例所確立的內地法院判決是否最終及不可推翻問題必須在正式審訊中處理的法律狀態，內地律師會更容易作出「單一化」的理解，而香港律師則會傾向於持有「多層次」的、更具「開放性」的理解。

不過，在實際上，即使是在內地，對特定法律問題的判斷出現因時因地因人而異的情況也不少見。比如夫妻共同財產的問題，對於特定財產取得究竟是夫妻雙方共同財產還是一方個人財產，在有明確的司法解釋前，不同的法院，甚至相同法院的不同法官，都可能作出不同的裁判。按理，

即使是內地律師也不應對任何法律問題作出過度「單一化」的理解。但無論如何，根據個人觀察，筆者確實發現內地律師比普通法律師更容易對法律問題作出更為「單一化」的理解。也許是在糾問式訴訟制度下，在理念上無論當事人是否提出主張或抗辯，法官均應主動適用本應適用的法律，從而更容易形成人們的一種對法律觀點理應「單一」的期待。正是在這種期待的影響下，內地律師會更容易傾向於認為法律規則「就是」甚麼，而不僅是「可能是」甚麼。

三、香港法院和法官對內地法院判決的態度？

（一）是否存在香港法院和法官的態度？

從本書所討論的判例看，在內地法院判決是否為最終及不可推翻判決問題上，貌似體現了香港法院的一種對內地法院判決態度「逐漸友好」的趨勢。而在所看到的一些內地文章中，以及在與一些相關學者、司法工作人員的討論中，筆者也注意到出現了這樣的一種看法——香港法院和法官的態度開始有所轉變，不再那麼歧視或敵視內地判決。有的觀點甚至把這種態度同香港回歸多年、兩地融合等因素拉上直接關係，認為此乃大勢所趨，香港法院和法官也不得不予認可。然而，筆者認為，上述觀點既不準確，也不妥當，理由如下：

其一，上述觀點將問題歸結為（至少在一定程度上歸結為）「香港法院和法官的態度」問題。所謂「香港法院和法官的態度」的說法，大概是假設了香港法院存在一種「一統化」的「集體」態度。但實際上，這樣的假設是否成立？這樣的態度是否存在？筆者認為，這樣的假設在相當程度上體現了內地法律觀念的影響，甚至有「以己度人」之嫌。在內地，糾問式訴訟制度、對統一法律觀點的追求（在制度上體現為審判委員會、法院系統的專業問題會議、司法解釋等制度），均更容易產生人們對司法機關形成一統化集體態度的期待，也確實更容易形成這樣態度。這也體現了一種習慣於由法官來主導的觀念。然而，在香港普通法司法制度下，不僅不存在類似上述的內地特有制度，而且法官們在實際上更是相互獨立、各自為政，恐怕較難為形成這種一統化集體態度提供充分的條件，這正是由當事人而非法官來擔任主導（正所謂當事人主義）的對抗式訴訟制度的特點。

其二，這種對主觀態度的判斷，本身就具有很大的主觀性。無論在早期判例中的「敵視」，還是後來的「友好」，實際上都屬對法官主觀態度的判斷。法官的主觀態度，旁人本來就無從得知，充其量只是猜測。筆者通過對所有這些涉及內地法院判決的香港判例進行了仔細研讀，也無從發現存在這些主觀態度的確鑿證據。

其三，退一步說，即使基於在「法官共同體」內的相互影響，香港法

院和法官對內地法院判決確實存在某種態度，筆者仍然反對把問題歸結為香港法院和法官們的態度問題。理由在於，一方面即使確實能夠形成並存在這種態度，在香港的法律制度下，其「一統化」和「集體化」的程度也要遠遠低於內地的情況；另一方面，更重要的是，把問題歸結為態度問題，會導致對問題的真正成因產生錯誤的判斷，從而也無法「對症下藥」，以正確的方式和途徑解決問題。

（二）當成態度問題：對問題的誤判及其後果

即使在 Chiyu 案中，張澤祐法官採用了諸如「內地《民事訴訟法》下的再審制度不是簡單的上訴程序，⋯⋯如果一個內地法院作出的判決被提起抗訴，該法院即必須進行再審，其顯然保留了變更其原判決的權力」「這表明該內地判決並非最終及不可推翻」等陳述，更明確採用了 "Not final and conclusive" 的標題，無論其判詞在內容上如何明確，對內地法院判決的態度如何「強硬」，但是相信也不會有香港的法官或律師會貿然認為：張法官在態度上一般性地敵視內地法院判決。他們只會認為，這不過只是一名法官在一項非正審聆訊程序中所作出的判詞。一方面，其所處理的問題既未經過充分的爭辯，所作出的裁判結果亦未經過更高級別法庭的確認；另一方面，張法官的裁判也在很大程度上受到該案當事人的主張和論證的影響。同樣地，也不能因為在一些個案中，原告人通過缺席判決程序或簡易判決程序成功地執行了內地法院判決，就認為香港法院和法官對內地法院判決持友好態度。

對問題的誤判，必然導致解決手段的錯配。不準確地將問題當成香港法院和法官的態度問題，也必然導致無法通過正確的方式和途徑解決問題，甚至導致採用適得其反的錯誤方式和手段。實際上，在一些內地學者和法律工作人員的論述中，也可以看到由於不準確地將問題歸結為香港法院和法官的態度問題，結果就出現了請香港法院和法官改變態度的呼籲。這種呼籲，不僅讓香港法律界感覺無的放矢、莫名其妙，更無助於問題的解決，甚至未必有利於兩地法律專業之間的交流和互動。

一個典型的例子，是在李祐榮案中，擔任內地法律專家證人的王亞新教授一方面為法庭提供了非常全面的關於內地審判監督制度的法律意見，但另一方面又在法律意見的最後部份作出了以下的陳述：

「考慮到香港特別行政區政府和內地的當局都正在謀求做出能夠促進兩地經濟交流與發展的有關安排這種努力，萬一法院的判例在事實上卻形成了十分不利於這種共同努力的司法政策，將可能帶來十分負面的影響或後果。在這個意義上，則不得不説本案的處理將會超越個案的正義，而具有一般政策的含義。鑒於最後這一點涉及公共利益或政策的考慮，本意見書的結論依然是：對於本案原審判決，應當認為屬最終和不可推翻的判決。」（見該判決第 30 段）

針對王教授的上述論述，張澤祐法官以專門的篇幅並採用了「專家證人的職責範圍」標題作出了以下評價：「專家證人無論是法律或其他方面的專家的功用是向法庭提供專業的知識，讓法庭參考後可以作出一個正確的判決，除此之外，專家證人不應該就其他議題發表個人意見。制定政策是政府機關的職責，法庭在審理案件時不會推行某種司法政策，只會就案情作出裁決。王教授以上所表達的意見可能是因不熟悉專家證人在本港訴訟程序上的職責或是出於關注內地與香港判決雙互執行的問題，但這並不是專家證人職責的範圍。本席需要強調本席提出這點並不是批評王教授，而是有需要重申專家證人職責的範圍。」（見該判決第 31 段）

王教授的上述觀點在學術及政策上固然具有相當的道理，但其論述並非遵循香港相關法律制度下的「遊戲規則」，不僅被指為超出職責範圍，更無從達到目的。

筆者認為，要有效地處理內地法院判決在普通法上的法律地位問題，改變香港法院和法官的「態度」，只能對問題的成因及解決的方式和途徑進行準確的了解。具體而言，就是要準確掌握香港普通法制度下的「遊戲規則」，採用普通法的方式和途徑，方可能有效地達到目的。

（三）對抗式訴訟制度下的正確方式：當事人在個案中主張及充分論證

普通法法域普遍採用的對抗式訴訟制度，又稱當事人主義訴訟制度。顧名思義，就是以當事人為中心，由當事人起主導作用。一般認為，在對抗式訴訟制度中，當事人的主導主要體現在訴訟程序的時間控制及案件的調查取證上。而事實上，這種當事人的主導也同樣體現在法律的適用上。儘管嚴格而言，案件的主審法官理應正確適用法律，即使當事人未主張適

用所應適用的法律，法官也有權並且有一定的職責主動適用。比如在伍威禁制令案中，被告人並未主張原告人據以起訴的內地法院判決具有既判力，但法官也主動考慮了此問題（該判決第 94 段）（該案簡評見本書簡評案例二）；又如在林哲民第一案中，當事人及原訟法官均未主張或適用不容反悔法原則，上訴法庭則主動引用該原則處理該案（該判決第 16 段）（該案評論見本書第四回）；再如在李祐榮案中，被告人並沒有在上訴中主張內地法院判決不是最終及不可推翻判決，但法官亦主動處理該問題（該判決第 35 段）（該案相關評論見本書第六回（上））。

相反，儘管如果法官未主動適用所應適用的法律，其裁判也可能會在上訴程序中被視為適用法律錯誤而被推翻，法官也同樣可以不主動適用當事人未主張適用的法律，或以當事人就有關法律問題不存在爭議而不予處理。比如，在陳國柱訴陳桂洲案中，法庭即直接按照雙方當事人的共識，採納了內地判決並非最終及不可推翻判決或不屬具有既判力判決的法律觀點並作為處理該案爭議的前提（該案判決第 4 段）（該案簡評見本書簡評案例二）；又如在 Yick Tat 案中，被告人以內地法院判決為具有既判力判決為由申請剔除原告人的起訴，根據普通法，內地法院判決具有既判力須以該判決為最終及不可推翻判決為條件，但雙方當事人均未提及最終及不可推翻的問題，法官亦在未考慮此條件的情況下作出了內地法院判決為具有既判力判決的裁判（該判決第 1 段、第 16 段、第 60 段、第 82 段）（該案簡評見本書簡評案例五）。可以想像，假如此二案件被進一步上訴，前述裁定或觀點均有可能在上訴程序中被視為適用法律錯誤而被推翻。然而，要強調的是，對「適用法律錯誤」的認知，內地法律人與香港法律人亦會有所不同。對於一名內地律師或法官來說，「適用法律錯誤」具有更為「嚴厲」的意義，其否定評價更為強烈，法官也更容易被標籤為「犯錯」，屬「紀律」問題。但對於香港律師或法官來說，雖然同樣為「適用法律錯誤」，但在觀念上並不會過度嚴厲。案件因適用法律錯誤而被推翻，香港法官會認為不過是其工作的固有內容而已，一般不會認為是「犯錯」，不過是工作問題而不是紀律問題。

基於對抗式訴訟制度的上述特點，當事人的主張，包括法律適用問題上的主張，就尤為重要。影響法官最終裁判觀點的因素，首先並不是法官自己的態度，而是當事人的主張，更準確的說，是當事人代表律師的訴訟主張和陳詞，其中就包含了當事人代表律師的論辯水平和力度。筆者在本

書中對二十多年來涉及內地法院判決是否最終及不可推翻判決問題的香港判例進行了評論，發現在這些案件中，需要主張內地法院判決為最終及不可推翻的一方，多數並未能在此問題上進行有力的舉證和論證。作為例外的是李祐榮案。在該案中，之所以能出現鍾安德法官的支持內地法院判決構成最終及不可推翻判決的異議判詞，相信在很大程度上要歸功於原告人一方的有力爭論，一方面提供了王亞新教授論證充分而全面的法律意見，另一方面又在法律上進行了深入的爭論（比如提供了 Nintendo 案判決，將判例依據擴大至 Chiyu 案以外的判例）。作為評論這些判例的個人體會，筆者更傾向於認為，內地法院判決在普通法下所處於的不利法律狀態，首先並非基於法官態度的原因，而是由於當事人及其代表律師爭論力度的緣故。

據上，筆者認為，要改變內地法院判決在香港普通法上的地位，最直接有效的方式和途徑，並不是羣眾式的呼籲，而是要在香港訴訟制度的既有框架內，按照其既有「遊戲規則」，在恰當的時點——個案中的訴訟程序，以恰當的身份——代表律師而不是專家證人，採用恰當的方式——全面、充分、有據的訴訟主張及論證，全面、有力的專家證人法律意見，據理力爭，促使法官在最大程度上採納內地法院判決理應為最終及不可推翻判決的觀點，並成為判例規則。這也是在普通法民事訴訟制度下，法官可改變內地法院判決法律地位的正常的、唯一的，並且是最具權威性的途徑。

四、關於論證思路的建議

（一）在法律（先例規則）上進行徹底論證

1. 否定 Chiyu 案的裁判觀點

儘管後來的判決已經回避或通過闡釋改變了 Chiyu 案的裁判觀點，但 Chiyu 案作為內地法院判決在普通法上難以獲得承認和執行的源頭案例，對其裁判觀點進行更徹底的檢討和否定，會更有利於改變內地法院判決在普通法上的地位。Chiyu 案的裁判觀點至少存在以下的問題：

其一，Chiyu 案的判詞，將判斷境外判決是否最終及不可推翻的標準，局限於判決是否有可能被原審法院推翻。單獨觀之，這是一個非常廣泛的標準，不僅被其他判例明確確認為構成最終及不可推翻判決的缺席判決也被涵蓋其中（從而可被認定為不構成最終及不可推翻判決），甚至連香港及其他普通法法域的許多本來具有終局性的判決亦可被涵蓋其中。顯然，香港普通法並沒有一概採用這一標準，從 Nouvion 先例本身的判詞看亦存在可斟酌的空間，結合其他判例則更可加以限縮。

其二，導致 Chiyu 案判詞出現上述情況，主要原因在於其對 Nouvion 先例的引用，存在比較明顯的斷章取義。在引用的判詞範圍上，Nouvion 先例的四位審理法官均發表了判詞，Chiyu 案判詞僅引用了兩位法官的一小部份判詞。在內容上，Nouvion 先例所處理的是西班牙法院特別簡易判決（remate judgment），對於該判決，綜合四位法官的判詞，除了指出特別簡易判決可被原審法院重新審理並予以改變或廢除外，同時也強調了另外兩項因素：（1）在據以作出特別簡易判決的程序中，法院並非對案件的全部是非曲折（merits）進行審理，而被告人也僅被允許提出特定的抗辯理由（而不是全面抗辯）；（2）原審法院可基於當事人的任意申請，而重新對案件進行全面審理。然而，Chiyu 案對於特別簡易判決的此兩項特點，均隻字未提。

基於以上的論證缺陷，Chiyu 案的裁判觀點並非無懈可擊，因此對其重新審視並予以否定也具有相當的可能性。

2. 將審判監督程序論證為相當於普通法的上訴程序

無論是 Nouvion 先例，還是 Chiyu 案（引用 Nouvion 先例），均明確確立了判決不因可被上訴而視為並非最終及不可推翻的判決。因此，一個重要的可採用論證思路是，將審判監督程序論證為相當於普通法的上訴程序。在李祐榮案中，鍾安德法官在其異議判詞中就是主要採用了這一論證思路。通過將審判監督程序的再審條件、時限、再審機構與香港的上訴制度進行比較，鍾法官認為審判監督程序如同香港的上訴程序，從而不應被視為並非最終及不可推翻判決（關於鍾法官的論證，詳見本書第六回）。

可以特別指出的是，從內地法律的角度看，上訴與再審的區別，主要在於：（1）可上訴的判決並非生效判決，不可進入強制執行程序，而可被提起再審的判決則為生效判決，並可被強制執行；（2）法院對案件進行再審，必須以法院裁定予以再審為前提。而這兩項再審制度的特點，實際上與香港法律中的上訴制度更為吻合。根據香港法律，判決一旦作出，原則上即生效並可強制執行，此與內地的可再審判決相同，反而不同於內地的可上訴判決。而對於已生效的判決，則可根據上訴的條件而區分為當然權利上訴（appeal as of right）與須取得上訴許可（leave a to appeal）的上訴，後者亦與內地可再審判決的情形相同，而不同於可上訴判決。

3. 重新審視 Nouvion 先例的裁判觀點

Nouvion 先例作為普通法上最終及不可推翻判決問題的非常重要的先例，要對其所確立的關於最終及不可推翻判決的規則作出準確的理解，就必須繞開 Chiyu 案判決對 Nouvion 先例判詞的斷章取義式引用，對其重新審視並進行全面的分析。

在李祐榮案的異議判詞中，鍾安德法官認為內地法律中的再審程序與 Nouvion 先例中的特別簡易判決上訴程序完全不同，內地法院判決與特別簡易判決也不同，從而 Nouvion 先例不應適用於內地法院判決（見李祐榮案判決第 73 段）。然而，對於內地法院判決及審判監督制度下的再審程序如何不同，鍾法官並未結合 Nouvion 先例的判詞作深入分析。在中國銀行案中，杜法官則對 Nouvion 先例中 Lord Watson 的判詞重新進行了闡釋，將「一個最終及不可推翻的判決，必須是在宣告該判決的法院為最終及不可改變（must be final and unalterable in the court which pronounced it）」的表述，理解為「一個判決是最終及不可推翻的判決，如果宣告該

判決的法院不能自願地改變該判決（a judgment is final and conclusive if it is unalterable voluntarily in the court which pronounced it）」，即加入了「自願地」的表述。

鍾法官與杜法官的上述判詞，無疑都是對 Nouvion 先例判詞進行重新審視的嘗試，然而其分析仍可更為深入。鍾法官只是指出 Nouvion 先例不適用於內地法院判決，並未對 Nouvion 先例相關判詞展開分析；杜法官則仍然只涉及 Nouvion 判詞中關於最終及不可推翻判決三項考慮因素中的其中一項，即判決是否可由原審法院重新審理。如前所述，綜合 Nouvion 先例四位法官的判詞，對於該先例所處理的特別簡易判決，考慮的因素並不限於原審法院是否可重新審理一項，同時也包括（1）在據以作出特別簡易判決的程序中法院是否對案件進行全面審理，以及（2）在上訴程序中法院是否基於當事人的任意申請即須對案件重新進行全面審理。強調此二項因素對爭取改變內地法院判決在普通法上的地位尤為重要，理由如下：

其一，根據內地審判監督制度，絕大多數可再審的判決，均屬經過一般訴訟程序（普通程序和簡易程序）作出的判決。而無論是在普通程序還是在簡易程序中，無論是事實問題還是法律問題，案件的爭議均經過法院的全面審理。這也是內地法院判決與 Nouvion 先例中的特別簡易判決的重大不同之處。

其二，根據內地審判監督制度的發展沿革，法院在再審程序中對案件的審理事項範圍也呈現出有所限縮的趨勢，也就是說，在再審中法院一般不對案件進行全面的重新審理。這也是內地法院判決與 Nouvion 先例中的特別簡易判決的另一項差異。

其三，在 Nouvion 先例中的三項考慮因素中，恰恰是 Chiyu 案所引用的考慮因素（即判決是否可由原審法院重新審理並予以改變或廢除）對內地法院判決最為不利。即使是採用杜法官在中國銀行判詞中的觀點，將 Nouvion 先例的觀點調整為最終及不可推翻判決是原審法院不能「自願地」改變的判決，內地法院判決仍然可能被視為不構成最終及不可推翻判決。理由在於，根據審判監督制度的相關規定，原審法院的院長始終是享有再審決定權的主體之一。若不能徹底否定原審法院是否能改變原判決這項考慮因素，內地法院判決始終存在被認定為不構成最終及不可推翻判決的空間。因此，強調另外兩項考慮因素，以擴大內地法院判決可能被認定為最

終及不可推翻判決的依據，甚有必要。

4. 以 Nintendo 案和 Vanquelin 先例為依據充分論證

如上所述，在 Nouvion 先例中的三項考慮因素中，判決是否可被原審法院改變是對內地法院判決不利的一項考慮因素。若能更徹底地排除此項考慮因素，則將更能有助於內地法院判決被認定為構成最終及不可推翻判決的可能。此外，基於 Nouvion 先例的判決不因可被上訴而視為並非最終及不可推翻判決的裁判觀點，固然可以採用類似於鍾安德法官在李祐榮案中的論證，將審判監督制度理解為上訴制度。然而，由於鍾法官的判詞僅為異議判詞，尚不構成有約束力的判例規則，僅依賴將審判監督制度相當於上訴制度的論證恐怕並不足夠。更重要的是，在 Nouvion 先例中，Lord Herschell 和 Lord Watson 在說明此項規則時，均指出是指判決可被上訴至「更高級別法院」（appealable to a higher tribunal 或 subject of appeal to a higher court）。因此，若判決可被上訴，但是由原審法院對上訴進行審理，該判決仍有可能被視為不屬此論述中的「可被上訴」，從而被視為並非最終及不可推翻。而在內地審判監督制度下，再審案件也很可能是由原審法院審理，因此即使將審判監督程序制度論證為上訴制度，但內地法院判決仍有可能被視為不符合上述的「可被上訴」判決。若能論證即使由原審法院對判決的上訴進行審理，該判決也仍然屬最終及不可推翻判決，則更有機會確保內地法院判決被視為最終及不可推翻的判決。Nintendo 案和 Vanquelin 先例的裁判觀點，正好為更徹底地排除判決是否可被原審法院改變的考慮因素，以及將「可被上訴」理解為包括上訴由原審法院審理的情形提供了有力的論證依據。詳述如下：

其一，Nintendo 案所處理的是一項美國法院的缺席判決，即相當於香港法律中的因欠缺行動而作出的判決（default judgment）（也簡稱為「缺席判決」）。根據美國法律，該缺席判決即可由原審法院重新進行審理，即使如此，根據 Nintendo 案的裁判觀點，這也足以構成最終及不可推翻的判決。其中的理由在於，即使法院就該案件最終作出的是缺席判決，也未對案件進行全面審理，但被告人本來是有權提出全面的抗辯並由法院進行全面審理，只是被告人自己欠缺行動，而不是被告人無機會提出抗辯。

其二，十分重要的是，Nintendo 案的上述裁判觀點，要溯源至作為其判例依據的 Vanquelin 先例。Vanquelin 先例，是在 Nouvion 先例之前的判

例，而 Nouvion 先例並未引用 Vanquelin 先例，這就為通過協調（reconcile）的方式對 Nouvion 先例的裁判觀點進行限縮創造了可能性。要通過協調使 Vanquelin 先例與 Nouvion 先例並存，其中最有可能的方式，就是將 Nouvion 先例中關於判決是否可由原審法院改變的考慮因素排除在外。

其三，不僅要對審判監督制度與上訴制度進行比較，更要對內地法院判決與普通法制度中的缺席判決進行比較。以香港法律中的缺席判決為例，在香港缺席判決程序中，不僅法院未對案件進行全面審理，而且在判決作出後，作出判決的法院有權主動（on its own motion）將該判決作廢（《高等法院規則》第 13 號命令第 9 條規則、第 19 號命令第 9 條規則）或變更（《高等法院規則》第 1B 號命令第 2 條規則）。此外，缺席判決經上訴後進行的審理，是完全的重審（de novo），即在上訴程序中要對案件重新進行全面的審理。從缺席判決的這些特點看，內地法院判決在實質上所具有的終局性，實際上要大大強於香港法律中的缺席判決。

（二）內地法律專家證人

上述的充分論證，除了需要代表律師的高水平陳詞外，還必須由論證充分、能有效協助法庭了解內地相關法律的專家證人法律意見（書面法律意見及在正式審訊中接受盤問）加以配合和支持。現就內地法律專家證人法律意見，提出如下意見：

其一，避免論證焦點局限於內地法院判決是否可被原審法院改變。就目前涉及內地法院判決最終及不可推翻問題的判例而言，似乎內地法律專家證人所出具的意見，主要局限於審判監督制度本身。這應該與當事人將內地法院判決是否為可被原審法院改變的問題作為論證重點有關。在此情況下，主張內地法院判決為最終及不可推翻的一方，也只能盡力說明該個案中的內地法院判決不會被原審法院改變。實際上，在內地審判監督制度的現有規定下，要作此論證非常困難，甚至也不太客觀。畢竟原審法院的院長享有決定再審的權力，上級法院及檢察院亦有權啟動再審，並且沒有時間限制。因此最終也只能變成論證判決被原審法院改變的機會不高。這樣就大大降低了內地法律專家證言的說服力。畢竟，在採用判決是否可被原審法院改變的標準下，只要判決有可能被原審法院改變，在概念上就可以被視為不構成最終及不可推翻。Chiyu 案的判詞也正是採用了這樣的觀

點：「如果一旦提出抗訴，無論其如何罕見（rare the circumstances may be），內地法院即必須進行再審，則其顯然保留了變更其裁判的權力」（該判決第 20 段）。因此，徹底解決之道，是要超越判決是否可被原審法院改變的標準，將論證重點擴大至內地法院判決的其他因素上。

其二，結合前文關於應強調（1）內地法院判決是基於全面審理而作出的判決，及（2）在再審中內地法院一般不會對案件進行全面的重新審理的建議。內地法律專家的法律意見應將說明的重點擴展到據以作出內地法院判決的審判程序以及再審審理的事項範圍，而不僅是局限於誰可以進行再審的問題。

其三，在一些判例的判詞中，均提到內地審判監督程序的相關法律一直在發生變化，而因此不能依賴過去案件中的認定。據此，內地法律專家的法律意見應該可以儘量精確地闡述內地審判監督制度及其變化，特別是在 2012 年《民事訴訟法》後最高人民法院頒佈的相關司法解釋，更全面地加以說明，也可以指出現有規定與過去案件中所認定的情形有哪些不同。不過，也要指出的是，儘管有關審判監督制度的法律規定在不斷發展，但就決定再審的權力主體而言，一直以來其實並沒有太大的變化。但專家證人通過詳細的說明，會更能凸顯再審制度實際上是與普通法中的上訴制度雷同。

其四，內地法律專家亦可提供權威的統計數據，以說明再審制度在實務中被適用的實際情況。儘管從 Chiyu 案「無論其如何罕見」的判詞看，這樣的數據可能作用不大，但在其他一些案件中，提供適當的數據也能增加法律意見的說服力（比如江平教授在 New Link Consultants Ltd 案中的法律意見，該案簡評見本書簡評案例一）。但也需要指出，近幾年由於巡迴法庭制度的推行，再審案件的數字和比例應有所回升。也許這在觀感上會給以內地法院判決的終局性有所減弱的印象。但是，只要能將論證的重點擴大至是否可被原審法院改變的其他因素，甚至確立判決是否最終及不可推翻不再以是否可被原審法院改變為標準，則即使案件再審的比例再高，也不會影響內地法院判決構成最終及不可推翻判決的可能。再者，若將再審案件數據與香港上訴案件的數據進行比較，相信內地再審案件的比例一定低於香港上訴案件的比例。

最後要特別強調，內地法律專家的法律意見，在香港的訴訟程序中只

是證據，充其量只能起到輔助的作用。在對抗式訴訟制度下，最重要的始終在於當事人及代表律師的論證，亦即陳詞（submission）。內地法律專家法律意見的分量，首先要取決於當事人及代表律師能夠準確確定需由內地法律專家處理的問題和事項。這要求當事人的專業團隊具備相當的專業水平，並必須對有關問題有足夠深入的研究。

五、通過司法解釋加強內地法院判決的終局性？

《協議管轄判決安排》第 1 條第 4 款規定：「當事人向香港特別行政區法院申請認可和執行判決後，內地人民法院對該案件依法再審的，由作出生效判決的上一級人民法院提審。」此款規定的緣由，在於內地和香港雙方就《協議管轄判決安排》進行磋商時，香港一方表示對內地法院判決可能因存在審判監督制度而不符合普通法的最終及不可推翻要求有所擔憂，最高人民法院為了消除香港一方的擔憂，同意在《協議管轄判決安排》中加入此規定，並以司法解釋頒佈（見香港立法會「CB（2）1365/06-07（02）號文件」）。

從香港一方的擔憂及此項規定的內容可知，香港一方當時是採用了Chiyu 案關於最終及不可推翻判決認定標準的裁判觀點，即認為內地法院判決是否最終及不可推翻判決取決於判決是否可被原審法院改變。從磋商的結果看，香港一方是接受只要內地法院判決在再審時是由原審法院的上級人民法院審理，內地法院判決即能符合普通法的最終及不可推翻要求。以此看來，是否意味只要最高人民法院頒佈一項司法解釋，明確規定對任何經香港法院承認和執行的判決進行再審時均由上一級法院審理，即能掃清內地法院判決在香港根據普通法承認和執行的障礙？

無可否認，若最高人民法院頒佈上述司法解釋，相信可在相當大程度上增加內地法院判決被香港法院認定為構成最終及不可推翻判決的機會。然而，這一解決方法仍然存在若干問題。

其一，這一方法雖然可以解決由基層人民法院至各地高級人民法院所作出判決的問題，但卻不能解決最高人民法院所作出判決的最終及不可推翻問題。理由在於，最高人民法院所作出判決不可能由更高級的人民法院進行再審。

其二，為了解決香港法院的裁判觀點所引起的問題，由最高人民法院頒佈在實質上修改了既有民事訴訟制度的司法解釋，在途徑上似乎有手段與目的之間不符合比例原則之嫌。此舉對於內地民事訴訟制度而言，可謂牽一髮而動全身，作為手段是否妥當必須謹慎考慮。假若今日最高人民法院通過此方式以掃除香港法院關於最終及不可推翻問題裁判觀點所引起的

障礙，他日香港法院在案例中又出現新的阻礙內地法院判決承認和執行的其他裁判觀點，最高人民法院是否應繼續「配合」？

其三，更嚴重的是，由最高人民法院頒佈此司法解釋，從內地法律的角度看是否具有充分的法律依據，在法律上是否妥當，也存有疑問。《協議管轄判決安排》司法解釋的上述規定，是以本身是以《基本法》第95條為依據達成的司法互助安排的《協議管轄判決安排》為基礎的，在法律上具有充分的依據。然而若最高人民法院「憑空」頒佈一項一般性地適用於任何經香港法院承認和執行的內地法院判決的司法解釋，恐怕就不存在相應的法律基礎。

其四，認為通過司法解釋可以解決最終及不可推翻要求的問題的，只是負責《協議管轄判決安排》磋商的香港相關部門及其人員（具體而言即律政司），而不是司法機構或法官。即使在立法機關也是在立法會議員接受這種觀點的基礎上通過《內地判決條例》，但在香港的普通法制度下，他們的接受對法院和法官在審理具體個案時所採用的裁判觀點也難有直接影響。實際上，從立法會的有關文件看，所體現的觀點，基本上不過是Chiyu 案的裁判觀點，也未能看到有關判例被經過深入研究的迹象（見香港立法會「CB（2）122/05-06（04）號」「CB（2）1365/06-07（02）號文件」「CB（2）1202/05-06（02）號」等）。因此，香港有關方面接受最高人民法院頒佈司法解釋為有效解決方法的觀點，其可靠性也不無疑問。

由此可見，通過司法解釋的途徑解決香港普通法上的最終及不可推翻判決的問題，必須謹慎考慮。無可否認，解決內地法院判決在香港的承認和執行問題，最徹底直接的方法，莫過於兩地達成全面的判決互認司法互助安排，而兩地的有關部門也正在積極努力達成這一目標。然而，在最終的全面結果達成之前，解決內地判決在香港的承認和執行遭遇障礙的問題，最理想的方法仍然在於通過個案判例，確立認可內地法院判決不因審判監督制度而不構成最終及不可推翻判決的判例規則。

附錄一

相 關 判 例

Chiyu Banking Corporation Ltd. v. Chan Tin Kwun

[1996] HKCFI 418; [1996] 2 HKLRD 395; HCA 11186/1995 （12 July 1996）

1995, No. A11186

IN THE SUPREME COURT OF HONG KONG

HIGH COURT

_____

BETWEEN

CHIYU BANKING CORPORATION LIMITED Plaintiff

AND

CHAN TIN KWUN   Defendant

_____

Coram : Hon Mr Justice Cheung in Chambers

Date of hearing : 12 July 1996

Date of delivery of judgment : 12 July 1996

_____

J U D G M E N T

_____

The application

1. This is an application by the Defendant to stay the proceedings on the basis that -

    (i) proceedings are pending in the People's Republic of China ("PRC"); and

    (ii) the most appropriate forum for the trial of this action is the PRC.

The background

2. The Plaintiff is a bank. On 18th March 1994, it commenced an action in the Fujian Intermediate People's Court ("the Intermediate Court") in the PRC against the Defendant as the guarantor of the debt of one of its customers, Hua Da Decoration & Furniture Co. ("Hua Da") pursuant to a guarantee dated 15th January 1991.

3. The Plaintiff's case was that the Defendant executed the guarantee in favour of the Plaintiff in consideration of the Plaintiff granting banking facilities to Hua Da.

4. Judgment was obtained against the Defendant on 19th January 1995 in the Intermediate Court in the sums of US$40,764.78 and US$8,769.

5. The Defendant appealed to the Fujian Higher People's Court but the appeal was dismissed on 30th July 1995 and the decision of the original court was affirmed.

6. The Defendant is a Hong Kong resident. The present action was commenced against him. The cause of action is based on the judgment obtained from the Intermediate Court.

The Protest

7. The dismissal of the appeal in PRC, however, is not the end of the matter. On 18th October 1995, the Defendant presented a petition to the Fujian People's Procuratorate for a retrial of the action conducted by the Intermediate Court.

8. On 14th March 1996, the Fujian People's Procuratorate presented a report to the Supreme People's Procuratorate requesting it to lodge a protest.

9. Under the legal system in PRC, another state organ, the Procuratorate exercises a supervisory function over civil adjudication by the courts: Article 14 of the Civil Procedure Law of 1991 ("the Civil Procedure Law"). Under Article 185, the Procuratorate may lodge a protest to the court in respect of a judicial decision. The circumstances in which the protest may be lodged are set out in Article 185, namely,

   (i) the main evidence to substantiate the original judgment or ruling was insufficient;

   (ii) the law which was applied in the original judgment or ruling was incorrect;

   (iii)the People's Court was in violation of the statutory procedure which have affected the correctness of the judgment or ruling;

   (iv)the judicial members in trying the case committed embezzlement, accepted bribes, practised favouritism or make a judgment that perverted the law.

   It is for the Supreme People's Procuratorate to lodge the protest but under Article 185, the Fujian People's Procuratorate is entitled to refer the matter to the Supreme People's Procuratorate for it to lodge a protest.

10. Under Article 187, the court, upon receipt of the protest, is required to conduct a retrial of the action.

11. This procedure is well recognised. Mr Li Ping, the Plaintiff's expert on Chinese law, stated at para.11 of his affidavit that "if such protest is made a retrial will be ordered." Legal literature on this topic can be found in -

   《中國訴訟制度法律全書》：楊柄芝、李春霖，法律出版社

   "A Comprehensive Law Book on PRC's Legal Procedure System" by Yang Bing Zhi and Li Chun Lin. Published by Falu Publishing House and

   《抗訴制度通論》：周士敏，中國政法大學出版社

   "PRC's System on Protest against the People's Court - General Discussion" by Shou Shi Min. Published by University of Politics & Law Publishing House.

The Defendant's argument

12. The Defendant submitted that in view of the steps taken by the Procuratorate, the present action should not be allowed to proceed further: if a protest is in due course lodged, the Intermediate Court will have to order a retrial with the possibility of the court reaching a different result on the case. Staying the present proceedings would avoid multiplicity of the action.

Forum non conveniens

13. I will briefly deal with *forum non conveniens* first. The leading authority on stay of proceedings on this basis is **Spiliada Maritime Corp. v. Consulex Ltd.**[1987] 1 AC 460 in which Lord Goff at page 476 held that :

> "The basic principle is that a stay would only be granted on the ground of *forum non conveniens* where the court is satisfied that there is some other available forum having competent jurisdiction which is the appropriate forum for the trial of the action, i.e. in which the case may be tried more suitably for the interest of all the parties and the ends of justice."

14. Bokhary JA in **S. Megga Telecommunication Ltd. v. Etowaru Co. Ltd.** [1995] 2 HKC 761 stated that,

> "This was not stated as merely a factor to be taken into account when deciding whether or not to exercise a discretion to stay proceedings on the ground of *forum non conveniens*. It goes to whether the discretion exists."

Relevance of forum

15. Mr Kerr, Counsel for the Plaintiff, said that the Plaintiff had already accepted that the Fujian Court was the proper forum for the determination of the dispute. That was the reason why proceedings were commenced there in the first place. However, the dispute having been adjudicated, the question of forum is no longer of relevance. The Plaintiff is now relying on the judgment obtained from the Intermediate Court by suing on it.

Recognition of foreign judgment

16. The real issue in this application is whether the Chinese judgment is final or conclusive.

17. Dicey & Morris in The Conflict of Laws at page 461 had this to say :

> "Subject to the exceptions hereinafter mentioned and to rule 55 (International Conventions), a foreign judgment in personam given by the court of a foreign country with jurisdiction to give that judgment in accordance with the principles set out in rules 36 to 39 which is not impeachable under any of rules 42 to 45 may be enforced by an action or counterclaim for the amount due under it if the judgment is
>
> (a) for a debt or definite sum of money not being a sum payable in respect of taxes or other charges of a like nature or in respect of a fine or other penalty; and
>
> (b) final and conclusive but not otherwise,
>
> provided that a foreign judgment may be final and conclusive though it is subject to an appeal and though an appeal against it is actually pending in the foreign country where it was given."

What is a final and conclusive judgment

18. One must apply Hong Kong law to determine whether a judgment is final and conclusive. In **Gustave Nouvion v. Freeman & Another** [1889] 15 AC 1, the Privy Council considered what is a final and conclusive judgment. Lord Herschell at page 9 had this to say :

> "......it must be shown that in the court by which it was pronounced conclusively, finally, and for ever established the existence of the debt of which it is sought to be made conclusive evidence in this country, so as to make it res judicata between the parties. If it is not conclusive in the same court which pronounced it, so that notwithstanding such a judgment the existence of the debt made between the same parties be afterwards contested in that court, and upon proper proceedings being taken and such context being adjudicated upon, it may be declared that there exists no obligation to pay the debt at all, then I do not think that a judgment which is of that character can be regarded as finally and conclusively evidencing the debt, and so entitling the person who has obtained the judgment to obtain a decree from a court for the payment of that debt."

And at page 10, the law lord continued :

"...... Although an appeal may be pending, a court of competent jurisdiction has finally and conclusively determined the existence of a debt, and it has nonetheless done so because the right of appeal has been given whereby a superior court may overrule that decision. There exists at the time of the suit a judgment which must be assumed to be valid until interfered with by a higher tribunal, and which conclusively establishes the existence of the debt which is sought to be recovered in this country. That appears to be in altogether a different position from a 'remate' judgment where the very court which pronounced the 'remate' judgment (not the Court of Appeal) may determine, if proper proceedings are taken, that the debt for which this 'remate' judgment is sought to be used as conclusive evidence has no existence at all."

Lord Watson, at page 13, said this :

"...... but no decision has been cited to the effect that an English Court is bound to give effect to a foreign decree which is liable to be abrogated or varied by the same court which issued it. All the authorities cited appeared to me, when fairly read, to assume that the decree which was given effect to had been pronounced causa cognita and that it was unnecessary to enquire into the merits of the controversy between the litigants, either because this had already been investigated and decided by the foreign tribunal, or because the Defendant had due opportunity of submitting for decision all the pleas which he desire to state in defence. In order to its receiving the fact here, a foreign decree need not be final in the sense that it cannot be made the subject of appeal to a higher court; but it must be final and unalterable in the court which pronounced it; and if appealable, the English Court will only enforce it, subject to conditions which may save the interest of those who have the right to appeal."

The Plaintiff's submission

19. Mr Kerr submitted that the Chinese law experts of both parties agreed that the judgment is final and conclusive, although I note that the Defendant's expert said that the judgment is final and conclusive "for the time being". Mr Kerr further submitted that the Intermediate Court is now functus. It does not retain any power for retrial until the protest is lodged. This procedure is akin to an appeal procedure which does not affect the conclusive nature of the judgment.

Not final and conclusive

20. Based on the material before me, the supervisory function of the Supreme People's Procuratorate and the protest system are not simply an appeal process. The Intermediate Court judgment is final in the sense that it is not appealable and it is enforceable in China, but it is not final and conclusive for the purpose of recognition and enforcement by the Hong Kong Courts because in the words of Lord Watson, it "is not final and unalterable in the court which pronounced it". It is liable to be altered by the Intermediate Court on a retrial if the Supreme People's Procuratorate lodge a protest in accordance with the Civil Procedure Law. If upon protest being made, rare the circumstances may be, a Chinese Court has to retry the case, then, clearly it retains the power to alter its own decision. As Lord Watson said at page 13 of Nouvion :

> "There is no real difference in principle between the case of a court retaining power to alter a decree by an order in the same suit and the case of its retaining power to defeat the operation of that decree by an order pronounced in another suit relating to the same debt."

21. Mr Kerr referred to **Colt Industries Inc v. Sarlie** (No.2) [1966] 1 WLR 1287 in which Lord Denning M.R. at page 1291 held that :

> "The appeal itself does not render it not final and conclusive, nor should the possibility of leave to appeal. It seems to me that the proper test is this : is the judgment a final and conclusive judgment of a court of competent jurisdiction in the territory in which it was pronounced. The relevant territory here is the State of New York. Applying this test, there was here a final and conclusive judgment."

In my view, Lord Denning's decision does not in any way contradict the principle in Nouvion.

22. Although no protest has been lodged yet, the procedure had actually been invoked. This demonstrated that the judgment is not final and conclusive. To allow the present action to continue would not be satisfactory because the Plaintiff is not suing on the guarantee but on the judgment itself which is not final and conclusive. There is a possibility that the judgment may be varied if the application to the Supreme People's Procuratorate is successful, and the debt for which the present judgment is sought to be used as conclusive evidence may have no existence at all.

Proceedings stayed

23. In the circumstances, the only course available to me is to stay the present proceedings pending the outcome of the decision of the Supreme People's Procuratorate. I give leave to the Plaintiff to, firstly, apply to remove the stay if the application is rejected by the Supreme People's Procuratorate and secondly, to seek further directions if the decision of the Supreme People's Procuratorate is still not reached within the next six months.

Variation of the consent orders

24. The Defendant further seeks to vary the consent order in which monies realised in the disposal of the Defendant's property and currently held by his solicitor as stakeholder be released to him. The consent order was reached on the Plaintiff's application for a Mareva injunction against the Defendant.

25. I am not prepared to accede to this request in view of the fact that the Supreme People's Procuratorate is still considering its decision and there is, at the moment, a valid judgment obtained against the Defendant. The status quo should be maintained. Mr Wong seeks reliance on **Mercedes Benz AG v. Leiduck**[1995] 3 HKC 1. I cannot see how the case can assist him. The factual circumstances of the cases are completely different.

(P. Cheung)

Judge of the High Court

Representation:

Mr John Kerr, inst'd by M/s Koo & Partners, for Plaintiff

Mr Brian C.W. Wong, inst'd by M/s David F.K. Yeung & Partners, for Defendant

Wuhan Zhong Shuo Hong Real Estate Co. Ltd. v. The Kwong Sang Hong International Ltd.

[2000]HKCFI 769; HCA 14325/1998 （12 June 2000）

HCA 14325/1998

IN THE HIGH COURT OF THE

HONG KONG SPECIAL ADMINISTRATIVE REGION

COURT OF FIRST INSTANCE

ACTION NO. 14325 OF 1998

———————

BETWEEN

WUHAN ZHONG SHUO HONG REAL ESTATE   Plaintiff

COMPANY LIMITED

（湖北省武漢中碩虹房地產開發有限公司）

AND

THE KWONG SANG HONG INTERNATIONAL LIMITED   Defendant

（香港廣生行國際有限公司）

———————

Coram: Hon Yeung J in Chambers

Date of Hearing: 12 June 2000

Date of Decision: 12 June 2000

————————————

REASONS FOR DECISION

————————————

1. In 1995, the Plaintiff commenced proceedings in the Higher People's Court of Hubei Province and obtained judgment against Defendant one year later in 1996. Both parties then appealed against the judgment of the Higher People's Court of Hubei Province to the Supreme People's Court.

2. On 28 May 1998, the Supreme People's Court dismissed the appeal by the Defendant. The Supreme People's Court also reduced the amount of the judgment sums granted by the Higher People's Court of Hubei Province in favour of the Plaintiff.

3. The Defendant satisfied, be it not voluntarily part of judgment sums awarded by the Supreme People's Court leaving a balance of about HK$2.9 million and RMB8.3 million.

4. In the present proceedings, the Plaintiff seeks to enforce the outstanding balance of the judgment in Hong Kong.

5. In its defence, the Defendant raises a number of matters. It is suggested firstly that the judgment of the Supreme People's Court is not final and conclusive in that the Supreme People's Procuratorate exercises a supervisory function over civil adjudication and if the Supreme People's Procuratorate lodges a protest against the judgment of a court, such judgment can be altered by the court.

6. In any event, the Defendant said that he had applied to the Supreme People's Court to alter its earlier decision.

7. The Defendant also alleges that the judgment granted by the Supreme People's Court was obtained by fraud and the granting of such judgment was against natural justice and/or contrary to public policy.

8. For the purpose of the present proceedings, it is not necessary to deal with the allegations of fraud and/or natural justice and/or public policy.

9. However, it is the Defendant's contention that the Defendant had in August of 1998 applied to the Supreme People's Court for a retrial and in January 1999 applied to the Supreme People's Procuratorate to protest against the judgment of Supreme People's Court and that the Supreme People's Procuratorate had decided to review the judgment of the Supreme People's Court on the basis that there was no sufficient evidence to establish the material facts and/or the wrong law had applied and/or that the lawful procedure had not been followed.

10. The Defendant's contention was initially based on a letter dated of 25 November 1999 addressed to the Defendant from the Supreme People's Procuratorate.

11. In the circumstances, the Defendant applies for stay of proceedings on the basis that there is a possibility of a retrial and/or that the earlier judgment of the Supreme People's Court may be nullified.

12. The Defendant relies on the case of **Chiyu Banking Corporation Ltd v. Chan Tin Kwan** [1996] 2 HKLR 395.

13. Cheung J in the Chiyu Banking Corporation Ltd case granted the application of the Defendant to stay the proceedings pending the decision of the Supreme People's Procuratorate to protest against the judgment granted by the court.

14. Cheung J took the view that under the Civil Procedure Law in China, if the Supreme People's Procuratorate lodges a protest, the court can alter its decision on a retrial. As the court retains the potential to modify its own decision, the judgment is not final and conclusive. He was the view that it would be inappropriate to allow an action based on a foreign judgment to continue when the judgment itself was not final and conclusive.

15. In order for a foreign judgment to be enforced in Hong Kong, one of the essential ingredients is that the judgment in question is final and conclusive.

16. There are authorities to the effect that a judgment is not final and conclusive if the court which pronounces it has the power to rescind or vary it subsequently.

17. There are also authorities to the effect that a judgment does not cease to be final merely because it may be the subject of an appeal to a higher court or because an appeal is actually pending, unless a stay of execution has been granted in the foreign country pending the hearing of the appeal.

18. On the issue of whether the judgment in question is final and conclusive, the parties' experts slightly differ in their opinions. The exact nature and effect of the protest by the Supreme People's Procuratorate on the judgment has not been scrutinized at a trial in Hong Kong.

19. As I have observed in the course of counsel's submission, it is not

appropriate for me at this stage to resolve this dispute or even to express any strong view on it. Such matter can only be resolved at the trial when the experts are properly questioned so as to enable the court to make a finding of fact on the issue.

20. But suffice it for me to say that if it is established that the judgment in question is not final and conclusive, the proper order to make is to dismiss the action and not just to stay the action. If it is the Defendant's contention that the judgment in question is not final and conclusive, perhaps it should have applied to have this issue dealt with in order to dismiss the Plaintiff's claim and not to stay the proceeding.

21. I accept that in certain circumstances when the issue of whether the judgment is final and conclusive is yet to be decided, it may be appropriate to stay the proceedings pending such decision in order to avoid the multiplicity of actions and to save costs. The court has a discretion under its inherit jurisdiction.

22. But the discretion of the court must be exercised judicially. The court must take into consideration the entire background of the case. The court must also balance the interests of the parties, in particular, the impact on each party of the decision to stay or not to stay the proceedings.

23. It has been 5 years since the Plaintiff commenced the proceedings against Defendant in the Higher People's Court of Hubei Province. More than two years has elapsed since the Supreme People's Court dismissed the Defendant's appeal in May 1998. Part of the judgment, had been satisfied, though I have been told, that it was satisfied only with the sums paid into court by the Defendant. To that extent, such satisfaction of the judgment cannot be said to be voluntary.

24. The Defendant only applied to the Supreme People's Procuratorate to protest against the judgment of the Supreme People's Court in January 1999. There is no conclusive indication as to when the Supreme People's Procuratorate will commence the process of the review and when such process will be concluded, although the latest information suggests that the Supreme People's Procuratorate is still reviewing the case due to its complexity.

25. There is also indications from the Supreme People's Court that it is in the course of reviewing and handling the Defendant's application for a retrial.

26. Mr Tang also draws the court's attention to the fact that the Defendant has not applied for a stay of execution on the judgment in the Supreme People's Court even though the civil procedure code in China permits such a course to be taken.

27. The Plaintiff, of course, is entitled to a swift determination on the issue of whether the judgment can be enforced in the Court of Hong Kong.

28. If a decision on the issue is to be made against the Plaintiff, it can of course commence a fresh action on the substantive claim rather than the enforcement of a foreign judgment.

29. On the present pleadings, even if the issues relating to the conclusiveness and finality or otherwise of the judgment in question were to be decided in favour of the Plaintiff, the court still have to resolve the further issues of whether the judgment was obtained by fraud and whether the granting of the judgment was against natural justice and/or contrary to public policy.

30. On the other hand, if the Defendant can establish at the trial that the judgment in question is not final and conclusive as Miss Ng has so confidently submitted to this court, then the Plaintiff's action will be dismissed, and to that extent, there will be no prejudice to the Defendant to allow the case to proceed to trial.

31. Bearing in mind the status of court's diary, even if the case were to proceed with some degree of urgency, it is unlikely that it will come up for trial in less than six months' time.

32. All these factors are against the application for a stay.

33. But there can be no doubt that if the Supreme People's Court was to alter its earlier decision, there would be no basis upon which the Plaintiff could successfully enforced the judgment. If the case is not stayed, the Defendant will have to make substantial effort and incur significant costs in the preparation of the case for trial as the issues involved, I am convinced, are extremely difficult and complicated.

34. If the Supreme People's Court were to make a decision in favour of the Defendant after the Court in Hong Kong had made a decision against it, it would create huge prejudice and injustice to the Defendant.

35. I appreciate that there is no time limit within which the Supreme People's Court can order a retrial and the Supreme People's Procuratorate can make a protest. If a successful party has to wait until all avenue to challenge a judgment of the court is exhausted, the wait can be infinite, a point made by the Professor Nauping Lin in his Article "A Vulnerable Justice: Finality of Civil Judgments in China."

36. But the information available to this court at this stage suggests that the Supreme People's Court and the Supreme People's Procuratorate have taken steps pursuant to the Defendant's request for a retrial and for an action based on the protest. One of the experts anticipates and suggests that the decision by them will be known within about 6 months.

37. On the other hand, if an order for stay is granted, the only prejudice to the Defendant is a further delay which is the only complaint made by Mr Tang.

38. I appreciate that delay of justice is denial of justice.

39. Mr Tang had complained that there had been substantial delay on the part of the Defendant. I am not persuaded that is so. After all, it has just been two years from the time when the Supreme People's Court granted its judgment and the evidence suggests that within three months, the Defendant had applied to the Supreme People's Court for a retrial and within about 7 months, an application had been made to the Supreme People's Procuratorate for a protest.

40. Having balanced the interests of the parties based on the available information, I am persuaded that a stay of proceedings for a period of 6 months would be right. But the case must be allowed to proceed to trial after the six months' period expires.

41. On the very narrow issue that I have to resolve, the appropriate order to make is that the action will be stayed for a period of six months and after the period is expired, the matter will be listed for a checklist hearing before the listing judge with a view to set the case down for trial.

W YEUNG

Judge of the Court of First Instance

of High Court

Representation:

Mr Ronald Tang, instructed by Messrs Ng & Shum, for the Plaintiff

Miss Margaret Ng, instructed by Messrs Sit, Fung, Kwong & Shum, for the Defendant

Tan Tay Cuan v. Ng Chi Hung

[2001] HKCFI 512; HCA 5477/2000 （5 February 2001）

HCA5477/2000

IN THE HIGH COURT OF THE

HONG KONG SPECIAL ADMINISTRATIVE REGION

COURT OF FIRST INSTANCE

ACTION NO.5477 OF 2000

––––––––––––

BETWEEN

TAN TAY CUAN   Plaintiff

AND

NG CHI HUNG   Defendant

––––––––––––

Coram: Hon Waung J in Chambers

Date of Hearing: 5 February 2001

Date of Judgment: 5 February 2001

––––––––––––

J U D G M E N T

––––––––––––

1. This is an appeal by the defendant from a summary judgment ordered by the master against the defendant in favour of the plaintiff in respect of a claim by the plaintiff based on a judgment on 27 March 2000 issued by the Higher People's Court of Fujian Province. The way the judgment came about was as follows.

2. The plaintiffs and the defendant entered into an agreement in relation to transfer of shareholding in certain company for a certain price. It is alleged that the defendant had failed in the obligation under the agreement and there was an outstanding amount payable to the plaintiff of some RMB5,000,000 odd. The proceedings were therefore issued by the plaintiff in the Intermediate People's Court of Xiamen, Fujian Province against the defendant. The judgment was given in favour of the plaintiff.

3. Then, as usual, pursuant to the two trial procedures under the laws of the People's Republic of China, the matter was taken up to the Higher People's Court of Fujian Province and where the judgement, as described earlier, was given on 27 March 2000. This is the subject of the proceedings that had been brought by the plaintiff in Hong Kong.

4. The governing principle in relation to an action based on the foreign judgment is if the foreign judgment sued on is final and conclusive, then the Hong Kong court would enforce it. The issue debated today before me is whether the judgment of the Higher People's Court of Fujian Province of 27 March 2000 is a judgment that is final and conclusive. It is a vexed question and it is by no means easy.

5. The material before me is somewhat unsatisfactory. But what is clear, however, by a reading of the relevant code, that is, Chapter 16, with the governing words of "Supervision of Trial Procedure" which starts from Article 177 and runs on to Article 188, is that under the Chinese legal system there is an elaborate procedure for retrial. There are different routes to retrial. One of the routes is under Articles 178 and 179, and the other route is under Article 185. Under the route of Articles 178 and 179, one of the parties can ask for retrial, either from the original court or from a higher court and, if any of the five conditions are satisfied, then the court must order a retrial. One of them, for example, is the wrong application of the law; another one is not following the correct procedure. Article 185 also has a number of grounds which are slightly different from Article 179 grounds, but there the supervision involves the Supreme People's

Procuratorate, a special legal person not known in our system.

6. In the judgment of Cheung J, in the case of **Chiyu Banking Corporation Ltd v. Chan Tin Kwun** [1996] 2 HKLR 395, the dispute is over the involvement of the Supreme People's Procuratorate and the question of the finality of the judgment turns on Article 185 and, to a certain extent, also the larger provisions of Chapter 16. Cheung J refused to order summary judgment and held that on the basis of the material before him, there was an arguable case of the judgment of being not final and conclusive. He therefore stayed the action.

7. Here, of course, it is a very different consideration. But the exercise, to a certain extent, is equally vexing and difficult. I have extensive material put before me by different experts, I am not sure to what extent they throw conclusive light on the matter. Looking at it in a round, it seems to me that the matter is plainly arguable. That is to say, the legal system in place in China is such that the judgment of the Higher People's Court of 27 March 2000 is arguably not a final and conclusive judgment because it is a judgment which by their procedure is capable of being corrected on review and on retrial. There is a reference, for example, in Article 182 to the two year period for application for retrial.

8. My conclusion, therefore, is that summary judgment ought not to have been given. The matter really is sufficiently complicated to merit it going to trial.

9. I just pause to also point out, that we are of course not dealing in abstract about the Chinese legal procedures. We also have uncontested the evidence that there was an application which was made by the defendant to the Supreme People's Court of China in Beijing, which ordered that the lower court should deal with the application, review and deal with it. It is pertinent to note the Supreme People's Court did not reject the application for retrial or dismiss it, which seems to suggest that there are possible good grounds for retrial. Of course, once the grounds have been established, as I read Article 179, then the court has no discretion but to order retrial. So, it is plainly at present that the Higher People's Court has been directed by the Supreme People's Court to consider the application for a retrial and to deal with it. A retrial may take place. It does not necessary mean that it will take place but certainly it may take place.

10. Having regard to the system in the PRC, as revealed by the Code (which

the parties and the courts have looked) in Chinese, at pages 49, 68 and 69 of Bundle C, it seems to me that the only sensible order that should be made is to allow the appeal and give unconditional leave to defend to the defendant.

11. The costs in the lower court shall be costs in the cause and the costs before me shall be costs to the defendant in any event.

（William Waung）

Judge of the Court of First Instance

High Court

Representation:

Mr Kivil Ip of Messrs Richards Butler, for the Plaintiff

Mr Louis Chan, instructed by Messrs Fung, Law & Ng, for the Defendant

林哲民經營之日昌電業公司 訴 林志滔

[2001] HKCA 470; [2001-2003] HKCLRT 133; CACV 354/2001 (18 December 2001)

CACV000354/2001

CACV354/2001

香港特別行政區

高等法院上訴法庭

民事司法管轄權

民事上訴

案件編號：民事上訴案件 2001 年第 354 號

（原本案件編號 1999 年第 9585 號）

———————

原告人（上訴人）　林哲民經營之日昌電業公司

對

被告人（答辯人）　林志滔

———————

主審法官：高等法院首席法官梁紹中

　　　　　高等法院上訴法庭法官胡國興

　　　　　高等法院上訴法庭法官張澤祐

聆訊日期：2001 年 12 月 12 日

宣判日期：2001 年 12 月 18 日

———————

判案書

———————

由高等法院上訴法庭法官胡國興宣讀上訴法庭判案書：

序言

1. 2001 年 1 月 4 日，當本案在原訟法庭鍾安德法官席前開始審訊時，因應被告提出的申請，鍾法官命令：原告在本訴訟中所有有關口頭租務協議及其相關的損失、損害及 / 或賠償的指控 / 濟助請求，均被撤銷。另外，鍾法官亦命令有關被告唆使員工毆打原告的訴訟，即使不應被撤銷，亦應被擱置。原告現在上訴，要求推翻鍾法官的命令，並要求重新排期審訊本案。

有關事實

2. 本案涉及原告與被告之間兩人的口頭租務協議，有關的物業是位於東莞市黃江鎮龍見田管理區的廠房。據「索償申請書」（即「申索陳述書」）所說，被告承諾將其正在該廠房加建的一層租給原告的東莞分公司。原告聲稱被告毀約，並沒有於指定日期提供該廠房的消防證以及其他批准文件，亦沒有提供足夠的工人宿舍，依約只收取低於市價的租金。被告更無理地切斷廠房及工人宿舍的水電供應，又佔用原告的工人宿舍。被告在 1999 年 4 月 23 日單方面發出通知終止租約。當原告正在撤離被告的廠房時，被告的電工衝入並揮拳毆打原告。

3. 本案的傳訊令狀連同申索陳述書於 1999 年 6 月 11 日發出。本案的被告為在東莞成立的「東莞榮豐錶業有限公司」（「榮豐」）的法定代理人。1999 年 7 月 12 日榮豐以原告身份在東莞市人民法院起訴恒昌電子（深圳）有限公司（「恒昌」），而恒昌的法定代理人是本案的原告林哲民。

4. 兩案分別在香港及東莞同時進行。林哲民向東莞法院提出反對該法院審理東莞的案件，不果。他也在該案中提出反訴。2000 年 11 月 13 日，東莞市人民法院就該東莞案件發出一份民事判決書。簡單而言，東莞市人民法院裁定榮豐勝訴而恒昌敗訴。

5. 據該民事判決書的內容，可見與訟雙方在該案中的訴因及爭議點，與本案雙方所提出的訴因及爭議並無分別。

6. 在該民事判決書中，也很清楚指出該案的處理情況，如下：

> 「本院受理後，依法組成合議庭，於 1998 年 8 月 25 日、10 月 19 日、2000 年 3 月 24 日、6 月 12 日、9 月 21 日、10 月 20 日公開開庭進行審理。原告法定代表人林志滔及其委托代理人黃惠忠、廖東江到庭參加訴訟，被告經傳票傳喚，法定代表人林哲民於 1999 年 8 月 25 日、10 月 19 日、

2000 年 3 月 24 日、6 月 12 日到庭參加訴訟，而 2000 年 9 月 21 日和 10 月 20 日兩次開庭未到庭。本案現已審理終結。」

7. 在該民事判決書中，東莞市人民法院就雙方的爭議點作出以下的裁定：

(1) 從開出的支票看，恒昌已默認了租金價格，且該價格在同地區內屬中下水平，合理合法。恒昌對每月租金計算持異議，但始終未能舉證。

(2) 恒昌要求對非法停水、停電賠償，但恒昌亦未能舉證。

(3) 經查，源豐在東莞市龍見田管理區投資開辦榮豐，恒昌雖辯稱榮豐以源豐的名義通知恒昌終止租賃關係欠妥，但恒昌收到此通知書之後，於 1999 年 5 月 24 日開始搬走了大部份機械設備，恒昌的行為表示同意解除廠房租賃協議，終止廠房租賃關係。

(4) 恒昌未按約定於 1999 年 8 月 1 日前將全部機械設備搬走，辯稱是榮豐阻止恒昌搬走機械設備，榮豐反駁恒昌拒不辦理結算手續，且將未搬走的機械設備鎖着，恒昌之辯稱缺乏充份的證據和理由，因此恒昌反訴原告非法扣留資產，理由不成立。

(5) 恒昌反訴稱，榮豐唆使電工行兇，應賠償恒昌醫藥費、工資損失，被告缺乏充份的證據，且此訴與本案糾紛是兩類不同的法律關係，本案不應對此訴進行辦理，被告可另行起訴。

(6) 恒昌辯稱榮豐必須對 1999 年 5 月份起廠房不能依期交付使用違約賠償，缺乏證據，理由不成立。

8. 該法院判決榮豐的大部份索償申請勝訴，而駁回恒昌關於賠償安裝電話費用的反訴請求、關於賠償扣留資產做成損失、和另租橫江廠房空置做成損失的反訴請求。該民事判決書在末段說：

「如不服本判決，可在判決書送達之日起 15 日內，向本院遞交上訴狀，並按對方當事人的人數提出副本，上訴於東莞市中級人民法院。」

鍾法官的判決理由

9. 在鍾法官 2001 年 1 月 30 日的判案書中，鍾法官援引數項法律典籍，然後作出以下裁決：

(1) 「涉及土地或與土地有關的協議的糾紛，應以該土地所處的地方法律為適用法律，或以與該協議有密切關連的法律（通常是指涉案土地所處的地方的法律），為通用法律。」 （判案書第 11 頁 A-D 行）

(2) 「東莞人民法院對此糾紛行使司法管轄權，依香港法律而言，並無不妥⋯⋯

　　（判案書第 11 頁 F-G 行）

(3) 恒昌在東莞的案件中提出抗辯及反申索及出庭應訊，「恒昌應被視為已接受了東莞人民法院的司法管轄權。」 （判案書第 12 頁 E-F 行）

(4) 「東莞人民法院的裁定，相對於本案的與訟雙方而言，具約束力，（或應被視為具約束力）。」 （判案書第 12 頁 I-K 行）

(5) 本案原告和被告為香港法例第 46 章《外地判決（限制承認及強制執行）條例》第 5 條所指，分別為恒昌及榮豐的「利害關係人。」 （判案書第 12 頁 R-S 行）

(6) 結論是，「原告在本訴訟中，所有有關口頭租務協議及 / 或其相關的損失，損害或 / 及賠償的指控 / 濟助請求，均應被撤銷。」 （判案書第 13 頁 J-K 行）

原告的上訴理由

10. 在原告的長達 23 頁的上訴通知書中，他舉出多項理由，支持他的上訴。本上訴可以說是純牽涉法律問題，故上訴通知書和原告人所提出的無關宏旨的事實，及他暗示鍾法官的行為不當的論調，本庭不擬作出處理，只是指出，原告對鍾法官採用無禮、情緒化和尖酸的言詞及指謫，對他的上訴並無任何益處，而又無關，徒然浪費本庭時間；上訴某一法官的裁決，當然是會指出該法官的判決在何處犯錯，但並無需要以不禮貌及尖酸刻薄的言詞指謫法官。

香港法律承認東莞法院的判決

11. 原告人提出，香港法例第 319 章《外地判決（交互強制執行）條例》只適用於英聯邦國家的外地判決，這是對的。但是，被告並不是運用該條例登記東莞人民法院該判決意圖在香港強制執行該判決。普通法把承認和執行外地判決作出不同的處理。強制執行外地判決是一件事，而承認外地判決又是另一回事。不論所涉外地判決是否可以在香港以登記的方式強制執行，這要視乎該判決是否為第 319 章內所包括的判決，但外地判決卻受普通法所承認，而阻止與訟雙方在香港的法院就該判決的訴因再進行訴訟。（參閱 *Dicey & Morris* 第 467 頁 14R-001 段和第 512 頁第 19R-109 段，*Halsbury's Laws of England*, 4th Ed Reissue 第 8(1) 冊 , 第 997 段第 4 附註和第 998 段第 8 及 10 附註）。

12. 香港法例第 319 章第 10 條也有如下規定：

「 （1） 除本條條文另有規定外，本條例的條文所適用的判決，或假若
根據判決須付一筆款項則本條例會適用的判決，不論該判決可
否予以登記，或如可予登記則不論是否已登記，香港的任何法
院須承認在基於同一訴因的一切法律程序中，該項判決為訴訟
各方之間不可推翻的判決，而在任何該等法律程序中，可援引
該項判決作為辯護或反申索。

　 （2） ……

　 （3） 就任何判決中有所決定的任何法律或事實問題而言，本條不得
被視為阻止香港任何法院承認該項判決是不可推翻的，但該判
決必須是在本條例生效日期前會被如此承認的。」

以上的條文，顯示第 319 章並不影響普通法對外地判決的承認及普通法的
不容反悔法可基於外地判決而適用，而明顯地指出，香港法律承認的外地
判決可援引作為辯護的用途。

東莞法院的判決是否最終及不可推翻的判決

13. 原告在他的上訴通知書及 2001 年 12 月 10 日的陳詞骨幹中，唯一對本
上訴有關的，就是稱東莞法院的判決並非最終及不可推翻的判決。這
是本上訴的關鍵。

14. 從上述第 9(1)、(2)、(3) 及 (5) 段中，可見鍾法官對於東莞案件及本案
所涉爭議的適用法律、東莞法院及香港法庭對本案的司法管轄及審判
權，和本案原告和被告是否分別為恒昌和榮豐的「利害關係人」等問
題，作出了裁決。本庭認為鍾法官就該等事項的裁決是正確無誤的。
原告可以爭議的，就是鍾法官判決中所說「東莞人民法院的裁定，相
對於本案的與訟雙方而言，具約束力（或應被視為具約束力）」是否
正確。這問題的答案並非單基於是否兩案的訴因及爭議是否一樣，而
是要解決東莞法院的判決是否最終及不可推翻的判決。

15. 在本庭未處理這個問題之前，要明白鍾法官為甚麼要命令撤銷本案。
他是根據《高等法院規則》第 18 號命令第 19 條規則及 / 或法庭的固
有司法權而撤銷本案的。根據該規則，如原告的訴訟是沒有成功的機
會，則容許他繼續進行訴訟，就會構成他濫用法庭程序，或案件所涉
的是瑣碎無聊的訴訟。但是，只是在申索是清楚及明顯地會敗訴或法
庭不應審理案件的情況下，法庭才可以運用該規則的權力，這是確定
已久的法律 （見《2001 年香港民事程序》[1] 第 289 頁第 18/19/6 段）。

16. 唯一鍾法官可以撤銷本案的原因，就是不容反悔法（estoppel）適用於本案：如東莞法院的判決對本案的與訟雙方具約束力，雙方都不能就該案的訴因及爭議再在香港法庭訴訟，因而法庭不審理本案。

17. 不容反悔法只可在判決是最終及不可推翻的判決的情況下適用。在本案而言，有關判決是東莞法院的判決，是外地的判決。如外地的判決是就該案件的爭議點作出是非曲直的判決，而判決是最終及不可推翻的判決，則對與訟雙方來說，判決是已有了最終的結論，雙方都不能對判決就事實或法律方面進行任何質疑，或在另外一案中就同樣的訴因或爭議再次訴訟。參閱 *Dicey & Morris* 第 475 頁第 14R-018 段、第 476-477 頁第 14R-021 段、第 512 頁第 14R-109 段。

18. 在**集友銀行對陳天君**（譯音）[2] 一案中，原訟法庭張澤祐法官（當時的官階）在處理一宗福建中級人民法院的判決時，指出該判決不是最終及不可推翻的判決。該案的情況特殊：被告是原告銀行一名借貸客戶的擔保人，他擔保原告借給該客戶的債務。1995 年 1 月 19 日，福建中級人民法院就原告的索償，判決被告須償還 4 萬多美元給原告。就此判決，被告上訴到福建高級人民法院，但上訴在 1995 年 7 月 30 日被駁回。原告在香港以福建中級人民法院的判決為訴因提出訴訟，要被告償還該款項。1995 年 10 月 18 日，被告向福建人民檢察院遞交呈請書，要求福建中級人民法院重審該案。1996 年 3 月 14 日，福建人民檢察院向最高人民檢察院提交報告，要求後者提出抗訴。因為該抗訴程序已展開，可能招致福建中級人民法院要重審該案，故張法官認為該法院的判決並不是最終及不可推翻的判決。

19. 本庭認為，張法官在該案的裁決是正確及合法合理的。但所要注意的是，在該案中，與訟雙方在張法官席前，都有提出中國法律專家的意見為證據。該等意見指出，檢察院對法庭的民事判決有監督的職能，它可以對判決作出抗訴，招致福建中級人民法院重審該案；而抗訴的程序亦已展開。故張法官接納該案被告的申請，把香港案件的程序擱置，以等候該抗訴程序的進行。

結論

20. 在該案中可見，因為國內法制的結構，檢察院對民事訴訟可以提出抗訴而使原審法庭把案件重審，故國內法院的判決不是最終及不可推翻的判決。但是該案的情況與本案的不同，因為該案有專家證據，證明當時有關的國內法律，張法官的裁決有證據支持。本案的雙方卻沒有就國內的法律提出證據，故法庭不知道現時國內的法律在這方面是否如前一樣，抑或是有所變更。

21. 在本案中，原告現時 他已就東莞的判決作出上訴。但是，這上訴並不表示該判決不是最終的判決。這是普通法的慣例（參閱 *Dicey & Morris* 第 478 頁第 14-024 段），亦是香港法例第 319 章第 3(3) 條所承認的。該第 3(3) 條規定，「即使在原訟法院的國家的法院中，針對有關判決的上訴仍未了結，或仍有可能針對有關判決提出上訴，該判決仍須當作最終及不可推翻。」而且在本案中，也沒有證據顯示原告有採取任何步驟，向人民檢察院要求抗訴。雖然如此，但是因為被告向鍾法官申請撤銷本案，要清楚無疑地證明本案受不容反悔法的約束，被告就有舉證責任，證明東莞的判決是最終及不可推翻的判決。在鍾法官席前，被告沒有提出這類的證據，故鍾法官作出撤銷本案的命令，在這方面是錯誤的，是沒有所需的證據支持的。況且，被告在本案延遲至開審的第一天才作出撤銷的申請，鍾法官是不應接納申請的（見《1999 年最高法院實踐》，第 1 冊 3 第 348 頁第 18/19/3 段，**Halliday v Shoesmith** [1993] 1 WLR 1，第 5 頁 C-D 行）。故此本庭命令上訴得值，把鍾法官撤銷本案的命令及訟費令撤銷，把案件發還原訟法庭另外一位法官審理。

22. 本庭亦作出暫准命令，本上訴訟費及 2001 年 1 月 4 日在鍾法官席前所招致的訟費，由被告負擔。

(梁紹中)　　　(胡國興)　　　(張澤祐)

高等法院首席法官　高等法院上訴法庭法官　高等法院上訴法庭法官

原告人（上訴人）：無律師代表

被告人（答辯人）：無律師代表

1　Hong Kong Civil Procedure, 2001.

2　**Chiyu Banking Corporation Limited** v **CHAN Tin Kwun**, HCA 1168 of 1995 (12 July 1996, unreported, Cheung J)

3　*The Supreme Court Practice, 1999*, Volume 1

林哲民日昌電業公司 訴 張順連

[2002] HKCA 4101; [2001-2003]HKCLRT 230; CACV 1046/2001 (12 July 2002)

CACV 1046/2001

香港特別行政區

高等法院上訴法庭

民事司法管轄權

民事上訴

案件編號：民事上訴案件 2001 年第 1046 號

（原高院民事訴訟案件 2000 年第 9827 號）

————————

原告人　林哲民日昌電業公司

對

被告人　張順連

————————

主審法官：　高等法院上訴法庭法官胡國興

　　　　　　高等法院原訟法庭法官鍾安德

聆訊日期：　2002 年 5 月 22 日

判案書日期：　2002 年 7 月 12 日

————————

判案書

————————

由高等法院原訟法庭法官鍾安德頒佈上訴法庭判案書：

1. 原告（上訴人）不服高等法院原訟法庭任懿君法官在 2001 年 5 月 9 日作出的判決，向本庭提出上訴。任法官在當日命令剔除本訴訟的申索陳述書及撤銷本訴訟。為方便理解任法官作出上述命令的原因及本庭對本上訴的裁決，本庭先將本訴訟的性質及過程作出簡述，如下。

2. 原告在 2000 年 11 月 6 日提出本訴訟，指被告（答辯人）違反與他曾訂定的有關深圳市龍崗區橫崗鎮一廠房的租用合約，並煽動橫崗鎮村民霸佔他工廠設備及資產。原告要求被告賠償有關損失。

3. 被告在 2000 年 11 月 28 日，依據高等法院規則第 18 號命令第 19 條規則提出申請，要求剔除本訴訟的申索陳述書。聆案官在 2001 年 1 月 16 日經聆訊後，作出以下命令：

「 除非原告人在 28 日內將廣東省深圳市龍崗區人民法院的判決作廢，否則剔除索償聲請書（即高等法院規則所指的申索陳述書）第 1 至 4 項。」

本訴訟的申索陳述書的第 1 至 4 項申索為：

「 1. 退回所交的租金，人民幣 7,500.00 元
2. 工場裝修費，人民幣 10,871.00 元
3. 搬遷費，人民幣 4,000.00 元
4. 維持工資，人民幣 16,000.00 元。」

共折合港幣 35,860.00 元。至於申索陳述書中的第 5 至 8 項申索，則未被列入上述命令。原告不服，在 2001 年 2 月 3 日向原訟法庭提出上訴。

4. 2001 年 5 月 9 日，該上訴在任法官席前進行聆訊。在該聆訊前數天（即 2001 年 5 月 5 日），被告在法庭呈交存檔一份標題為「交相上訴通告」的文件，要求原訟法庭在 2001 年 5 月 9 日「重新聆訊被告人於 2000 年 11 月 28 日以傳票方式申請剔除原告人的索償聲請書（即高等法院規則所指的申索陳述書）及撤銷本訴訟」。

5. 因此，在 2001 年 5 月 9 日聆訊時，任法官需處理的共有兩項申請，即原告在 2001 年 2 月 3 日提出的上訴，及被告在 2001 年 5 月 5 日提出的所謂「交相上訴通告」。

6. 任法官在他 2001 年 5 月 9 日的「判案書」中，並未清楚指出法庭如何處理被告方提出的所謂「交相上訴通告」。根據高等法院規則第 58 號命令第 1(2) 條規則，來自聆案官的判決、命令或決定的上訴，須以通知書方式通知送達另一方，而根據第 58 號命令第 1(3) 條規則：

「除非法庭另有命令，否則通知書必須在遭上訴的判決、命令或決定

作出後 14 天內發出，並必須在發出後 5 天內送達。」

7. 因此，被告方的「交相上訴通告」是在法定期限屆滿後才提出。高等法院第 3 號命令第 5(1) 條規則賦予法庭延展或縮短有關期限的權力。雖然如此，如前所述，任法官並沒有在判案書中，清楚顯示曾行使有關的酌情權，延展有關的上訴期限。

8. 在原訟法庭未行使其酌情權情況下，本庭可依據情況，自行決定應如何行使該酌情權。根據 2002 年香港民事程序 (*Hong Kong Civil Practice* 2002) 中第 3/5/2 段：

   "...... application to enlarge the time for an appeal when the litigant has had his trial and lost, will not generally be granted unless there is material on which the court can exercise its discretion (*Ratnan v Cumarasamy* [1965] 1 WLR 8; [1964] 3 ALL ER 933 PC and see *Chiu Sin-chung v Yu Yan-yan Angela* [1993] 1 HKLR 225)." （中文譯本請參閱附件註一）

9. 被告從未解釋為何未在法定期限內提出該所謂「交相上訴通告」。而代表被告的劉大律師，在本上訴聆訊時，亦非常公正地承認，被告方在提出該通知時，可能對有關法律規定有所誤解。基於以上兩點，本庭認為假如原訟法庭是基於上述的「交相上訴通告」而撤銷此訴訟，這判決缺乏充分的理據。因此，單就此點，原訟法庭在 2001 年 5 月 9 日決定撤銷本訴訟的命令是錯誤的。本上訴亦應因此而得直。

10. 除被告方提出的所謂「交相上訴通告」外，在 2001 年 5 月 9 日的聆訊時，原訟法庭應處理的，只為原告在 2001 年 2 月 3 日提出的上訴。該上訴針對的是聆案官在 2001 年 1 月 16 日作出的剔除申索陳述書中第 1 至 4 項申索的命令，即使原訟法庭駁回原告提出的上訴，亦無合理理據剔除申索陳述書中的所有申索及／或撤銷本訴訟。涉及剔除申索陳述書中第 5 至 8 項申索的原訟法庭命令，亦應因此而被撤銷。

11. 任法官在 2001 年 5 月 9 日的判決中，並沒有清楚指出，聆案官在 2001 年 1 月 16 日的命令是否正確，但由於任法官在當日撤銷了本訴訟，他理應是同意聆案官在 2001 年 1 月 16 日所作出的命令。

12. 任法官在其「判案書」中說：

   「驟眼看來，這 [申索陳述書] 不應該在香港司法管轄範圍內，或者說是不適合香港司法管轄範圍內裁定這個毀約行為，因為所涉及的內容發生在深圳。……

   根據龍崗區人民法院在 2000 年 12 月 15 日的判決，有以下的聲明：

『被告 [即本案的原告] 經本院合法傳喚，無正當理由拒不到庭，本案現已審理終結。』

……本席認為此案交由香港的法庭審理是不妥當的，因為涉及的內容是在深圳的房地產，而在當地已經興起訴訟……」

13. 有關涉及大陸房地產租務合約的糾紛，是否應在香港提出訴訟這一點，本庭曾在 **林哲民經營之日昌電業公司對林志滔**（2001 年民事上訴第354 號）一案中作出判決。在該上訴中，原告亦在香港提出訴訟，指該案的被告違反口頭租務協議。有關的糾紛，未在香港法院進行審訊前，已在東莞市人民法院審理完結。上訴法庭在考慮過 Chiyu Banking Corporation Ltd v Chan Tin Kwun, HCA 1186 of 1995 一案後，裁定東莞市人民法院的判決，並非最終及不可推翻的判決。因此，原訟法庭不應引用「不容反悔法」（estoppel）而撤銷該訴訟。

14. 在本訴訟中，聆案官並沒有在 2001 年 1 月 16 日即時撤銷本訴訟，而僅在其命令中要求原告在 28 天內將龍崗區人民法院的判決作廢。因此，本庭在對本上訴作出判決時，須考慮聆案官是否正確地行使酌情權作出以上的命令。

15. 原訟法庭在 **Chiyu Banking Corporation** 一案作出的裁決，是基於國內民事法中有關「抗訴制度」（System of Protest）的法律而作出。在該案的「判案書」中有關的判詞為：

"Under the legal system in PRC, another state organ, the Procuratorate exercises a supervisory function over civil adjudication by the courts: Article 14 of the Civil Procedure Law of 1991 ("*the Civil Procedure Law*"). Under Article 185, the Procuratorate may lodge a protest to the court in respect of a judicial decision. The circumstances in which the protest may be lodged are set out in Article 185, namely,

(i) the main evidence to substantiate the original judgment or ruling was insufficient;

(ii) the law which was applied in the original judgment or ruling was incorrect;

(iii)the People's Court was in violation of the statutory procedure which have affected the correctness of the judgment or ruling;

(iv)the judicial members in trying the case committed embezzlement, accepted bribes, practised favouritism or make a judgment that perverted the law.

It is for the Supreme People's Procuratorate to lodge the protest but under Article 185, the Fujian People's Procuratorate is entitled to refer the matter to the Supreme People's Procuratorate for it to lodge a protest.

Under Article 187, the court, upon receipt of the protest, is required to conduct a retrial of the action.

This procedure is well recognised. Mr Li Ping, the Plaintiff's expert on Chinese law, stated at para. 11 of his affidavit that 'if such protest is made a retrail will be ordered.' Legal literature on this topic can be found in -

《中國訴訟制度法律全書》：楊柄芝、李春霖，法律出版社

"A Comprehenisve Law Book on PRC's Legal Procedure System" by Yang Bing Zhi and Li Chun Lin. Published by the Falu Publishing House and

《抗訴制度通論》：周士敏，中國政法大學出版社

"PRC's System on Protest against the People's Court - General Discussion" by Shou Shi Min. Published by University of Politics & Law Publishing House.

What is a final and conclusive judgment

One must apply Hong Kong law to determine whether a judgment is final and conclusive. In *Gustave Nouvion v Freeman & Another* [1889] 15 AC 1, the Privy Council considered what is a final and conclusive judgment. Lord Herschell at page 9 had this to say:

'...... it must be shown that in the court by which it was pronounced conclusively, finally, and for ever established the existence of the debt of which it is sought to be made conclusive evidence in this country, so as to make it res judicata between the parties. If it is not conclusive in the same court which pronounced it, so that notwithstanding such a judgment the existence of the debt made between the same parties be afterwards contested in that court, and upon proper proceedings being taken and such context being adjudicated upon, it may be declared that there exists no obligation to pay the debt at all, then I do not think that a judgment which is of that character can be regarded as finally and conclusively evidencing the debt, and so entitling the person who has obtained the judgment to obtain a decree from a court for the payment of that debt.'

And at page 10, the law lord continued:

'...... Although an appeal may be pending, a court of competent jurisdiction has finally and conclusively determined the existence of a debt, and it has nonetheless done so because the right of appeal has been given whereby a superior court may overrule that decision. There exists at the time of the suit a judgment which must be assumed to be valid until interfered with by a higher tribunal, and which conclusively establishes the existence of the debt which is sought to be recovered in this country. That appears to be in altogether a different position from a 'remate' judgment where the very court which pronounced the 'remate' judgment (not the Court of Appeal) may determine, if proper proceedings are taken, that the debt for which this 'remate' judgment is sought to be used as conclusive evidence has no existence at all.'

Not final and conclusive

Based on the material before me, the supervisory function of the Supreme People's Procuratorate and the protest system are not simply an appeal process. The Intermediate Court judgment is final in the sense that it is not appealable and it is enforceable in China, but it is not final and conclusive for the purpose of recognition and enforcement by the Hong Kong Courts because in the words of Lord Watson, it 'is not final and unalterable in the court which pronounced it'. It is liable to the altered by the Intermediate Court on a retrial if the Supreme People's Procuratorate lodge a protest in accordance with the Civil Procedure Law. If upon protest being made, rare the circumstances may be, a Chinese Court has to retry the case, then, clearly it retains the power to alter its own decision. As Lord Watson said at page 13 of Nouvion:

'There is no real difference in principle between the case of a court retaining power to alter a decree by an order in the same suit and the case of its retaining power to defeat the operation of that decree by an order pronounced in another suit relating to the same debt.'"

（中文譯本請參閱附件註二）

16. 香港以外國家或地區的法律，以普通法而言，屬香港法院對事實的裁斷。*Phipson on Evidence*（2000 年）第 15 版第 37-58 段，對此點有以下的陳述：

"Foreign law must, in general, be proved *on oath*, either orally or, in some cases, by affidavit; and not by the mere certificates of experts, though this strictness has occasionally been relaxed ......

Formerly, in all cases, *previous decisions* upon the same point of foreign law and even between the same parties were not admissible, for being a question of fact it must be decided on evidence and not on authority, in addition to which the law is continually liable to change. However, in civil proceedings, a previous decision on a question of foreign law is now given some status as a precedent. By section 4(2) to (5) of the Civil Evidence Act 1972 a previous decision of a superior court on a question of foreign law (which is reported in a citable form) may be tendered as evidence of that law and will be presumed to be a correct statement of that law until the contrary is proved."

（中文譯本請參閱附件註三）

17. Phipson 一書中所指的，是英國法律（特別是《1972 年民事證據法令》）對外地法律的處理方法。香港亦有類似英格蘭法令的法律條文。根據香港法例第 8 章《證據條例》第 59 條：

「 (2) 凡就香港以外任何國家或地區關乎任何事宜的法律的任何問題，已在第 (4) 款所述法律程序中獲裁定（不論是在本部的生效日期之前或之後獲裁定），則在任何民事法律程序中（在可對該國家或地區關乎該事宜的法律予以司法認知的法庭席前進行的法律程序除外）-

　　(a) 在首述的法律程序中就該問題所作的任何裁斷或決定，如以可引述的形式作報導或記錄，則可接納為證據，以證明該國家或地區關乎該事宜的法律；及

　　(b) 如為上述目的援引如此作報導或記錄的上述裁斷或決定，則除非相反證明成立，否則該國家或地區關乎該事宜的法律須當作與該裁斷或決定相符……」

「 (5) 為施行本條的規定，就第 (2) 款所述問題所作的裁斷或決定，如是以書面形式在一份報告、謄本或其他文件內作報導或記錄，而該報告、謄本或其他文件在假如該問題是有關香港法律的問題時可在香港進行的法律訴訟程序中被引述作為根據，則在並僅在上述情況下，該裁斷或決定須當作為以可引述的形式作報導或記錄。」

　　18. 第 59 條第 4(a) 段的英文本規定：

" (4) The proceedings referred to in subsection (2) are the following, whether civil or criminal, namely -

(a) proceedings at first instance in the High Court or in the Supreme Court of England as constituted by section 1 of the Courts Act 1971 （1971 c. 23 UK）;"

19. 根據香港法例第 1 章《釋義及通則條例》第 3 條：

"'High Court'（ 高 等 法 院 ） means the High Court of the Hong Kong Special Administrative Region established by section 3 of the High Court Ordinance (Cap. 4)."

「 『高等法院』（High Court）指《高等法院條例》（第 4 章）第 3 條所設立的香港特別行政區高等法院。」

20. 而香港法例第 4 章《高等法院條例》第 3 條則規定：

"There shall be a High Court of the Hong Kong Special Administrative Region consisting of the Court of First Instance and the Court of Appeal."

「現設立香港特別行政區高等法院，由原訟法庭及上訴法庭組成。」

21. 因此，根據以上各條款，雖然在本訴訟中，並無有關「抗訴制度」的證據，基於第 8 章第 59 條的條文，本庭亦可採納原訟法庭在 Chiyu Banking Corporation 一案的「判案書」中有關此點的裁斷，作為本庭對本上訴作出裁決時的證據。

22. 但第 8 章中第 59 條第 4(a) 段的中文本，與英文本的有所不同。該中文本為：

「 在由《1971 年法院法令》（1971 c. 23 UK）第 1 條所組成的英格蘭高等法院或最高法院中的原訟法律程序；」

根據中文本，第 59 條第 4(a) 段所指的「高等法院或最高法院」均為英格蘭的法院，而非分別指香港高等法院和英格蘭的最高法院。假如中文本是第 59 條第 4(a) 段的真正意義，本庭不可採納香港高等法院原訟法庭在 **Chiyu Banking Corporation** 的裁斷，作為「抗訴制度」的證據。

23. 第 59 條第 4(a) 段的中文本的意義與英文本的意義出現分歧，本庭認為，英文本所載的意義是真正的意義，即 "High Court" 是指香港特別行政區的高等法院。原因如下：

（1）第 59 條第 4(a) 段的英文本，明確指明有關的法律程序是 "proceedings at first instance"（原訟法律程序）。該條款亦明文指定，有關法院是 "...... the High Court or the Supreme Court of England ......"（「……高等法院或英格蘭的最高法院……」）。根據英格蘭的 1971 年法院法令第 1 條：

"The Supreme Court shall consist of the Court of Appeal and the High Court, together with the Crown Court established by this Act."

（中文譯本請參閱附件註四）

在英格蘭而言，最高法院中負責原訟法律程序的法院，基本上是高等法庭（High Court）和英皇法院（Crown Court）。因此，假如第 59 條第 4(a) 段僅指英格蘭法院的原訟法庭程序（無論是在英格蘭高等法院或英皇法院的法律程序），該條款只須訂明有關的法律程序是：

「在由《1971 年法院法令》……第 1 條所組成的英格蘭最高法院中的原訟法律程序」

已經足夠。另方面，假如第 59 條第 4(a) 段是專指英格蘭高等法院中的原訟法律程序，便無須訂明有關原訟法律程序是 "...... the High Court or the Supreme Court of England ...."（……高等法院或英格蘭的最高法院……）中的原訟法律程序，而只須直接規定是 "...... the Supreme Court of England ......"（英格蘭的最高法院）的原訟法律程序；

（2）第 59 條第 4(b) 和 4(c) 段，分別涉及第 4(a) 段「所述的法律程序所產生的上訴」及「在終審法院席前進行的法律程序」。因此，第 59 條第 4(a) 至 (c) 段所指的法律程序，應該是分別在香港高等法院中的兩級法庭及香港終審法院席前的法律程序。

24. 香港法例第 1 章第 10B(3) 款規定：

「凡條例的兩種真確本在比較之下，出現意義分歧，而引用通常適用的法律釋義規則，亦不能解決，則須在考慮條例的目的和作用後，採用最能兼顧及協調兩文本的意義。」

25. 如前所述，本庭裁斷第 59 條第 4(a) 段的英文本的真正意義是指，香港原訟法庭的裁決或決定，可被接納為有關香港以外國家或地區的法律的證據。

26. 本庭亦裁斷，第 59 條第 4(a) 段的中文本，在此點與英文本出現意義分歧。因此，本庭運用第 10B(3) 條賦予的權力，採用第 59 條第 4(a) 段英文本的意義，為該條文的真正意義。

27. 根據 **Chiyu Banking Corporation** 一案的裁斷，由於國內的法律容許有關方面提出「抗訴」，而「抗訴」經提出後，有可能引致裁決原訟的法院須對有關訴訟重行審理。因此，根據香港法律而言，該法院的判決，並非一最終及不可推翻的判決。

28. 第 8 章第 59 條第 (3) 款規定，除經法庭許可外，與訟的任何一方，不得援引有關的裁斷或決定。原告並無律師代表應訊，亦無接受法律訓練，在此情況下，原告沒有在本上訴聆訊前申請法庭許可，實可理解。本庭為能考慮與本上訴有關的事項，決定給予許可。

29. 此外，國內的法律亦沒有對提出「抗訴」的期限作出任何規定。基於以上各點，聆案官在 2001 年 1 月 16 日所作的命令，規定原告須在命令日起 28 天內將人民法院的判決作廢，並無充分的理據支持。而任法官在 2001 年 5 月 9 日駁回原告針對 2001 年 1 月 16 日命令而提出的上訴時，亦無解釋如此裁斷的理據。

30. 本庭因此裁定原告的上訴得直，命令撤銷任法官 2001 年 5 月 9 日及聆案官 2001 年 1 月 16 日的兩項命令。

31. 最後，本庭必須一提，與本上訴相關的兩事項：

（a）被告在本上訴聆訊時，要求本庭批予許可接納進一步證據呈堂，該進一步證據基本上涉及被告指龍崗區人民法院的判決，已在較早前完成執行程序。但此點與人民法院的判決是否一最終及不可推翻的判決，並無關係。因此，本庭認定這進一步證據與本上訴的爭議無關，把有關的申請撤銷。

（b）代表被告的劉大律師指 **Chiyu Banking Corporation** 一案中的被告，在該案聆訊時，已提出「抗訴」，但本訴訟的原告，從未提出「抗訴」。雖然如此，由於並無證據顯示，國內法律規定提出「抗訴」的期限，本庭認為單憑此點，不足以令本庭裁斷 **Chiyu Banking Corporation** 一案的裁決，不適用於本上訴。

32. 本庭作出暫許訟費命令，被告要支付予原告本上訴及在聆案官和原訟法庭席前涉及有關本上訴各爭議點的訟費。

（胡國興）　　　　　　　　　（鍾安德）

高等法院上訴法庭法官　　　高等法院原訟法庭法官

原告人：自行應訊

被告人：由黎錦文李孟華律師事務所轉聘劉煥新大律師代表

附件

[以下節錄以英文原文為準，中文譯本僅供參考。]

註一：

「…… 案件經過審訊而訴訟人於被判敗訴後申請延展期限以進行上訴，除非有資料讓法庭賴以行使其酌情權，否則法庭在一般情況下都不會批准（**Ratnan v Cumarasamy** [1965] 1 WLR 8; [1964] 3 ALL ER 933 PC 及 **Chiu Sin-chung v Yu Yan-yan Angela** [1993] 1 HKLR 225）。」

註二：

「根據中華人民共和國的法制，另一國家機關檢察院有權對民事審判活動實行法律監督：《1991 年民事訴訟法》（「民事訴訟法」）第 14 條。第 185 條則規定檢察院可在下述情況下對司法判決提出抗訴：

（i）　支持原判決或裁定的主要證據不足夠；

（ii）　原判決或裁定所採用的法律有錯誤；

（iii）　人民法院違反法定程序，影響了案件正確判決或裁定；

（iv）　審判人員在審理案件時有貪污受賄、徇私舞弊、枉法裁決行為。

雖然抗訴須由最高人民檢察院提出，但根據第 185 條，福建人民檢察院有權把有關事宜提交最高人民檢察院，以便最高人民檢察院提出抗訴。」

根據第 187 條，法院於收到抗訴後須對案件再行審理。

這項程序已是眾所周知。原告人的中國法律專家李平（譯音）在其誓章第 11 段指出「如抗訴被提出，法院會指令再審該案。」有關這方面的論述可見於下列法律文獻：

《中國訴訟制度法律全書》：楊柄芝、李春霖，法律出版社，和

《抗訴制度通論》：周士敏，中國政法大學出版社

何謂最終及不可推翻的判決

我們必須根據香港法律來判定一項判決是否最終及不可推翻。英國樞密院曾在 **Gustave Nouvion v Freeman & Another** 一案 [1889] 15 AC 1 考慮何謂最終及不可推翻的判決這問題。Lord Herschell 在判案書的第 9 頁有以下論述：

「…… 必須有證據顯示，在本國擬用來確證該筆債項存在的判決，經由宣布該判決的法庭作出後，該項判決便不可推翻、最終及永久地確立

該筆債項的存在，以致對訴訟各方而言，債項的存在已成既判事情（res judicata）。若這判決在宣布判決的法庭並非不可推翻，那麼即使法庭已作出判決，但相同的訴訟各方日後依然有可能在同一法庭，就債項是否存在提出爭議，而法庭經過恰當的法律程序審理該項爭議後，有可能宣布訴訟的其中一方根本沒有義務償還債項。在這情況下，本席認為，這樣性質的判決便不能看作是最終及不可推翻地確實證明了該筆債項，致使獲得該判決的人因而有權向本國法庭要求作出償付債項的命令。」

在該判案書的第 10 頁，Lord Herschell 續說：

「…… 雖然案件可能正待上訴，但具有司法管轄權的法庭已最終及不可推翻地裁定這筆債項確實存在。儘管這項裁定有可能會被較高級的法庭推翻，然而法庭還是作出了判決，因為訴訟任何一方都有權向較高級的法庭提出上訴。這項判決未被較高級的法庭推翻之前，在本案訴訟期間都必須視為有效，並且不可推翻地確立了在本國所擬追討的債項確實存在。這種判決看來跟『出售財產』判決的性質截然不同。宣布該項『出售財產』判決的法庭（並非上訴法庭），如經過恰當的法律程序審理有關案件後，就該筆現擬以這項『出售財產』判決為不可推翻的證據來證明的債項，可能會裁定根本並不存在。」

並非最終及不可推翻

根據本席在本案所得資料，最高人民檢察院的監督職能和抗訴制度並非僅是一項上訴程序。從中級人民法院的判決是不可上訴，及在中國是可以強制執行這個角度而言，中級人民法院的判決是一項最終判決。然而，就香港法院承認和強制執行判決這目的而言，這並非一項最終及不可推翻的判決，因為引用 Lord Watson 所言，這判決「在宣布判決的法庭並非是最終和不可更改的」。如最高人民檢察院根據《民事訴訟法》提出抗訴，則案件在中級人民法院經過再行審理後，判決是可以被更改的。即使提出抗訴的情況或許很罕有，但一旦抗訴提出後，中國的法院便須再行審理該案，這樣，中國法院顯然保留着改變其決定的權力。誠如 Lord Watson 在 Nouvion 一案第 13 頁所言：

「法庭保留權力，在同一訴訟中發出命令，以更改先前的一項判決，與法庭保留權力，在另一宗與同一筆債項有關的訴訟中發出命令，使先前的判決無法執行，兩者在原則上都沒有實質分別。」

註三：

「一般來説，外地法律必須經宣誓來證明，宣誓可以是用口頭形式，或在某些案件以誓章形式作出，而並非單靠專家的證書來證明，雖然，法庭以往亦曾偶然放寬這項嚴格的規定……

以前，在所有案件，同一項有關外地法律問題的先前判決，即使對訟的各方相同，都不可以在另一案件中接納為證據。這是因為涉及外地法律的問題屬於事實問題，必須基於證據而非案例來作出裁斷，而且有關法律亦可能在不斷轉變。但現在，在民事法律程序中，有關外地法律問題的先前判決已享有某些類似法律先例的地位。根據英國《1992年民事證據法令》第4(2)至(5)條，高級的法庭就外地法律問題所作的先前判決（經已用可引述的形式報導）可被提出作為該項法律的證據，而這判決亦會被推定為該項法律的正確陳述，直至相反證明成立為止。」

註四：

「最高法院由上訴法院和高等法院，連同由本法令所設立的英皇法院所組成。」

李祐榮　訴　李瑞群

[2005] HKCA 657; [2007] 2 HKLRD 749; CACV 159/2004 (9 December 2005)

CACV 159/2004

香港特別行政區

高等法院上訴法庭

民事司法管轄權

民事上訴

案件編號：民事上訴案件 2004 年第 159 號

（原高等法院民事訴訟 2003 年第 1075 號）

————————

原告人　　李祐榮

與

被告人　　李瑞群

————————

審理法官：高等法院上訴法庭法官張澤祐

高等法院上訴法庭法官袁家寧

高等法院原訟法庭法官鍾安德

聆訊日期：2005 年 10 月 25 日

判案書日期：2005 年 12 月 9 日

————————

判案書

————————

上訴法庭法官張澤祐：

案情

1. 本案的原告人及被告人是兄妹關係，雙方曾經在內地清遠市合作經營工廠，根據原告人所說雙方其後同意工廠由被告人經營，而被告人需要給予原告人 $199,000 作為補償。原告人指由於被告人沒有履行協議給予他有關款項，他於是在 2002 年 2 月 27 日在清遠市清城區人民法院（「清城法院」）向被告人索償該筆款項。被告人在該宗案件的答辯理由是有關的工廠是她獨立投資及經營的。清城法院於 2002 年 5 月 18 日對案件作出裁決，判原告人勝訴。

2. 被告人不服判決，向清遠市中級人民法院（「清遠中院」）提出上訴。該法院於 2002 年 9 月 11 日駁回被告人的上訴及維持清城法院的原判。

3. 被告人仍不服清遠中院的判決，向廣東省高級人民法院（「廣東高院」）提出民事申訴。廣東高院命令清遠中院對案件提出覆查。經覆查後清遠中院於 2002 年 12 月 28 日駁回被告人的申請。

4. 原告人在清遠中院頒發 2002 年 9 月 11 日的判決後，在同年 10 月 30 日向香港區域法院提出申索，要求被告人償還 $199,000。原告人是根據清城法院 2002 年 5 月 18 日的判決向被告人提出索償。原告人並於同年 11 月 28 日提交傳票，要求區域法院以簡易程序判他勝訴。

5. 區域法院於 2003 年 2 月 19 日將案件轉交高等法院原訟法庭審理。原訟法庭聆案官於 2003 年 12 月 9 日駁回原告人的申請。原告人提出上訴。原訟法庭暫委法官陳江耀於 2004 年 5 月 25 日判原告人上訴得直，陳法官根據原告人的再經修訂的申索陳述書，判原告人可獲 $192,861 連利息。

6. 被告人就陳法官的命令向上訴法庭提出上訴。

外地判決

7. 原告人雖然已在清城法院取得判決，但他仍可以根據在清城法院所提出的訴因即被告人沒有根據協議支付有關的補償作為在向香港法院提出訴訟的訴因。他亦可以根據清城法院的判決作為向本港法院提出訴訟的訴因。若果他根據清城法院的判決作為訴因，他必須證明有關的判決是一項最終及不可推翻的判決。由於《外地判決（交互強制執行）條例》（香港法例第 319 章）不適用於內地法院的判決，故此原告人不可以根據這條例登記有關的判決及在香港執行這個判決。

最終及不可推翻的判決

8. 由於原告人所持的訴因是清城法院的判決，本上訴的重要爭議點是這判決是不是一項最終及不可推翻的判決。雖然原告人在經修訂的申索陳述書內指出有關的判決是最終及不可推翻的判決，但雙方從未在陳法官席前就這議題作出陳述。被告人在陳法官席前是沒有律師代表的。由於本案涉及公眾重要性而被告一方並沒有律師代表，因此上訴法庭邀請了法庭之友袁國強資深大律師協助法庭及於上次聆訊時批准雙方提交專家證人的證供。原告人提交了一份清華大學王亞新法學教授（民事訴訟法學）的法律意見書。被告人説由於她財政有困難，故此沒有聘請專家提供意見。

9. 若果一名原告人根據外地判決作為香港訴訟的訴因，他需負上舉證責任去證明有關的判決是最終及不可推翻的，而有關的責任包括提交外地法律專家意見書來支持有關的申請。本案的原告人在原訟法庭審訊時並沒有提交任何內地法律專家意見書去支持有關的申請。

Nouvion v. Freeman

10. 香港法庭在考慮香港以外法院的判決是不是一項最終及不可推翻的判決時是根據適用於香港的國際私法原則。本港適用的案例是英國上議院法庭 *Nouvion v. Freeman*[1889] 15 App. Cas. 1 一案。Lord Herschell 法官在該案有以下的裁決：

「 法官閣下，原告人在請求我國法院承認一個外國判決時提出，藉着該外國判決他就有充分的權利取得判決，以執行其追討債務的命令。本案唯一有爭議的問題是，在上述的情況下，在我國法院，該外國判決是否足以令原告人有權以他作為已故的衡特信先生（Mr. Henderson）之債權人的身份取得執行償債命令的判決。

法官閣下，毫無疑問，現時我國法院會承認外國判決的效力。法院要承認這樣一個判決判的效力，並把它視作具有足以確定該債項的效力，究竟是基於甚麼原則？這無需查究，依賴的是在威廉對鍾斯一案中佰萊男爵（Parke B.）及愛特信男爵（Alderson B.）在闡釋有關法律時提出的觀點：「當有司法管轄權的法院在裁定某人欠另一人若干數額的款項時，給付該款項的法律責任便隨之而生，[債權人]可以以此責任為訴因提起債務之訴從而執行該判決。」然而，上訴人的代表大律師已承認，亦必須承認，會獲承認的判決之必具條件法律已有所規定，它必須是通過有司法管轄權的法院作出裁決所產生的，並且是最終及不可推翻之判決。一個外國法院作出的判決在頒佈時若僅僅是了結並且最終地解決了某個法律程序中的爭議，這事實本身並不足以使該判

決成為一個最終的、不可推翻的並且可藉以在我國法院請求執行的判決。

法官閣下，我認為，若要確定原審國法院作出的是這樣的一個判決，就必需顯示這判決在該法院作出時，它已不可推翻地、最終地及永久地確定了該債務的存在，並可請求我國法庭將該債務承認為不可推翻的證據，進而承認為與訟各方之間的既判事實。若這判決在該外國法院作出時並非一個不可推翻的判決，以致縱使有該判決，與訟各方日後仍可在該法院就債務存在與否進行爭辯，而法院通過恰當的法律程序，經審裁後又可能宣判債務並不存在，不須繳付，那麼，我不認為這種判決可以算是一個已最終及不可推翻地證明了債務存在的判決。

我認為我國法院在執行外國判決時應遵從以下原則：在有司法管轄權的法院中，無論與訟人有否充分利用甚或放棄他們的任何權利，只要與訟各方均可按固有的程序就案情的是非曲直全面進行爭辯，法院經審裁後判定了某項債務或責任的存在及作出了最終裁決，並且各方日後不得在該法院提出爭議，而只能通過在上級法院進行上訴時才能提出質疑。在這樣一種情況下才可說，我們因認同該外國法院的裁決而願意承認該判決事實已確定了債項或責任的存在。但就本案的情況而言，請求本院審裁是否執行的是一個較近於確定債項或責任不存在的判決，而該外國法院日後仍然可能宣告該債項或責任並不存在，對我來說我國法院執行外地判決的最基本原則並不足以處理這情況。……法官閣下，還有一種說法是，這樣的一項判決，縱使有待上訴，它實在與一個在我國法院經過訴訟而取得的判決相似，我認為兩者之間有着至關重要的區別。雖然仍有待上訴，但有司法管轄權的法院已最終及不可推翻地裁定了該債務的存在；因為就算上訴權的賦予使該決定可能被上級法院推翻，這裁定畢竟是最終及不可推翻的。在訴訟展開時存在着一項判決，該判決在未被上級法院干預之前必須被假設為有效判決，並且必須假設其已不可推翻地確定了當事人欲在本國追討的債務的存在……

11. 該案的原告人是引用西班牙法院頒佈的判決作為他在英國法院向被告人提出申索的訴因。該案顯示西班牙訴訟法律程序有兩種：首先原告人可以根據「簡易程序」獲得一項「remate 判決」。除非該判決在上訴時被推翻或更改，它是一項最終的判決。但敗訴的一方亦可以在同一法院引用「普通程序」就同一議題提出訴訟。有關的判決是「plenary（正規的判決）判決」。這判決會令法庭之前頒佈的「remate 判決」無效。另外，在「普通程序」勝訴的一方亦可向對方追討之前因在「簡易程序」敗訴而履行「remate 判決」支付給對方的款項。

12. 該案的原告人是根據一項「remate 判決」作為在英國法院提出訴訟的訴因。英國上議院法庭指這裁決不是一項最終及不可推翻的裁決。該法庭亦指出就算原告人未能在英國執行這外國判決也不會構成任何不公義的情況，因為這名原告人是可以依賴原本的訴因在英國興訟。但若果這名原告人是依賴外國判決作為在英國提出訴訟的訴因，他必須符合有關的條件。

內地民事訴訟

13. 簡單來說，內地民事訴訟實行兩審終審制度，這是指一件民事案件經過兩級法院的審判，案件的審判即宣告終結的制度。根據這制度，一件民事案件經第一審人民法院審判後，當事人如果不服，有權依法向上一級人民法院提出上訴，上一級人民法院對上訴案件審理後作出的判決和裁定是終審判決、裁定當事人不得再提出上訴，見：譚兵主編《民事訴訟法學》第 115-116 頁。

「審判監督」制度

14. 雖然根據這個制度已審的判決是終審的判決，但根據《民事訴訟法》第 16 章，內地同時實行「審判監督」制度，以下三個途徑可啟動有關的制度：

1. 案件的當事人可根據《民事訴訟法》第 178 條，在認為已經發生法律效力的判決有錯誤時，可向原審人民法院或者上一級人民法院申請再審。《民事訴訟法》第 179 條規定，若果當事人的申請符合下列情況之一，人民法院應當再審：

(1) 有新的證據，足以推翻原判決、裁定的；

(2) 原判決、裁定認定事實的主要證據不足的；

(3) 原判決、裁定適用法律確有錯誤的；

(4) 人民法院違反法定程序，可能影響案件正確判決、裁定的；

(5) 審判人員在審理該案件時有貪污受賄，徇私舞弊，枉法裁判行為的。

人民法院對不符合前款規定的申請，予以駁回。

2. 根據《民事訴訟法》第 177 條，各級人民法院院長對該院已經發生法律效力的判決發現確有錯誤，認為需要再審的，應當提交審判委員討論決定。另外，最高人民法院對地方各級人民法院已經發生法律效力的判決及上級人民法院對下級人民法院已經發生法律效力的判決，發

現確有錯誤的，有權提審或者指令下級人民法院再審。

3. 根據《民事訴訟法》第 185 條，最高人民檢察院對各級人民法院已經發生法律效力的判決，上級人民檢察院對下級人民法院發生法律效力的判決，發現有下列情況之一應當按照審訊程序提出抗訴：

(1) 原判決、裁定認定事實的主要證據不足的；

(2) 原判決、裁定適用法律確有錯誤的；

(3) 人民法院違反法定程序，可能影響案件正確判決、裁定的；

(4) 審判人員在審理該案件時有貪污受賄，徇私舞弊，枉法裁判行為的。

另外，地方各級人民檢察院對同級人民法院已經發生法律效力的裁決、裁定，發現有前款規定情形之一，應當提請上級人民檢察院按照審判監督程序提出抗訴。

制度的影響

15. 本席了解上述的審判監督制度是因應國情需要及實踐「有錯必糾」原則而設立：見梁寶儉主編《人民法院改革理論與實踐》，《論審判監督制度的改革》作者曾秋山及王文忠。但同時，若一名原告人在香港法院依賴內地法院的判決作為在本港提出訴訟的訴因，正因這個審判監督制度而產生內地判決是否可視為最終及不可推翻判決的爭議。這就是由於有關的制度是超越了敗訴一方可就判決提出上訴的一般上訴制度。該審判監督制度賦予（1）當事人（2）法院本身及（3）另一個權力機關（即檢察院）權力去啟動程序令案件重新審理，經審裁後法院又可能宣判原審時裁定的債務並不存在。這正如 Lord Herschell 法官所說，這類的判決不可以算是一個證明了債務存在的已最終及不可推翻的判決。香港法庭曾在多宗案件處理有關的審判監督制度是否令內地法院的裁決不能被視為是最終及不可推翻的判決的爭議，但上訴法庭仍未在一宗正審的案件中就這議題作出最終的判決。這些案例包括：

(1) *Chiyu Banking Corporation Ltd. v Chan Tin Kwun* [1966] 1 HKLR 395;

(2) *Tan Tay Cuan v Ng Chi Hung*, unrep. HCA 5477/2000 （5/2/2001）；

(3) 林哲民經營之日昌電業公司對林志滔，CACV 354/2001 （18/12/2001）；

(4) 林哲民經營之日昌電業公司對林志滔，HCA 9585/1999（8/4/2003）；及

(5) 林哲民日昌電業公司對張順連，CACV 1046/2001 （12/7/2002）。

王教授的意見

16. 王亞新教授指出近年內地最高法院及最高檢察院頒佈以下的司法解釋正在逐步限制啟動審判監督程序：

1. 2001 年 8 月 14 日最高人民檢察院民事行政檢察廳頒佈的《關於規範省級人民檢察院辦理民事行政提請抗訴案件的意見》（「《意見》」）第一條第 5 款規定，「申訴人在人民法院判決、裁定生效二年之內無正當理由，未向人民檢察院提出申訴的案件」，省級檢察院應不予受理。（最高法院在同年 12 月 13 日以「最高法院通知」的形式向各級法院正式轉發了檢察院的這一文件。）

2. 2001 年 9 月 30 日最高人民檢察院通過了《人民檢察院民事行政抗訴案件辦案規則》（「《規則》」），規定自受理當事人申訴之日起 7 日內必須決定立案或不立案，立案後檢察院應調閱法院審判案卷，調閱後應在三個月內審查終結，決定是否抗訴並通知申請人（第 9、13、23 至 27，30）條等。

3. 2001 年 11 月 1 日最高人民法院以通知的形式頒佈印發了全國審判監督工作座談會《關於當前審判監督工作若干問題的紀要》（「《紀要》」），該紀要明確指出當前及今後審判監督改革的主要任務是：規範再審立案標準，將無限申訴變為有限申訴，將無限再審改為有限再審。還在有關民事抗訴的部份明確要求，對於「原審案件當事人在原審裁判生效二年內無正當理由，未向人民法院或人民檢察院提出申訴的案件」，即使檢察院提起抗訴，法院也不予受理（第 14 條）。

4. 2002 年 7 月 31 日最高人民法院頒佈並於同年 8 月 15 日起施行的《關於人民法院對民事案件發回重審和指令再審有關問題的規定》（「《規定》」）對發動審判監督程序進行再審的次數做了明確限制，即再審都只能以一次為限。

17. 王教授指出：

1. 清遠中院已於 2002 年 9 月 11 日做出被告人敗訴的終審判決，而被告對此不服而向廣東高院提出的申訴請求也於 2002 年 12 月 28 日被駁回。這個時間距今已約三年。

2. 被告人此後並未向檢察院提出申訴，並請求檢察院提起抗訴。根據上述發佈的有關司法解釋，時至今日被告已經不大可能再獲得通過檢察院抗訴啟動審判監督程序的機會。

3. 唯一為被告人剩下的啟動審判監督程序、推翻原審判決的渠道就在於通過法院依職權而發動再審（按照現行法規定，只有清遠中院院長向審判委員會提起再審、或廣東高院和最高法院才能指令該中級法院再審或自行提審）。但在上下各級法院觀念改變的背景及限制再審的一般司法政策下，指望本級法院主動對本案啟動審判監督程序幾乎是不可能的事情。而廣東高院和最高法院在無從知悉本案具體案情的情況下更無可能指令再審或自行提審。事實上，被告人只有採取不計成本地到各級人大或政府去上訪的行動，才有可能通過這些權力機關對法院實施的監督來推動法院依職權對本案提起再審，而這種可能性不僅在現實中微乎其微，而且也沒有任何證據表明被告人在長達兩年多的時間內從上訪這樣的渠道尋求過救濟。

18. 王教授亦指根據司法統計，近年啟動審判監督程序的案件比率在急劇下降。 在上述情況下，內地法院在執行如本案這樣的判決時，已經是不存在任何法律上的障礙，一般而言也不會有任何猶豫的。

19. 王教授認為本案的具體情況與香港法院迄今為止就是否承認執行內地判決而做出的一系列判例所涉及的案情都有不同，被告已經極少有可能或機會啟動審判監督程序去挑戰原審的裁判。因此，應該將本案原審生效判決視為最終和不可推翻的判決。

袁大律師的意見

20. 袁大律師對王教授意見的回應可以簡述如下：

1. 2001 年 8 月 14 日最高人民檢察院民事行政檢察廳頒發的《意見》尾段指出該條文僅供各省級人民檢察院參考，並非強制性之規範。即使撇開有關的規定是否有強制性，這意見只適用於省級人民檢察院而不適用於最高人民檢察院。根據《民事訴訟法》第 185 條最高檢察院對各級人民法院已經發生法律效力的判決裁定有權提出抗訴。

2. 最高人民檢察院 2001 年 9 月 30 日的《規則》雖然訂立了受理案件的條件及受理後的程序，但該規則並沒有訂立時限規定申訴人在特定時限之外作出的申訴不會被受理。

3. 除了檢察院可以提出的抗訴制度之外，法院本身根據《民事訴訟法》第 177 條是有提審及再審的權利。雖然廣東高院曾經命令清遠中院再審案件，但廣東高院亦擁有將案件提審的權力。

4. 對於 2001 年 11 月 1 日最高人民法院頒佈的《紀要》即原審案件當事人在原審裁決生效兩年內無正當理由未向人民法院或人民檢察院提出的申訴案件，即使檢察院提出抗訴法庭也不予受理，袁大律師指出這是可能與監督制度抵觸，他引用張衛平《民事再審：基礎置換與制度重建》《中國法學》2003 年第一期 102-115 頁，其中以下一段支持他的說法 （109 頁）：

「有的人也許會指出，關於當事人糾纏再審的難題，審判監督程序也可以設定有關的條件對此加以防止。例如，必須在一定期間內提起申訴、只能提起一次、法院再審後，當事人也不能再次申請再審。對檢察機關的抗訴也可以設定抗訴限制，例如，不得超過 4 年。但問題在於，我國的再審作為一種審判監督程序，是以審判權作為基礎的，啟動它的是國家司法機關的外部權力，對這種權力的行使如果從當事人這個方面來加以限制是沒有任何意義的，如果限制司法機關行使審判監督權，又與審判監督權本身的性質相違背。審判監督權行使的條件之一就是確有錯誤，否則審判監督權就沒有存在的根據。因此，只能通過再審之訴對審判監督程序的置換，通過對當事人權利行使的合理限制來防止糾纏再審的問題。」

被告人的立場

21. 被告人承認她並沒有再去申請啟動審訊監督的程序，她說原告人曾經恐嚇她，若她回內地會作出對她不利的行動，故此她沒有再回內地跟進這件案件。她在上訴時提出了針對「鎮領導」及清遠中院司法人員瀆職的指控。

本席的意見

22. 在本案上訴聆訊後原告人代表律師試圖以傳票形式要求本席接納王教授對袁大律師意見的回覆。本席不接納這項申請。

23. 本席認為本案不能單是依賴書面法律意見作出判決。原告人是引用簡易程序要求法院給予判決，法律規定若這類申請存有爭議點或涉及艱難的法律議題，法庭就不應頒佈簡易判決，而需給予被告人答辯機會，讓案件進行正式審訊然後才作出判決。

24. 本席認為本案最具爭議性的議題是內地的判決是否純是因為審判監督制度的存在而令判決不能成為最終及不可推翻的判決，抑或是需要視乎實際情況才可以決定有關的裁決是不是屬於這類的裁決。如果法庭要視乎實際的情況來作出判決，它應如何規範或界定這個情況？舉一個例子，如果就某一宗案件，所有審判監督制度內的渠道已經被運用

而內地法院最終維持原審的判決，但同時有證據顯示有關權力機構對某個法庭在某段期間所判決的案件重新調查及命令重審，而當事人的案件亦是該法庭在該段期間作出判決的，當事人雖然未能在兩年的期限之內要求有關權力機構重新處理這些案件，但本港法庭在這情況下是否仍因當事人未能符合王教授所指有關制度新運作的規定而裁定內地裁決是一項最終及不可推翻的裁決？若果本港法庭需要考慮案件的實際情況，本港法庭應以甚麼標準來界定內地近期司法解釋文件提出涉及就兩年期限的「正當理由」？

25. 在 *Nouvion* 一案，法庭沒有清楚說明到底是不是只要存在着一個可以推翻「remate 判決」的制度，法庭就已具備穩固的基礎去裁定這類判決不是最終及不可被推翻的判決。

26. 本港法庭需要考慮實際情況才作出決定的觀點無疑是有它的優點，但這樣做會出現該裁決可能和內地可使用審判監督權力的機關的實質決定有所不同，畢竟本港法庭只能就當時雙方提供的證據來作出法庭認為正確的判決。這正突顯了本港法庭採用這方式處理案件的難處，也突顯了一個原則性的議題即是本港法庭應否單方面認為在內地判決敗訴的一方再沒有可能依賴有關的審判監督制度去推翻有關的判決，就因而裁定這判決是一項最終及不可推翻的判決？鑒於內地審判監督制度的存在及內地法制沒有一項條文規定內地判決若在外地執行會在甚麼時間或情況下才被視為最終及不可推翻的判決，香港法庭應否作出一個價值判斷來裁定一宗案件在內地已經是沒有「正當理由」來啟動「審判監督」制度。在現階段，本席不需要深入探討這些問題或者作出確定性的裁決，因為本上訴只是一項有關簡易判決的上訴。

27. 本案涉及的議題明顯是一項具有公眾重要性的議題。雖然王教授對本席提供了珍貴的意見，但這也只是訴訟一方所提供的專家的書面意見。袁大律師作為法庭之友對案件持中立態度，他是以專業知識協助法庭，雖然他不是內地法律專家，但本席認為他對王教授的意見所作出的回應並不是泛泛之言，王教授是應該出庭作證、接受盤問及全面解釋他的意見。

28. 代表原告人的黃大律師亦依賴王教授的法律意見，要求本席駁回被告人的上訴。黃大律師更引用「因欠缺行動而作出的判決」（default judgment）的性質來支持內地判決是最終判決的說法。在 *Nintendo of America Inc. v. Bung Enterprises Limited* [2000] HKCFI 654; [2000] 2 HKC 629，香港原訟法庭認為雖然「因欠缺行動而作出的判決」會被同級法院撤銷，但這也不代表有關的判決不是最終及不可推翻的判決，除非被告人申請撤銷有關的判決，該判決仍是最終及不可推翻的判決。

本席認為審判監督制度是內地法制獨有的制度，本港法庭是否可以引用「欠缺行動而作出的判決」的性質來處理內地判決亦是本案具有爭議性的論點，法庭需要經過正式審訊才可以作出定斷。

29. 在這情況下，本席認為適當的做法是案件需要進行正式的審訊。雖然被告人在原審時申請法律援助被拒絕，但她上訴時並沒有再次申請法律援助，本席希望被告人再次申請法律援助及法律援助署可以援助被告人，使她可以提供另一份內地法律專家意見，以便香港法庭可就這議題作出一個全面的裁決。本席亦邀請律政司司長考慮加入本訴訟及協助提供內地法律專家意見。本席認為袁大律師在審訊時應該繼續以法庭之友身份協助法庭。

專家證人的職責範圍

30. 最後，本席有必要提出一點，希望律師及專家證人能夠清楚了解專家證人在本港法律程序上的職責範圍。王教授在他的意見書最後一段說：

「 考慮到香港特別行政區政府和內地的當局都正在謀求做出能夠促進兩地經濟交流與發展的有關安排這種努力，萬一法院的判例在事實上卻形成了十分不利於這種共同努力的司法政策，將可能帶來十分負面的影響或後果。在這個意義上，則不得不說本案的處理將會超越個案的正義，而具有一般政策的含義。

鑒於最後這一點涉及公共利益或政策的考慮，本意見書的結論依然是：對於本案原審判決，應當認為屬於最終和不可推翻的判決。」

31. 專家證人無論是法律或其他方面的專家的功用是向法庭提供專業的知識，讓法庭參考後可以作出一個正確的判決，除此之外，專家證人不應該就其他議題發表個人意見。制定政策是政府機關的職責，法庭在審理案件時不會推行某種司法政策，只會就案情作出裁決。王教授以上所表達的竟見可能是因不熟悉專家證人在本港訴訟程序上的職責或是出於關注內地與香港判決相互執行的問題，但這並不是專家證人職責的範圍。本席需要強調本席提出這點並不是批評王教授，而是有需要重申專家證人職責的範圍。

命令

32. 本席裁定被告人上訴得直，命令案件進行正式審訊。

訴費命令

33. 雖然原告人在經修訂的申索陳述書稱清城法院的判決是最終的判決，但在整個原訟法庭簡易程序的過程，他從沒有提交任何專家證供來支

持這論點，而有關的證供是必須及基本的。關於訟費的暫准命令是本席對本上訴訟費及陳法官席前的訟費不作出任何命令。

上訴法庭法官袁家寧：

34. 本席已閱讀過上訴法庭張澤祐法官及高等法院原訟法庭鍾安德法官各自草擬的判詞。本席認為，在香港法庭應用普通法的原則的情況下，應否視內地法院的判決為「最終及不可推翻」的判決，是一項複雜及影響深遠的爭議點，法庭沒有可能在一簡易程序的申請中作出判決。

35. 本席明白，本案的被告人沒有以上述的爭議點作為上訴理由之一，但原告人在申索陳述書中，要求被告人償還款項的唯一訴因，正是清城法院 2002 年 5 月 18 日的判決。有見及此，又考慮到被告人是沒有律師代表，本席認為，法庭不能當作上述爭議點沒有存在，亦不能只認定上述爭議點是局限於 *Chiyu Banking Corporation Ltd v Chan Tin Kwan* [1996] 2 HKLR 395 一案內所提及的規限。

36. 況且，原告人的中國法律專家證人的證據也顯示，內地法院到現時為止就審判監督制度對法院判決的影響，看來還在發展階段中，理論上及實行上的限制，還未塵埃落定。因此，本席認為香港法庭決不能在簡易程序的申請中，斷定在審判監督制度下的內地法院判決是否「最終及不可推翻的」判決。

37. 無論如何，本席認為，香港法院是否應該（1）由於該審判監督制度存在，絕對地否定內地法院的判決是「最終及不可推翻的判決」，或是（2）在甚麼情況下有關判決可被當作為「最終及不可推翻的判決」，這重要及影響深遠的決定，應由法院經詳細考慮過雙方的法律專家意見（包括他們經受盤問過的證供後）才作出決定，法庭並不能在一簡易程序的申請中立下判斷。

38. 本席補充一點，鑒於本港與內地商業來往日見頻繁，亦有不少香港商人在內地法院提出訴訟，本席期望可盡快有一訴訟，讓法庭可在雙方有律師代表及有中國法律專家證人的證據的情況下，作出裁決。既然本案的訴因僅是基於清城法院的判決，本席鼓勵法律援助處給予被告人法律援助，及替她聘請中國法律專家作出專家報告，好讓在正審時，雙方專家接受盤問。若能在本案作出這樣的安排，亦會惠及現時及將來的訴訟人。

39. 本席同意張法官的判決，被告人上訴得直，案件應進行正式審訊。

原訟法庭法官鍾安德：

40. 本訴訟的背景，已在上訴法庭張法官的判詞的第 1 至 6 段述及，不再在此重覆。

41. 導致本上訴的是 2004 年 5 月 25 日宣佈的判決。該判決是依《高等法院規則》第 14 號命令第 3（1）條規則作出。該規則的相關部份規定：-

「 除非 …… 被告人使法庭信納，就該申請所關乎的申索或部份申索而言，有應予以審訊的爭論點或有爭議的問題，或為其他理由該申索或該部份申索應予以審訊，否則法庭在顧及所申索的補救或濟助的性質後，可就該申索或該部份申索，作出公正的原告人勝訴被告人敗訴的判決」。

42. 在依第 14 號命令提出的申請中，被告人有令法庭信納，「有應予以審訊的爭論點 …… 或為其他理由該申索 …… 應予以審訊」的責任：參看 *Bank of India v Murjani and Others*[1990] 1 HKLR 586, *Re Safe Rich Industries Ltd.* [1994] HKLY 183, *Ng Shou Chun v Hung Chun San* [1994] HKCA 347; [1994] 1 HKC 155。

43. 被告人在上訴通知書中列載的上訴理由，可簡述為以下幾點 :-

（a）原訟法庭暫委法官在作出 2004 年 5 月 25 判決時，誤以為她在誓章中聲稱在國內的訴訟程序中，因懷孕從未出席任何聆訊。其實她在誓章中僅稱，在國內的「二審終審庭」聆訊時，因懷孕而未能出席應訊；

（b）原訟法庭暫委法官過於偏重原告人存檔的誓章，致在「判案書」中，就 2002 年 4 月 12 日的事情，作出錯誤的敍述；

（c）前（a）及（b）分段證明，暫委法官未清楚理解被告人存檔的誓章的內容；

（d）暫委法官以原告人代表律師提供的案例作出判決，對未能延聘律師代表的被告人不公平；

（e）原告人國內既已查封被告人的資產，企圖將之出售以支付判決債項，又同時在香港取得判決，對被告人不公。

44. 上訴理由的第 1 點（前第 43（a）段），是指暫委法官的判案書中的第 18，20，21 及 / 或 24 段。而相關誓章則為被告人分別在 2003 年 1 月 14 日，2004 年 1 月 2 日，2004 年 2 月 26 日及 2004 年 3 月 15 日存檔的誓章。本席在審閱過該等誓章後，認定暫委法官並無誤解其內容。

45. 上訴理由的第 2 點（前第 43（b）段），不具合理理據。從暫委法官的「判案書」的整體內容可知，暫委法官已公允及平衡地考慮過，與訟雙方就涉案案情及事實提出的證據及論據。

46. 基於以上各點，本席亦裁定上訴理由書的第 3 點（前第 43（c）段），並無理據。

47. 暫委法官在「判案書」中引用的法律典籍，例如 *Dicey and Morris: The Conflict of Laws* 第 13 版，及 *Ever Chance Development Ltd. v. Ching Kai Chiu trading as Wing Hung Hardwares & Machinery Co. and Others* HCA 8/1997 等均是涉及，以欺詐手段取得外地判決有關的法律原則。而暫委法官在考慮過有關的法律典籍及案例後說：-

「 因此，明顯的是如果被告人能夠證實有表面證據、有爭論餘地或可信的案情，指出清城法院及清遠中院的判決是用欺詐得到的，她便應該獲得准許在這個訴訟提出抗辯 ……

（「判案書」第 9 段）

從上文得知，暫委法官並沒有因此而在「判案書」中表示，單從法律論點而言，被告人已無抗辯理據。相反，暫委法官在其中已考慮過一個被告人未明確提出的抗辯理由。

48. 故此，本席亦認定，上訴理由書第 4 點（前第 43（d）段）並不成立。

49. 最後，並無證據證明或顯示，原告人在已獲付內地的判決債務的全數後，企圖在本訴訟取得雙重利益。因此，上訴理由書的第 5 點亦不成立（前第 43（e）段）。

50. 在本訴訟（包括本上訴）中，被告人自己並未以內地的民事訴訟制度中，設有「審判監督」的基制，容許對原審判提出抗訴這一點，作為本上訴的上訴理由。

51. 內地的「審判監督」制度，相對於本上訴的重要性，源起於 *Chiyu Banking Corporation Ltd. v. Chan Tin Kwun* [1996] 2 HKLR 395 一案。香港法庭在 *Chiyu Banking Corporation* 一案判定，香港法院在以外地判決為訴因的訴訟中，只會執行性質屬最終及不可推翻的外地判決。香港法院在 *Chiyu Banking Corporation* 一案的「判案書」，對內地的「審判監督」制度，有以下的描述：-

"Under the legal system in PRC, another state organ, the Procuratorate exercise a supervisory function over civil adjudication by the courts: Article 14 of the Civil Procedure Law of 1991 ("the Civil Procedure Law"). Under Article 185, the Procuratorate may lodge a protest to the court in respect of a judicial decision. The circumstance in which the protest may be lodged are set out in art. 185, namely,

(i) the main evidence to substantiate the original judgment or ruling was insufficient;

(ii) the law which was applied in the original judgment or ruling was incorrect;

(iii) the People's Court was in violation of the statutory procedure which have affected the correctness of the judgment or ruling;

(iv) the judicial members in trying the case committed embezzlement, accepted bribes, practised favouritism or [made] a judgment that perverted the law.

It is for the Supreme People's Procuratorate to lodge the protest but under Article 185, the Fujian People's Procuratorate is entitled to refer the matter to the Supreme People's Procuratorate for it to lodge a protest.

Under art. 187, the court, upon receipt of the protest, is required to conduct a retrial of the action."

（第 397 頁 A 至 D）。

高等法院基於上述事項，及英國上議院法庭在 *Nouvion v. Freeman* 一案的判決（詳見前第 10 至 12 段），在 *Chiyu Banking Corporation* 一案裁定，福建中級人民法院的判決，並非香港普通法所指的「最終及不可推翻」的判決。

52. 依香港法例第 8 章《證據條例》第 59 條（尤其第 59（2）條），在香港高等法庭以可引述形式報導或記錄的裁斷或決定，可接納為有關香港以外國家或地區的法律的證據：參看林哲民日昌電業公司對張順連 CACV 1046/2001（其中第 17 至 27 段）。

53. 就香港法院在 *Chiyu Banking Corporation* 一案有關內地「審判監督」制度的描述，原告人提交的專家意見書並沒有提出異議。被告人並未提交有關此點的專家意見書或其他證據。香港以外的國家或地區的法律，依香港法律而言，屬香港法院對涉案事實的裁斷：詳見 *Phipson on Evidence*（2005 年）第 16 版，第 1-42，33-57 及 33-58 段，及香港法例第 4 章《高等法院條例》第 33A（5）條。

54. 基於以上各點，本席認定內地「審判監督」制度，只可在規定的四種情況才可援引（見前第 51 段）。

55. 但是，除名稱有別之外，內地「審判監督」制度所涉的四種情況，與香港法律已確立的上訴理由，實質上並無不同：詳見 *Hong Kong Civil Procedure 2004*，第 59/1/48（第 828 頁）（"…… [where the] Court of Appeal is satisfied that the conclusion reached … is plainly wrong, it should intervene ……"），59/3/1（"…… whether the misdirection, misconception of evidence or other alleged defect in the trial has taken place, so that a new trial should be ordered……"），59/11/3（"Misdirection, where substantial wrong or miscarriage has been thereby occasioned"）至 59/11/8（"Improperly admitting or rejecting evidence, where some substantial wrong or miscarriage has been thereby occasioned"），59/11/15（"Discovery of fresh evidence"）至 59/11/18（"A slip or mistake in the proceedings"）及 59/11/23（"Some substantial wrong or miscarriage"）段。

56. 此外，香港法律亦賦予法院在裁定上訴得直時，頒令訴訟應重新審訊的權力：詳見《高等法院規則》第 59 號命令第 11 條規則，及 *Hong Kong Civil Procedure 2004*，第 59/1/47 及 59/11/2 至 59/11/21 段。

57. 原訟法庭在其自身頒佈的命令未完備及登錄前，亦具自行重新審訊訴訟的權力：詳見 *Hong Kong Civil Procedure 2004*，第 20/11/1，20/11/6，20/11/7，20/11/8 及 59/1/53 段。

58. 即使有前第 55 至 57 段所述的情況，以香港的法律而言，香港法院的判決，仍屬「最終及不可推翻」的判決。並無資料顯示，香港法院的判決，依普遍適用的國際私法原則，在外地被視為不屬「最終及不可推翻」的判決。

59. 本席因此認定，單就「審判監督」制度所涉的四種情況而言，並不足以令內地的判決，被裁定為不屬「最終及不可推翻」的判決。

60. 前第 14.2 至 14.3 段述及，內地《中華人民共和國民事訴訟法》（「《民事訴訟法》」）第 177 及 185 條。因該等條款並未在 *Chiyu Baking Corporation* 一案，或原告人提交的專家意見書中述及，不屬第 8 章第 59 條所指的可接納的證據。

61. 即使《民事訴訟法》第 177 及 185 條屬可接納的證據，其性質亦與前第 54 至 59 段所述的相同。本席在本判案書的論據亦適用於該等條款。

62. 法庭之友在本上訴作出的陳詞亦稱，就原審法院再審的權力而言，內地「審判監督」制度，有兩點可被視為與香港的法制有實質不同之處 :-

　　(a) 除內地民事訴訟所涉的與訟人外，(1) 各級人民法院院長，(2) 上級人民法院及 (3) 人民檢察院，均可依上述的四種情況，向

原審人民法院或上一級人民法院申請再審;

（b）由各級人民法院院長或最高人民法院提交,提審或指令的再審,
單就《民事訴訟法》而言,並無指明的時限（詳見其中第 177 條）。
人民檢察院依《民事訴訟法》提出抗訴,亦無指明的時限（詳見其中
第 185 條）。

63. 但無論抗訴是否由與訟其中一方提出（前第 62（a）段）,或是否在
某時限內提出（前第 62（b）段）,以在本上訴所呈交的證據而言（即
Chiyu Banking Corporation 一案的判決的有關指述,及原告人呈交的專
家意見書）,任何抗訴申請,只可在前述的四種情況其中一種已被確
立時,才會被接納及導致頒令再審。

64. 故此,內地「審判監督」制度可經由第三者（例如最高人民法院或人
民檢察院）提交、提審或指令,亦不足以影響此結論。因為無論抗訴
申請由何方提出,仍需符合前第 51 及 59 段所述的四種情況。本席因
此仍維持在前第 58 及 59 段所作的結論。

65. 除與訟其中一方提出再審申請外,《民事訴訟法》並未列明提出再審
申請的時限:詳見其中第 182 條。表面看來,這一點與香港的法律原
則不同。但實際上,香港法院亦具延展法律程序（包括上訴程序）的
時限的權力:詳見《高等法院規則》第 3 號命令第 5 條規則及第 59 號
命令第 15 條規則及 *Hong Kong Civil Procedure 2004*, 第 3/5/1 至 3/5/3
及 59/15/1 段。因此,即使香港法院的判決,亦可能在規定時限屆滿後,
被頒令撤銷及重審。

66. 在本上訴,原告人呈交的專家意見書述明,內地在不同場合提出的司
法解釋,已對申請再審的時限作出規定。其中包括:-

（1）2001 年 8 月 14 日最高人民檢察院民事行政檢察廳頒佈的《關於
規範省級人民檢察院辦理民事行政提請抗訴案件的意見》規定,內地
判決,裁定生效兩年之內無正當理由,未向人民檢察院提出申訴的案
件,省級人民檢察院應不予受理;

（2）2001 年 9 月 30 日通過的《人民檢察院民事行政抗訴案件辦案規
則》規定,自受理與訟其中一方申訴之日起 7 天內,檢察院必須決定
立案或不立案。立案後檢察院應調閱法院審判資料,並應在 3 個月內
審查終結,決定是否抗訴;

（3）2001 年 11 月 1 日最高人民法院頒佈的《關於當前審判監督工作
若干問題的紀要》指出,有關民事抗訴的部份明確要求,對於「原審
案件當事人在原審裁判生效二年內無正當理由,未向人民法院或人民

檢察院提出申訴的案件」，即使檢察院提起抗訴，法院也不予受理；

    （4）2002 年 7 月 31 日最高人民法院頒佈《關於人民法院對民事案件發回重審和指令再審有關問題的規定》，再審只能以一次為限。

67. 有關《民事訴訟法》未列明申請時限這一點，本席已在前第 65 段討論。本席認為，前第 66 段所述的專家意見書，已進一步確定，被告人未能在本上訴中顯示，就重審內地判決這一點，「有應予以審訊的爭論點 …… 或為其他理由 …… 應予以審訊 …… 」。

68. 本席在作出此裁斷時，亦考慮到被告人在內地曾提出的上訴，已在 2002 年 9 月 11 日被中級人民法院駁回，而她曾向中級人民法院請求申訴，亦在 2002 年 12 月 28 日被駁回。她在本上訴聆訊時承認，自該日起計近三年的期間，並未向任何內地機關作出抗訴申請。她亦沒有表示將會這樣做。

69. 法庭之友在其「補充陳詞撮要」中，作出了對上述各司法解釋的評論（詳見其中第 3 至 9 段），例如最高人民檢察院頒佈的意見（前第 66(2) 段），僅供各省級人民檢察院參考用，或該意見只列明適用於各省級人民檢察院，而不適用於頒佈該意見的最高人民檢察院，或最高人民法院頒佈的記要（前第 66(2) 段），只適用於人民檢察院提出的申請，不適用於各級人民法院等。本席認為這些論據：-

    （a）不足以影響本席在前第 64 及 67 段作出的結論；

    （b）無論如何，過份着重純理論性而未顧及本上訴所涉案情的合理可能性。

70. 有關英國上議院在 *Nouvion* 一案所作的判決，香港原訟法庭曾在 *Biard Laboratoires SA v. Rosumi Ltd.* HCMP 252/1997 一案中論及。該案的判案書認定，*Nouvion* 一案的判決，是基於其涉案事實而作出。*Biard Laboratoires* 一案，涉及在香港依法國里昂上訴法院（依法國的《新民事程序法》（New Code of Civil Procedure）第 484 及 488 條）頒令的中期判令（interim decision）而提出的訴訟。該案的原告人已依香港法例第 319 章《外地判決（交互強制執行）條例》將法國法院的判令登記，但該案的被告人，以依第 319 章第 3（2）(a) 及 6(1)(a)(i) 條而言，該中期判令並非「最終及不可推翻的判決」為由，要求香港法院撤銷該登記。祈彥輝法官（當時官階）在判案書論及 *Nouvion* 一案時說：-

"5. Final and conclusive. The Defendant contends that the order of the Commercial Court was not final and conclusive because of the nature of the order which was made and the nature of the proceedings in which it was made. ......

6. I cannot accept this argument ......

9. [The Defendant] relied on the decision of the House of Lords in Nouvion v. Freeman (1889) 15 App. Cas. 1. ......

10. However, the *House of Lords' conclusion on the facts* of that case *do not assist me* in determining whether the *ordonnance de refere* in the present case was final and conclusive. In both the remate and "plenary" proceedings, the issue was whether one of the parties was indebted to the other. *The remate proceedings did not conclusively resolve that issue.* It resolved only some of the questions which bore on that issue. In the present case, the issue in the proceedings in the Commercial Court was wholly unrelated to the underlying dispute between the parties. The issue was whether, irrespective of the merits of the underlying dispute, French law permitted the Defendant to countermand the cheques. The conclusion of the Commercial Court that the Defendant was not permitted under French law to countermand the cheques was final and conclusive because it did not depend on the merits of the underlying dispute between the parties. ......"
（上文獲強調處，由本席後加）。

基於上述（及其他）原因，法庭拒絕被告人撤銷判令登記的申請。

71. 原訟法庭在 *Nintendo of America Inc. v. Bung Enterprise Ltd.* HCA 1189/2000 一案，亦論及外地判決是否「最終及不可推翻的判決」這一點。該訴訟所涉的是美國加洲法院頒佈的缺席判決（default judgment）。有關 *Nouvion* 一案的判決，原訟法庭在 *Nintendo of America* 一案的判決書說：-

"8. The defendant relied on the observation of Lord Watson in Nouvion v Freeman (1889) 15 App. Cas. 1 at page 13 that the Court would refuse to recognise a judgment because it is not final and conclusive on the ground that 'it might be at any time recalled or modified by the Court of Session on just cause shown'. However I am of the view that *the observation must be looked at in the context of the judgment* which Lord Watson had to consider. In Nouvion's case, the Court would have to consider *a judgment of the Spanish Court which was known as a 'remate' judgment* which was a judgment after consideration of limited issuesand which was *liable to be reconsidered in 'plenary' proceedings* where the whole merits of the matters might be gone into. Likewise the order of the Court of Session spoken of by Lord Watson as one which the Court would not recognise was one which the Court had retained the power to alter.

9. The defendant also relied on the observation of Lord Diplock in The Sennar (No. 2) where he said (at 494A):

'It is often said that the final judgment of the foreign court must be "on the merits". The moral overtones which this expression tends to conjure up may make it misleading. What it means in the context of judgments delivered by courts of justice is that the court has held that it has jurisdiction to adjudicate upon an issue raised in the cause of action to which the particular set of facts give rise, and that its judgment on that cause of action is one that cannot be varied, re-opened or set aside by the court that delivered it or any other court of co-ordinate jurisdiction although it may be subject to appeal to a court of higher jurisdiction.'

......

10. However it is **well established** that for the purpose of enforcement by an action in Hong Kong, a **foreign judgment may be final and conclusive** even though it is [a] *default judgment liable to be set aside* in the very Court which rendered it (*see Dicey & Morris The Conflict of Laws* 13th edition paragraph 14-021). In Vanquelin v Bouard [1863] EngR 977; (1863) 15 C B (N S) 341, Erle C J held that it was no defence to an action based on a judgment given by a Court in France that the judgment was a judgment by default for wanting of an appearance by the defendant in the Court and by the law of France, the judgment would become void as of course on an appearance being entered. In so holding, the Chief Justice said (at page 367-368):

'I apprehend that every judgment of a foreign court of competent jurisdiction is valid and may be the foundation of an action in our courts, though subject to the contingency, that, by adopting a certain course, the party against whom the judgment is obtained might cause it to be vacated or set aside. But **until that course has been pursued,** the **judgment remains in full force** and capable of being sued upon.'

Thus the fact that the judgment is a judgment by default whereby the Court may have the power to set it aside is no ground for saying that the judgment is not final and conclusive for this purpose. The defendant cannot improve its position by refusing to comply with the procedural requirement of the foreign Court or refusing to defend an action properly brought against him in a foreign Court.

11. In my view the *apparent conflict* between the observation of Lord Diplock quoted above and the observation of Erle C J *could be reconciled*. In my view when Lord Diplock said 'its judgment on that cause of action is one that cannot be varied, re-opened or set aside by the Court that delivered it or any other Court of co-ordinate jurisdiction' *he was referring to cases where the Court delivering the judgment had intended that the effect of its judgment was merely provisional* such as in cases when the Court had reserved the jurisdiction to vary or set aside the judgment." （上文獲強調處，由本席後加）。

72. 法庭之友在其書面陳詞撮要亦說 :-

「…… 因被告欠缺抗辯而取得的判決（default judgment）可被頒佈該判決的法院撤銷，但在普通法上仍被視為最終及不可推翻之判決。（參看 Dicey & Morrison [The Conflict of Law], 13th edn., Vol. I, para. 14.021 (p.477; *Barclays Bank Ltd .v. Piacun* [1984] 2 Qd. R. 476, pp.477 (line 29) – 478 (line 60.）」

（其中第 15 段）。

73. Nouvion 一案所涉的 「remate 判決」，屬即使是正確的判決，仍可在 「plenary 判決」 中重新判定的判決。這種 「remate 判決」 與在本上訴所涉，可依「審判監督」而被命令重審的內地判決完全不同，更沒有證據顯示，本上訴所涉的內地判決在內地被視為暫准判決。

74. 在此情況下，本席認為 Nouvion 一案的判決，不適用於本上訴。

75. 基於以上各點，本席認定，內地判決不應純因有可能被頒令重審而被視為不屬「最終及不可推翻」的判決。這是因為同一可能性，亦適用於至少部份採用普通法法律原則的國家或地區（包括香港）（參看前第 56 至 58 段）。法庭之友在本上訴聆訊時亦同意，在裁定內地判決是否屬「最終不可推翻」的判決這一點時，香港法院不應只從純理論的角度考慮重審的可能性，而應兼顧涉案事實是否顯示有合理的可能性。

76. 法庭之友亦在本上訴聆訊時指，被告人有權在本訴訟審訊時，向原告人方的專家證人提出盤問。但單以這點，並不足以顯示，被告人已確立第 14 號命令第 3(1) 條規則規定的舉證責任：參看原訟法院在 *Eugene Jae-hoon Oh v. Kate Gaskell Richdale* HCA 380/2002 （尤其判案

書的第 23，27 及第 63 段）及上訴法庭在同案的上訴 CACV 162/2003
（2005 年 10 月 7 日的判案書）（尤其判案書的第 13(c) and (d), 18, 20,
29, 30 及 31 段）的判決。

77. 基於以上各點，本席更改本席在林哲民日昌電業公司對張順連一案中，
對內地「審判監督」制度是否導致內地判決不屬「最終及不可推推翻」
的判決的看法。

78. 本席必須指出，如前所述，香港以外國家或地區的法律，屬法院對涉
案事實的裁斷：詳見前第 53 段。因此，香港法院對此點的裁斷，往往
取決於在該訴訟中呈交的相關證據。亦基於此因，該等裁斷通常不具
概括的適用性。

79. 原告人在本上訴提交的專家意見書，是依本庭在 2005 年 5 月 20 日發
出的指示而預備的。如前所述（前第 8 及 53 段），被告人雖已有充分
機會在本上訴提交專家意見書，但她基於個人理由，並未依指示提交
有關資料。

80. 法庭之友亦在其書面陳詞撮要中指出，被告人聲稱內地法院的判決，
是原告人以欺詐手段取得。但此點不是被告人的上訴理由之一。此外，
本席審閱過原訟法庭的「判案書」及被告人呈交的資料。本席認定，
原訟法庭正確地裁定，被告人的指稱全不可信。

81. 故此，本席駁回本上訴。

上訴法庭法官張澤祐：

82. 本庭以大比數裁定被告人上訴得直及命令案件進行正式審訊。本庭作
出以下的暫准訟費命令：本庭對本上訴訟費及陳法官席前的訟費不作
出任何命令。

高等法院上訴法庭法官（張澤祐）

高等法院上訴法庭法官（袁家寧）

高等法院原訟法庭法官（鍾安德）

原告人：由梁鄧蔡律師事務所轉聘黃士翔大律師代表。

被告人：無律師代表，親自出席。

袁國強資深大律師，法庭之友。

Nintendo of America Inc v. Bung Enterprises Ltd.

[2000] HKCFI 654; [2000] 2 HKC 629; HCA 1189/2000 (21 March 2000)

HCA 1189/2000

IN THE HIGH COURT OF THE

HONG KONG SPECIAL ADMINISTRATIVE REGION

COURT OF FIRST INSTANCE

ACTION NO. 1189 OF 2000

BETWEEN

NINTENDO OF AMERICA INC   Plaintiff

AND

BUNG ENTERPRISES LTD   Defendant

Coram: Recorder Edward Chan, SC in Chambers

Date of Hearing: 15 March 2000

Date of Judgment: 21 March 2000

J U D G M E N T

1. In 1997 the plaintiff brought an action against amongst others, the defendant in the United States District Court Central District of California, Western Division in the United States of America under Case no. 97-8511GAF(VAPx). The subject matter of that action was the claim for contributory and vicarious liability for copyright infringement, trademark infringement and unfair competition in connection with the manufacture, marketing, sale and distribution of videogame copying devices. The action was defended by the defendant who also brought a counterclaim against the plaintiff. For the purpose of this hearing, it is conceded that the defendant had a meritorious defence in the US proceedings. The action proceeded to a stage where the Court in the United States had made certain order of discovery against the defendant which the defendant thought was too onerous and unfair. The defendant decided not to comply with the order and not to take any further part in the proceedings. As a result default judgment was entered against the defendant in September 1999. The defendant after consulting its lawyers in the United States decided to apply to set aside the default judgment and on 20 October 1999 succeeded in doing so on terms. The terms were that (a) the defendant would have to pay the sum of US$50,645.98 being the legal cost incurred by the plaintiff between 1 August 1999 to 14 October 1999 to the plaintiff before 29 October 1999; (b) providing all documents previously ordered by the Court to be disclosed by 22 October 1999; and (c) making all witnesses available for dispositions be taken in Los Angeles by 13 December 1999. The defendant did not consider that the terms of the order were right and fair and decided not to comply with the order. In particular the defendant considered that the imposition of the term of payment of US$50,645.98 was too onerous in that such payment would deprive the defendant with funds to continue to fund its litigation in the States. As a result the Court ordered judgment be entered against the defendant again on 15 December 1999.

2. By the terms of this judgment, the Court ordered that the plaintiff be entitled to recover the sum of US$7,480,980.00 and interest on the said sum as provided by law and cost from the defendant. The Court also granted an injunction against the defendant.

3. In this action brought by the plaintiff in Hong Kong, the plaintiff sought to recover from the defendant the amount of US$7,480,980.00 awarded by

the judgement of the Court in the United States. The plaintiff also asked for interest under Section 48 of the High Court Ordinance.

4. The plaintiff applied for summary judgment against the defendant.

5. It is trite law that a judgment of the Courts in the United States for a monetary sum may be enforced by an action suing on the judgment at common law in Hong Kong. There are a few requirements for the action to succeed. First the Court granting the judgment must have the jurisdiction to adjudicate on the cause giving rise to the judgement. Secondly the judgment must be final and conclusive according to the law of the Court granting the judgment, and in this case, it is California of the United States. Thirdly the judgment must not be impeachable according to the private international law here.

6. Insofar as jurisdiction of the Court in California is concerned, plainly that Court has the jurisdiction to adjudicate on the action brought by the plaintiff. To say the least, the defendant must have submitted to the jurisdiction of that Court by bringing a counterclaim and by using its procedure in applying to set aside the judgment of September 1999.

7. The main contention of the defendant in this case is that the judgment is not final and conclusive. The defendant contended that the judgment was not given by the Court after a consideration of the merits of the claim and in fact there was no investigation by the Court of the merits of the claim at all. It was also contended that the judgment was not final and conclusive because it may be set aside by the trial Court upon a reconsideration motion or overturned on appeal.

8. The defendant relied on the observation of Lord Watson in Nouvion v Freeman (1889) 15 App. Cas. 1 at page 13 that the Court would refuse to recognise a judgment because it is not final and conclusive on the ground that "it might be at any time recalled or modified by the Court of Session on just cause shown". However I am of the view that the observation must be looked at in the context of the judgment which Lord Watson had to consider. In Nouvion's case, the Court would have to consider a judgment of the Spanish Court which was known as a "remate" judgment which was a judgment after consideration of limited issues and which was liable to be reconsidered in "plenary" proceedings where the whole merits of the matters might be gone into. Likewise the order of the Court of Session

spoken of by Lord Watson as one which the Court would not recognise was one which the Court had retained the power to alter.

9. The defendant also relied on the observation of Lord Diplock in The Sennar (No.2) where he said (at 494A) :

"It is often said that the final judgment of the foreign court must be 'on the merits'. The moral overtones which this expression tends to conjure up may make it misleading. What it means in the context of judgments delivered by courts of justice is that the court has held that it has jurisdiction to adjudicate upon an issue raised in the cause of action to which the particular set of facts give rise, and that its judgment on that cause of action is one that cannot be varied, re-opened or set aside by the court that delivered it or any other court of co-ordinate jurisdiction although it may be subject to appeal to a court of higher jurisdiction."

In the same case, Lord Brandon commented on the issue whether a judgment which is procedure in nature could be final and conclusive on the merits. He said (at page 499E) :

"The argument in relation to the first contention was that the judgment of the Dutch Court of Appeal was procedural in nature in that it consisted only of a decision that a Dutch court had no jurisdiction to entertain and adjudicate upon the appellant's claim and did not pronounce in any way on the question whether the claim itself, or any substantive issue in it, if it were to be entertained and adjudicated on, would succeed or fail. In my opinion, this argument is based on a misconception with regard to the meaning of the expression 'on the merits' as used in the context of the doctrine of issue estoppel. Looking at the matter negatively a decision on procedure alone is not a decision on the merits. Looking at the matter positively a decision on the merits is a decision which establishes certain facts as proved or not in dispute; states what are the relevant principles of law applicable to such facts; and expresses a conclusion with regard to the effect of applying those principles to the factual situation concerned."

10. However it is well established that for the purpose of enforcement by an action in Hong Kong, a foreign judgment may be final and conclusive even though it is an default judgment liable to be set aside in the very Court which rendered it (see *Dicey & Morris The Conflict of Laws* 13th edition paragraph 14-021). In Vanquelin v Bouard [1863] EngR 977; (1863) 15

C B (N S) 341, Erle C J held that it was no defence to an action based on a judgment given by a Court in France that the judgment was a judgment by default for wanting of an appearance by the defendant in the Court and by the law of France, the judgment would become void as of course on an appearance being entered. In so holding, the Chief Justice said (at page 367-368) :

"I apprehend that every judgment of a foreign court of competent jurisdiction is valid and may be the foundation of an action in our courts, though subject to the contingency, that, by adopting a certain course, the party against whom the judgment is obtained might cause it to be vacated or set aside. But until that course has been pursued, the judgment remains in full force and capable of being sued upon."

Thus the fact that the judgment is a judgment by default whereby the Court may have the power to set it aside is no ground for saying that the judgment is not final and conclusive for this purpose. The defendant cannot improve its position by refusing to comply with the procedural requirement of the foreign Court or refusing to defend an action properly brought against him in a foreign Court.

11. In my view the apparent conflict between the observation of Lord Diplock quoted above and the observation of Erle C J could be reconciled. In my view when Lord Diplock said "its judgment on that cause of action is one that cannot be varied, re-opened or set aside by the Court that delivered it or any other Court of co-ordinate jurisdiction" he was referring to cases where the Court delivering the judgment had intended that the effect of its judgment was merely provisional such as in cases when the Court had reserved the jurisdiction to vary or set aside the judgment. Certainly he could not be referring to situations where the judgment was obtained in default of defence or when one party failed to appear and thus was liable to be set aside under Order 19 rule 9 or Order 35 rule 2.

12. In the present case, it would appear that after the default of the defendant, the Court in California directed the plaintiff's counsel to draw up the judgment and finding for the Court's consideration and the Court after consideration pronounced the judgment with finding of facts. The uncontradicted evidence before me is that it was possible to file a motion to alter or amend a judgment in that Court, however this would have to

be done within 10 days after entry of the judgment. The time for so doing had expired. Although there was also power under Rule 60 of the Federal Rules of Civil Procedure to obtain relief from a final judgment on some very narrowly defined grounds by filing a motion for such relief within a reasonable time, no step had been taken at all. All that the defendant had adduced before me by way of evidence was a statement from its attorney in the US that the defendant planned to seek reconsideration of the default judgment and planned to appeal if the reconsideration motion should fail.

13. In all the circumstances I am of the view that there is no triable issue that the judgment sued upon was a final and conclusive judgment on the merits in the sense that it was *res judicata* by the law of California and had determined the controversies between the plaintiff and the defendant in the proceedings in California.

14. It is also argued that the judgment ought not to be enforced here because the proceedings in which the judgment was obtained were opposed to natural justice in that the defendant was not given an opportunity to present its case on the merits before the Court in California. On the evidence put before me, I am of the view that there is completely no merit in this point. As I have briefly summarised above, the defendant instructed its attorney to apply to set aside the default judgment and had succeeded in so doing on terms. Plainly the defendant had ample opportunity of presenting its case on the setting aside of the order. The terms of the order setting aside the default judgment were known to the defendant. The fact that the defendant thought that the order was wrong does not mean that the judgment given in default of compliance with the order is rendered unenforceable because it was unfair. It was not suggested that there was no machinery of appeal against the terms imposed by the Court. However the defendant deliberately decided not to comply with the terms of the order well knowing that the consequence must be that default judgment might be entered against it. Indeed even though the order provided the opportunity for the defendant to make submission, according to the 2nd affirmation of Mr Leung Yiu Choy, the defendant had decided not to take up that opportunity. However from exhibit LYC-30 of the 3rd Affirmation of Leung Yiu Choy it would appear that the defendant's attorney in the US did take the opportunity of raising certain objections to the draft of the plaintiff's counsel before the judgment was finalised by the Court. In the circumstances, I am not convinced that

there is even a triable issue on whether the defendant was given a fair opportunity to present its case on merit.

15. The defendant further contended that the defendant was not given a fair opportunity to present its case on merit because the Court in California had ordered the defendant to pay a large sum of money as cost before the defendant would be allowed to continue to defend the action. It is said that this would tantamount to shutting out the defendant altogether because of the financial inability of the defendant to meet the payment. There are two answers to this contention. First, on the facts before me, the evidence filed in the Mareva proceedings did indicate that although the defendant as a company might not have the means of meeting the payment, the shareholders and directors of the defendant certainly would have the means of meeting such payment. Hence it is not a case that the defendant could not even raise the money to comply with the Court's order. Secondly in any case, I would consider that the question of the means of a party is something personal and peculiar to the litigant, and even though because of this personal financial constraint a party could not participate in the litigation it does not mean that in that litigation the litigant did not have the opportunity to present its case. It certainly has the opportunity although for reason peculiar to him, he would not be able to take it up.

16. However the defendant contended that breach of natural justice was not limited to the requirements of due notice of the hearing to a litigant and opportunity to put a case to the foreign Court. The defendant went on to contend that what happened in this case and particularly the way that the judgment was drawn up would indicate that there was a breach of the English Court's view of substantial justice in that the finding of facts recorded in the judgment as well as the assessment of the damages was not done by the Judge but was done by the plaintiff's attorney.

17. The defendant relied on the decision of Adams v Cape Industries Plc [1990] Ch 433. In Adams' case the plaintiff obtained a judgment against the defendant in the Court of Tyler in the USA and sought to enforce the judgment in England. The defendant resisted the claim on the ground that the Court of Tyler did not have jurisdiction. Also as an additional ground, the defendant contended that the way that damages was in fact assessed was done not by the Judge in the light of the evidence put before him as required by the laws of the United States but was done by

the plaintiff's counsel in a rather arbitrary manner. The Court of Appeal upheld the decision of Scott J and took the view that there was a breach of natural justice where the foreign legal system contains provisions for judicial assessment of damages and the system was not followed. The reason being that the defendant had a reasonable expectation that there would be a judicial assessment. The Court of Appeal further took the view that the situation was not saved by the fact that the defendant was notified of the assessment and further had the opportunity of applying to set aside the assessment subsequently and had chosen not to do so, because at the time of the service of the default judgment on the defendant, the defendant was not aware of the irregularity.

18. I think however the present situation was quite different from the case of Adams. It is to be noted that the relevant part of the order of 1 November 1999 merely said :

"counsel for Nintendo are ordered to prepared a judgment resolving the entire action and to submit that proposed judgment to the Court no later than November 8, 1999. Bung will have until November 15, 1999, to file any objections it may have to the proposed judgment. Thereafter, judgment will be entered in favour of Nintendo on its complaints and on Bung's counterclaims."

Even assuming that the judgment in its current form was in fact the same as the draft provided by the plaintiff's attorney, there is nothing to show that the Judge in the United States had not exercised his judicial function in approving the judgment. In fact, a cursory comparison of the judgment as approved and delivered by the Court and the draft submitted by the plaintiff's attorney indicated that there were very substantial revisions of the terms and contents on the part concerning the assessment of damages. Furthermore, the defendant was given the opportunity of actually seeing the draft judgment and as I have pointed out there was evidence to suggest that the defendant had raised objections to the issue of damages. In any case even assuming that the defendant had not done so, it was a case that the defendant had chosen not to make any representation on the quantum or indeed on any other part of the findings in the judgment.

19. The defendant had also drawn my attention to the Judge's reasoning on the issue of damages in the judgment and submitted that the reasoning

demonstrated that the Judge had acted rather arbitrarily in coming to his conclusion. In my view this contention merely serves to demonstrate that the Judge was wrong in his assessment and it is trite law that in an action brought to enforce a foreign judgment, it is not defence to say that the foreign Court was wrong.

20. In these circumstances, I do not think that the defendant had raised any triable issue and there will be summary judgment against the defendant in the sum of US$7,480,980.00. Insofar as interest is concerned, I think that interest in US dollar is somewhat lower than in Hong Kong dollar. In exercise of my discretion under Section 48 of the High Court Ordinance, I ordered that interest at the rate of 8% per annum be paid from the date of the writ until the date hereof. The plaintiff will also have his cost of the application.

21. There is also a summons for the continuation of a Mareva injunction obtained against the defendant returnable before me. On that issue the defendant would ask for 21 days to file affidavits in support of its application to resist and to set aside the injunction. I will give such direction, and I will further direct that the plaintiff be given 14 days to file any affidavits in reply. The plaintiff had indicated that if I should give summary judgment against the defendant the plaintiff is happy that the Mareva injunction be continued for 21 more days so as to enable the plaintiff to make preparation for execution. I will extend the Mareva injunction for 21 days from the day of handing down of this judgment. Of course the continuation of the injunction is without prejudice to the defendant's right to make an application to have it set aside. There will be no order as to cost for the application for direction and also for the continuation of the injunction before me.

(Edward Chan)

Recorder of the Court of First Instance

Representation:

Mr Douglas Clark, of Messrs Lovells, for the Plaintiff

Ms Linda Chan, instructed by Messrs Lau Pau & Co., for the Defendant

Bank of China Ltd v. Yang Fan

[2016] HKCFI 708; HCMP 1797/2015 （29 April 2016）

HCMP 1797/2015

IN THE HIGH COURT OF THE

HONG KONG SPECIAL ADMINISTRATIVE REGION

COURT OF FIRST INSTANCE

MISCELLANEOUS PROCEEDINGS NO 1797 OF 2015

———————

IN THE MATTER OF Section 21M(1) of the High Court Ordinance, Chapter 4 of the Laws of the Hong Kong Special Administrative Region

———————

BETWEEN

BANK OF CHINA LIMITED （中國銀行股份有限公司）　　Plaintiff

（suing in the name of Bank of China Ltd Rizhao Branch （日照分行） in the PRC）

and

YANG FAN （楊凡）　Defendant

———————

Before: Hon To J in Chambers

Date of Hearing: 14 January 2016

Date of Decision: 29 April 2016

———————

D E C I S I O N

———————

Introduction

1. This is the hearing of the Plaintiff's summons dated 27 July 2015 applying to continue an *ex parte Mareva* injunction (the "Continuation Summons") granted by Chow J on 24 July 2015 as extended by Mimmie Chan J on 31 July 2015; and the Defendant's summons taken out on 15 September 2015 to discharge the above injunction (the "Discharge Summons"). By consent, the two summonses were ordered to be heard together.

2. The injunction restrains the Defendant from disposing of his assets in Hong Kong up to the value of RMB 500 million pursuant to section 21M of the High Court Ordinance in support of five sets of proceedings commenced by the Plaintiff in the Shandong Provincial Higher People's Court and the Rizhao Intermediate People's Court.

The background

3. The Plaintiff is the Bank of China Limited. Its hierarchical structure is made up of provincial branches, city branches, and sub-branches. It is suing in the name of its Rizhao Branch, a city branch under the Shandong Provincial Branch. The Plaintiff, its Shandong Provincial Branch, its Rizhao Branch and two of its sub-branches, namely the Weihai Sub-branch and the Haiqu Sub-branch, are collectively referred to as the "Bank". The Weihai Sub-branch and the Haiqu Sub-branch, advanced funds to Lianghe Group Co Ltd ("Lianghe") and Shandong Chenghua Group Co Ltd ("Chenghua")under two loan agreements guaranteed by the Defendant, his wife and others. These loan agreements are respectively, the Lianghe Agreement and Chenghua Agreement.

4. The Defendant is a resident of the People's Republic of China (the "PRC") and legal representative of Chenghua. He was, until 19 May 2015, the chairman and executive director of National United Resources Holdings Ltd ("NURH"), a company listed on the Stock Exchange of Hong Kong Limited. He, his wife and others, are guarantors of the Lianghe Agreement and the Chenghua Agreement. Neither of them are directors or shareholders of Lianghe.

5. Under the Lianghe Agreement dated 6 September 2013, the Weihai Sub-branch provided a credit line to Lianghe totalling RMB 200 million. By a guarantee agreement of the same date, the Defendant and his wife guaranteed Lianghe's liability under the Lianghe Agreement (the "Lianghe Guarantee").

6. Under the Chenghua Agreement dated 28 December 2014, the Weihai Sub-branch advanced a loan of RMB 291.6 million to Chenghua. By a similar guarantee agreement of the same date, the Defendant and his wife guaranteed Chenghua's liability under the Chenghua Agreement (the "Chenghua Guarantee").

7. Both Lianghe and Chenghua defaulted under their respective loan agreements. The Defendant also failed to honour his obligations under the respective guarantees.

8. On 15 January 2015, the Weihai Sub-branch obtained three property preservation orders from the Rizhao Intermediate People's Court to freeze the bank deposits of Lianghe, Chenghua, the Defendant, his wife and others in the amount of RMB 31 million, RMB 49.5 million and RMB 49.5 million or their property of equivalent value. But the Defendant did not have substantial assets located in the PRC to meet the preservation orders.

9. On 2 March 2015, the Weihai Sub-branch commenced three actions at the Rizhao Intermediate People's Court against, *inter alia*, Lianghe, Chenghua, the Defendant and his wife under the Lianghe Agreement and the Lianghe Guarantee in respect of three loans under three invoices in the total sum of RMB125 million.

10. On 12 May 2015, the Rizhao Branch commenced another action in the Rizhao Intermediate People's Court against, *inter alia*, the Defendant for a debt of RMB 67.26 million under the Lianghe Agreement and the Lianghe Guarantee. This action was brought under the name of the Rizhao Branch instead of the Weihai Sub-branch due to a change in the Bank's policy which no longer authorised sub-branches to bring legal actions in their own name.

11. On 28 May 2015, the Rizhao Branch filed another claim with the Shandong Higher People's Court against, *inter alia*, Chenghua, Lianghe, the Defendant and his wife for a debt of RMB 291.6 million under the Chenghua Agreement and the Chenghua Guarantee.

12. On 1 June 2015, the Rizhao Branch obtained from the Rizhao Intermediate People's Court a property preservation order freezing the Defendant's bank deposit in the sum of RMB 80 or property of equivalent value.

13. In June 2015, unknown to the sub-branches, the Shandong Provincial

Branch entered into the following arrangement with Shandong Province Financial Assets Management Company Limited ("Shandong Assets Management"), an asset management company, to dispose of its and its sub-branches' non-performing assets. By an agreement dated 29 June 2015 (the "Batch Assignment"), the Shandong Provincial Branch assigned a batch of non-performing assets including the debts under the two loan agreements and guarantees (the "Subject Debts") to Shandong Assets Management. In turn, by an agreement dated 2 July 2015 (the "Subject Debts Assignment") Shandong Assets Management assigned the Subject Debts to Rizhao Steel Holding Group Co Ltd ("Rizhao Steel"). By an earlier agreement dated 24 June 2015 (the "First Authorisation"), Rizhao Steel authorised the Rizhao Branch to collect the Subject Debts in its own name by way of legal proceedings.

14. On 24 July 2015, the Rizhao Branch obtained an *ex parte Mareva* injunction from Chow J. The application was supported by affirmations filed by Li, the Weihai Sub-branch manager, and Zang, the Plaintiff's PRC lawyer representing the Rizhao Branch in its civil actions in the PRC against the Defendant and others. At the *ex parte* hearing, the assignment of the Subject Debts was unknown to both Li and Zang and was therefore not disclosed to the court. The case was presented on the basis that the Rizhao Branch had the right to sue for the Subject Debts as lender. The order granted at the *ex parte* hearing was continued by the order of Mimmie Chan J on 31 July 2015.

15. Upon reporting the progress of the Hong Kong proceedings to the Rizhao Branch, Li was informed by the deputy manager of the Rizhao Branch that the Subject Debts had been assigned by the Shandong Provincial Branch to Rizhao Steel and of the arrangement under which Rizhao Steel authorised the Rizhao Branch to collect the Subject Debts on its behalf. It is common practice of the Bank to deal with bad debts by assigning them to an asset management corporation. Such assignments are handled in strict confidence at head office and branch level and are usually not disclosed to the sub-branches.

16. On 6 September 2015, the Bank and Rizhao Steel entered into a second agreement to confirm the principal terms of the First Authorisation of 24 June 2015 (the "Second Authorisation").

17. On 10 September 2015, the Plaintiff filed an affidavit prepared by its solicitor ("Green's 1st Affidavit") in performance of its continuing duty of full and frank disclosure by informing the court of the assignment of the Subject Debts.

The applicable legal principles

18. The cases have shown that the following principles are applicable to an application for interim relief in aid of foreign proceedings under section 21M of the High Court Ordinance.

19. First, proceedings have been or are to be commenced in a place outside Hong Kong: *Pacific King Shipping Holdings Pte Ltd (In Compulsory Liquidation)* v Huang Ziqiang[1].

20. Second, such proceedings are capable of giving rise to a judgment which can be enforced in Hong Kong: *Pacific King Shipping Holdings Pte Ltd (In Compulsory Liquidation)* v Huang Ziqiang and *Beyonics Technology Ltd v Goh Chan Peng*[2]. As the proceeding is interlocutory in nature, the applicant seeking this relief is only required to show a good arguable case that the foreign judgment to be obtained will be final and conclusive without having to actually prove that such judgment will be final and conclusive: see the fourth principle set out below. That more onerous burden is to be discharged when actually seeking to enforce the foreign judgment in Hong Kong: see *Chiyu Banking Corp Ltd v Chan Tin Kwun*[3] and *Lee Yau Wing and Lee Shui Kwan*[4].

21. Third, under section 21M(4) of the High Court Ordinance, the relief may be refused if the court is of the opinion that the fact that it has no jurisdiction apart from this section makes it unjust or inconvenient to grant the relief: see *Beyonics Technology Ltd v Goh Chan Peng*.

22. Fourth, the court has to be satisfied that the basic requirements for granting the relief were met, if the substantive proceedings were brought in Hong Kong: see *Pacific King Shipping HoldingsPte Ltd (In Compulsory Liquidation) v Huang Ziqiang* and *Beyonics Technology Ltd v Goh Chan Peng*. In the case of a *Mareva* injunction application, these requirements involve demonstrating a good arguable case, that the Defendant has assets within the jurisdiction, a real risk of dissipation of assets which would render any judgment obtained nugatory, and balance in favour of granting the relief in that it is just and convenient to do so. The strict duty of full

and frank disclosure also applies.

23. Fifth, the court has to consider whether it is unjust or inconvenient to grant the interim relief sought: see *Refco Inc & Anor v Eastern Trading Co & Ors*[5]. The court has to bear in mind that the relief sought is in relation to and in aid of foreign proceedings. The considerations generally revolve around judicial comity, potential conflict as to jurisdiction, potential conflict in inconsistent or overlapping orders, etc. Such considerations do not arise on the facts of the present case.

24. Lastly, the Defendant must have assets within the jurisdiction.

Whether the parties had entered into a choice of Mainland court agreement

25. The principal basis of the Plaintiff's application is that the five on-going actions brought against the Defendant in the PRC courts will give rise to a judgment which may be enforced in Hong Kong under the Mainland Judgments (Reciprocal Enforcement) Ordinance, Cap 597 (the "Ordinance") or at common law. Mr Wong, argues that they are not for want of an exclusive jurisdiction clause in favour of any PRC court in the loan agreements or the guarantees.

26. Under section 5(1) of the Ordinance, a judgment creditor under a Mainland judgment may apply to the Court of First Instance within a certain time limit to have the judgment registered in the Court of First Instance. The Court of First Instance shall order the Mainland judgment to be registered if it meets the requirements set out in subsection (2). Undersection 14, a registered Mainland judgment shall, for the purpose of execution, be of the same force and effect as if it had been a judgment originally given in the Court of First Instance and entered on the day of registration. For the purpose of the present application, two requirements under section 5(2)(b) and (c) are pertinent. These are, respectively, that the parties had entered into a choice of Mainland court agreement; and that the Mainland judgment is final and conclusive as between the parties to that judgment.

27. A "choice of Mainland court agreement" is defined by section 3(2) of the Ordinance to mean "an agreement concluded by the parties to a specified contract and specifying the courts in the Mainland or any of them as the court to determine a dispute which has arisen or may arise in connection with the specified contract to the exclusion of courts of other jurisdictions."

28. The Plaintiff relies on clause 13 of the Lianghe Agreement and clause 15 of the Chenghua Agreement as the choice of Mainland court agreement. The relevant parts of these clauses are identical. Clause 13 of the Lianghe Agreement provides as follows:

「除當事人另有約定外，本協議、單項協議適用中華人民共和國法律。

除當事人另有約定外，在本協議、單項協議生效後，因訂立、履行本協議、單項協議所發生的或與本協議、單項協議有關的一切爭議，雙方可協商解決。協商不成的，任何一方<u>可以</u>採取下列第 3 種方式加以解決：

1. ……

2. ……

3. 依法向有管轄權的人民法院起訴。」

（Translation:

"Unless otherwise agreed by the Parties, this Agreement and individual agreement shall be governed in accordance with Chinese law.

Unless otherwise agreed by the Parties, after this Agreement and individual agreement become effective, where any dispute arises out of the establishment and performance of this Agreement, individual agreement or related to this Agreement and individual agreement shall be resolved through negotiation. Where negotiation fails, both parties <u>agree</u> to resolve the dispute by the **[third of the following methods]**:

1. ……

2. ……

3. File a lawsuit to the people's court with jurisdiction.")

（My amendment of the translation highlighted in bold print; my emphasis underlined.）

Clause 15 of the Chenghua Agreement provides:

「本合同適用中華人民共和國法律。

在本合同生效後，因訂立、履行本合同所發生的或與本合同有關的一切爭議，雙方可協商解決。協商不成的，任何一方<u>可以</u>採取下列第 3 種方式加以解決：

1. ……

2. ……

3. 依法向有管轄權的人民法院起訴。」

(Translation:

This Contract adopts Law of the People's Republic of China.

Both parties could settle all disputes in compromise which are resulted from concluding and performing this Contract or related to this Contract. Any party <u>can</u> choose the third way below to settle the case if there is no agreement upon negotiations:

1. ……

2. ……

3. Submit the case to the People's Court which has the jurisdiction.")

(My emphasis underlined.)

The translation of the two clauses provided by the Plaintiff's solicitors is inconsistent. For the same phrase 「可以」, it is translated as "agree to (resolve)" in one clause and "can choose … to (settle)" in another. The translation in Clause 13 of the Lianghe Agreement was nonsensical and necessitated my amendment highlighted in bold print above. In either case, the effect of these clauses is that upon failing to negotiate a settlement, the parties may or can institute proceedings in the PRC court which has jurisdiction.

29. The Plaintiff also relies on clause 14 of the Lianghe Guarantee and clause 12 of the Chenghua Guarantee as the choice of Mainland court agreement in its action against the Defendant in respect of his liability under the guarantees for the Subject Debts owed by Lianghe and Chenghua respectively. These clauses are identical and provide as follows:

「本合同適用中華人民共和國法律。

凡因履行本合同而產生的一切爭議、糾紛，雙方可先通過協商解決。協商不成的，雙方同意採用與主合同之約定相同的爭議解決方式。」

(Translation:

"This contract shall be governed in accordance with the Law of the

People's Republic of China.

Where any dispute arises out of the performance of this contract, both parties shall resolve such dispute through negotiation. Where negotiation fails, both parties agree to resolve the dispute by the same method stipulated in the Master Contract.")

In either case, there is express agreement that the parties shall adopt the same means to resolve their dispute as provided for under the Lianghe Agreement and Chenghua Agreement.

30. Thus, the question of whether the parties had entered into a "choice of Mainland court agreement" boils down to whether clause 13 of the Lianghe Agreement and clause 15 of the Chenghua Agreement give the PRC court jurisdiction over the parties' disputes to the exclusion of courts of other jurisdictions. This is a question of construction.

31. The thrust of Mr Wong's argument is that the word 「可以 (may)」 is permissive, not imperative, and does not confer exclusivity to any PRC court. Despite the inconsistency in the translation, I would treat in favour of the Defendant that the words 「可以」 should be translated as "may" or "can". In ordinary usage, "may" or "can" is permissive whereas "must" or "shall" is imperative. In accordance with such usage, the phrase 「可以」 will not generally be construed to be imperative. This is only the *prima facie* meaning. There are numerous examples where the word "may" is construed as imperative, and the word "must" or "shall" is construed as permissive even in statues, not just in documents or contracts. All depends on the context in which the word is used. Ultimately, it is a question of what is the intention of the parties who drafted the document.

32. The applicable principles in construction of document have been summarised by Lord Hoffmann in *Investors Compensation Scheme Ltd and West Bromwich Building Society* [1997] UKHL 28; [1998] 1 WLR 896 at 912-913 as follows:

"The principles may be summarised as follows.

(1) Interpretation is the ascertainment of the meaning which the document would convey to a reasonable person having all the background knowledge which would reasonably have been available to the parties in the situation in which they were at the time of the contract.

(2) The background was famously referred to by Lord Wilberforce as the 'matrix of fact', but this phrase is, if anything, an understated description of what the background may include. Subject to the requirement that it should have been reasonably available to the parties and to the exception to be mentioned next, it includes absolutely anything which would have affected the way in which the language of the document would have been understood by a reasonable man.

(3) The law excludes from the admissible background the previous negotiations of the parties and their declarations of subjective intent. They are admissible only in an action for rectification. The law makes this distinction for reasons of practical policy and, in this respect only, legal interpretation differs from the way we would interpret utterances in ordinary life. The boundaries of this exception are in some respects unclear. But this is not the occasion on which to explore them.

(4) The meaning which a document （or any other utterance） would convey to a reasonable man is not the same thing as the meaning of its words. The meaning of words is a matter of dictionaries and grammars; the meaning of the document is what the parties using those words against the relevant background would reasonably have been understood to mean. The background may not merely enable the reasonable man to choose between the possible meanings of words which are ambiguous but even （as occasionally happens in ordinary life） to conclude that the parties must, for whatever reason, have used the wrong words or syntax: see*Mannai Investments Co Ltd v Eagle Star Life Assurance Co Ltd* [1997] UKHL 19; [1997] A.C. 749.

(5) the 'rule' that words should be given their 'natural and ordinary meaning' reflects the common sense proposition that we do not easily accept that people have made linguistic mistakes, particularly in formal documents. On the other hand, if one would nevertheless conclude from the background that something must have gone wrong with the language, the law does not require judges to attribute to the parties an intention which they plainly could not have had. Lord Diplock made this point more vigorously when he said in *Antaios Compania Naviera SA v Salen Rederierna AB* [1985] A.C. 191, 201:

'....... if detailed semantic and syntactical analysis of words in a commercial contract is going to lead to a conclusion that flouts business commonsense, it must be made to yield to business commonsense.' "

These principles were repeated by Lord Hoffmann NPJ when delivering the judgment of the Court of Final Appeal in *Jumbo King Ltd v Faithful Properties Ltd & Ors*[6]. The first, fourth and fifth principles quoted above are particularly pertinent to the present case.

33. The question for this court is to ascertain the meaning which the loan agreements and guarantees would convey to a reasonable person having all the background knowledge which would reasonably have been available to the parties in the situation in which they were at the time of the contract, ie the factual matrix, and having regard to the ordinary meaning of the word "may". The factual matrix is as follows. The parties are PRC parties. The Plaintiff is a bank residing and operating in the PRC. The borrowers, ie the parties primarily liable, are residing and carrying on business in the PRC. The Defendant is a PRC resident residing in Rizhao, Shandong. The two loan agreements and the two guarantees were all executed in the PRC. The parties' contracted place of performance and the place of breach are in the PRC. The governing law of the loan agreements and guarantees is PRC law.

34. Like most contracts with PRC parties, the contracting parties would agree to resolve their disputes by mediation or negotiation and only upon failing that would they resort to litigation. Here, the parties specified the third of three means of dispute resolution as the manner in which their disputes are to be resolved. The first one is to submit to arbitration by an arbitration committee. The second one is to institute legal proceedings against the plaintiff in a PRC court. This option is only available to the Defendant and is inapplicable to the present case. The third one is to institute legal proceedings in a PRC court which has jurisdiction. Against the above factual matrix and the three means set out in the loan agreements, *prima facie*, it must be the parties' intention that the third means is the only means of dispute resolution agreed between the parties if they cannot resolve their dispute by mediation. This intention could be tested by asking what if one party wishes to proceed by the third means but the other party wishes to proceed by the first or second means or an unspecified means such as litigation in a jurisdiction outside the PRC. The first and second options must have been impliedly excluded by reason of the parties consciously

choosing the third option only out of the three specified options, whereas any other unspecified options would render the entire clause superfluous and meaningless. To litigate outside the PRC does not make sense in the light of the factual matrix. As submitted by Ms Lok, counsel for the Plaintiff, the Defendant's argument that these clauses are not exclusive jurisdiction clauses is artificial and disingenuous. If the Defendant genuinely takes the position that the clauses are non-exclusive jurisdiction clauses, he should forthwith confirm whether his solicitors have instruction to accept service such that proceedings can be commenced against him in Hong Kong where his assets are principally located. In the context of the two loan agreements, I am well satisfied that it was the parties' intention that they shall resolve their dispute by the third means. The phrase 「可以」 should be construed as having the imperative meaning as "shall". Accordingly, I find that clause 13 and clause 15 of the Lianghe Agreement and Chenghua Agreement are exclusive jurisdiction clauses.

35. The parties' intention under the two guarantees could not be any clearer. The *prima facie* intention as expressed by the words 「同意 (agreed)」 is that the means of dispute resolution as set out in the two loan agreements shall be adopted in respect of any dispute under the two guarantees. There is no other contrary meaning. Accordingly, I also find that clause 14 and clause 12 of the Lianghe Guarantee and Chenghua Guarantee are exclusive jurisdiction clauses.

Whether PRC judgment to be obtained will be final and conclusive

36. Whether a foreign judgment is final and conclusive has to be determined in accordance with the law of the jurisdiction in which the judgment is sought to be enforced: *Nouvion v Freeman & Another*[7]. Under Hong Kong law, to be final and conclusion a judgment must, in the words of Lord Watson in *Nouvion v Freeman & Another*, be final and unalterable in the court which pronounced it. The test is not whether the judgment is subject to appeal. In that case, Lord Herschell said[8]:

"....... it must be shown that in the court by which it was pronounced conclusively, finally, and for ever established the existence of the debt of which it is sought to be made conclusive evidence in this country, so as to make it res judicata between the parties. If it is not conclusive in the same court which pronounced it, so that notwithstanding such a judgment the existence of the debt made between the same parties be afterwards contested in that court, and upon proper proceedings being taken and such context being adjudicated upon, it may be declared that there exists no obligation to pay the debt at all, then I do not think that a judgment which is of that character can be regarded as finally and conclusively evidencing the debt, and so entitling the person who has obtained the judgment to obtain a decree from a court for the payment of that debt."

His Lordship continued[9]:

"....... Although an appeal may be pending, a court of competent jurisdiction has finally and conclusively determined the existence of a debt, and it has nonetheless done so because the right of appeal has been given whereby a superior court may overrule that decision. There exists at the time of the suit a judgment which must be assumed to be valid until interfered with by a higher tribunal, and which conclusively establishes the existence of the debt which is sought to be recovered in this country. That appears to be in altogether a different position from a 'remate' judgment where the very court which pronounced the 'remate' judgment （not the Court of Appeal） may determine, if proper proceedings are taken, that the debt for which this 'remate' judgment is sought to be used as conclusive evidence has no existence at all."

37. Lord Watson also said[10]:

"....... but no decision has been cited to the effect that an English court is bound to give effect to a foreign decree which is liable to be abrogated or varied by the same court which issued it. All the authorities cited appeared to me, when fairly read, to assume that the decree which was given effect to had been pronounced causa cognitâ, and that it was unnecessary to enquire into the merits of the controversy between the litigants, either because this had already been investigated and decided by the foreign tribunal, or because the defendant had due opportunity of submitting for decision all the pleas which he desire to state in defence. In order to its receiving the fact here, a foreign decree need not be final in the sense that it cannot be made the subject of appeal to a higher court; but it must be final and unalterable in the court which pronounced it; and if appealable, the English court will only enforce it, subject to conditions which may save the interest of those who have the right to appeal."

38. Both parties produced expert evidence on the issue of finality and conclusiveness of the PRC judgment. The Plaintiff filed three affirmations by Mr Zang, the PRC lawyer who handled the Plaintiff's litigations in the PRC (the "Plaintiff's expert"). The Defendant's solicitor filed an affirmation exhibiting a report by Mr Liu, also a PRC lawyer (the "Defendant's expert").

39. Mr Wong, counsel for the Defendant, criticises the reliability of opinion of the Plaintiff's expert on the basis that there is no indication that he had read the code of conduct in Appendix D as mandated by Order 38 rule 37B of the Rules of the High Court ("RHC") and queried his independence or impartiality as he is the Plaintiff's lawyer instructed to handle the PRC proceedings. He submits that the evidence of the Plaintiff's expert should not be admitted or, if admitted, should be given little weight. In reply, Ms Lok argues that the requirements of giving the expert declaration in Appendix D and the statement of truth apply only to expert witnesses who are called to give oral evidence or expert reports and is not applicable to witness affirmations made under oath pursuant to Order 38, rule 36(2). I agree with that submission. As is stated in *Hong Kong Civil Procedure 2015*[11], filing of an affidavit and its service on the other parties is as effective a means of securing the disclosure of expert evidence as is provided by Part IV of Order 38; and moreover, it would be highly impracticable to apply the provisions of Part IV of the Order to interlocutory proceedings in which evidence is normally given by affidavit. As for the question of impartiality, it is indeed a question of weight.

40. Though the Defendant's expert's reports were not given by affidavit and without prior leave having been sought pursuant to Order 38, rule 36(1), Ms Lok does not raise any serious challenge to their admissibility. In the exercise of my discretion, I admit them in evidence.

41. The opinions of the two experts are conflicting. I tested their opinion against each other's and against the authorities they cited. Despite having borne in mind Mr Wong's submission on impartiality, I prefer the Plaintiff's expert's opinion which is generally supported by the authorities whereas the Defendant's expert's opinion appears to be made up of bald assertions.

42. It is common ground between both experts that the PRC courts adopt a "two

tier adjudication system（兩審終審制）". This is so provided by articles 10 of 《中華人民共和國民事訴訟法》（《Civil Procedure Law of the People's Republic of China （2012）》)("the Code"). Articles 155 and 175 are pertinent. These articles provide:

「10. 人民法院審理民事案件，依照法律規定實行合議、迴避、公開審判和兩審終審制度。」；

「155. 最高人民法院的判決、裁定，以及依法不准上訴或者超過上訴期沒有上訴的判決、裁定，是發生法律效力的判決、裁定。」；

「175. 第二審人民法院的判決、裁定，是終審的判決、裁定。」

（Translation:

"10. When adjudicating civil cases, the people's courts shall apply the systems of collegial panel, recusal, public trial, and two trials and the second one is final."

"155. All judgments and rulings rendered by the Supreme People's Court, as well as judgments and rulings against which shall not be appealed according to law or have not been appealed within the prescribed time limit, shall be legally effective."

"175. The judgments and rulings of a people's court of second instance shall be final.")

The adjudication system of the PRC admits of only one appeal against a judgment of a court of first instance to a court of one level higher within the prescribed time limit. No further appeal is available upon conclusion of that appellate proceeding in the court of second instance. No appeal will be entertained upon expiry of time allowed for appeal. The judgments and rulings of the court of second instance and those of the court of first instance, if not appealed against, shall be legally effective. As the test of finality is not whether the judgment is subject to appeal, no argument has been advanced that a PRC judgment given by the court of first instance is not final and conclusive by reason of its being subject to appeal.

43. The thrust of the Defendant's expert's argument that PRC judgments lack finality is founded on the People's Procuratorate's right to lodge a protest（抗訴）against a judgment under the adjudication supervision regime（審判監督制度）available under the Code. He opines that once this protest

is invoked, the court that gave the judgment or ruling may have to re-try the case. Hence, He argues that PRC judgments are clearly not final and conclusive for the purpose of enforcement under Hong Kong law. The Plaintiff's expert argues that a re-trial by the court which passed the judgment does not necessarily follow a protest as matter of course.

44. Under the Code, apart from the appellate procedure, a legally effective judgment, against which no appeal is available, is amenable to review under the adjudication supervision system by the president of the relevant people's court or the Supreme People's Court under article 198, by the Supreme People's Procuratorate at the request of the local people's procuratorates under article 208 or the parties themselves under article 199, if certain requirements are met. The review by the people's courts and procuratorates is initiated by those bodies on their own initiative upon discovery of errors in the judgment or ruling. The review by the parties is initiated by the parties if they believe there is an error in the judgment or ruling. They have to petition to the court of the next higher level. The review by the parties may only be made under thirteen circumstances specified in article 200. These circumstances are essentially insufficiency of evidence, error in law, violation of statutory procedure which has affected the correctness of the judgment or ruling and misconduct of judicial members in trying the case. The review by procuratorates may only be made under those thirteen circumstances and circumstances involving endangering national interest or social public interest.

45. Articles 198, 199 and 208 are relevant. They provide as follows:

「198. 各級人民法院院長對本院已經發生法律效力的判決、裁定、調解書，發現確有錯誤，認為需要再審的，應當提交審判委員會討論決定。

最高人民法院對地方各級人民法院已經發生法律效力的判決、裁定、調解書，上級人民法院對下級人民法院已經發生法律效力的判決、裁定、調解書，發現確有錯誤的，有權提審或者指令下級人民法院再審。

199. 當事人對已經發生法律效力的判決、裁定，認為有錯誤的，可以向上一級人民法院申請再審；當事人一方人數眾多或者當事人雙方為公民的案件，也可以向原審人民法院申請再審。當事人申請再審的，不停止判決、裁定的執行。」；

「208. 最高人民檢察院對各級人民法院已經發生法律效力的判決、裁

定，上級人民檢察院對下級人民法院已經發生法律效力的判決、裁定，發現有本法第二百條規定情形之一的，或者發現調解書損害國家利益、社會公共利益的，應當提出抗訴。

地方各級人民檢察院對同級人民法院已經發生法律效力的判決、裁定，發現有本法第二百條規定情形之一的，或者發現調解書損害國家利益、社會公共利益的，可以向同級人民法院提出檢察建議，並報上級人民檢察院備案；也可以提請上級人民檢察院向同級人民法院提出抗訴。

各級人民檢察院對審判監督程序以外的其他審判程序中審判人員的違法行為，有權向同級人民法院提出檢察建議。」

(Translation:

"198. If the president of a people's court at any level discovers that a legally effective judgment, ruling or mediation agreement made by his court indeed contains an error and deems it necessary to have the case retried, he shall refer it to the judicial committee for discussion and decision.

If the Supreme People's Court discovers that a legally effective judgment, ruling or mediation agreement made by a local people's court at any level indeed contains an error, or if a people's court at a higher level discovers that a legally effective judgment, ruling or mediation agreement made by a people's court at a lower level indeed contains an error, they shall have the power to bring the case up for trial by themselves or direct the people's court at a lower level to conduct a re-trial.

199. If the parties concerned believe that there is an error in a legally effective judgment or ruling, they may apply to the people's court at the next higher level for a re-trial. If one party to the case comprises a large number of persons, or both parties to the case are citizens, they may also apply to the people's court of original instance for re-trial. However, the execution of the judgment or ruling shall not be suspended during the application."

"208. If the Supreme People's Procuratorate discovers that a legally effective judgment or ruling made by a people's court at any level involves any of the circumstances under Article 200 of this Law, or if a people's procuratorate at a higher level discovers that a legally effective judgment or ruling made by a people's court at a lower level involves any of the circumstances under Article 200 of this Law, or the mediation agreement endangers the national interest or the social public interest, the Supreme People's Procuratorate or the said people's procuratorate at a higher level shall lodge a protest.

If a local people's procuratorate at any level discovers that a legally effective judgment or ruling made by a people's court at the same level involves any of the circumstances specified under Article 200 of this Law, or the mediation agreement endangers the national interest or the social public interest, the people's procuratorate may raise procuratorial suggestions to the people's court at the same level and report them to the people's procuratorate at the higher level for record-filing, or request the people's procuratorate at a higher level to lodge a protest to the people's court at the same level.

The people's procuratorates at all levels shall have the right to raise procuratorial suggestions to the people's courts at the same level regarding any illegal acts of judicial officials in judicial procedures other than the trial and supervision procedure.")

46. Having set out these statutory provisions, I now turn to the authorities referred by Mr Wong which he says the courts have expressed reservations over the finality of PRC judgments in the context of summary judgment applications. It should be noted that the statutory provisions cited above are effective on 1 January 2013, some seven to seventeen years after the authorities referred to by Mr Wong.

47. *In Chiyu Banking Corp Ltd v Chan Tin Kwun*[12], the plaintiff obtained a judgment from the Fujian Intermediate People's Court against the defendant under a guarantee. The Defendant's appeal to the Fujian Higher People's Court was dismissed. He presented a petition to the Fujian People's Procuratorate seeking a re-trial by the intermediate court. The procuratorate presented a report to the Supreme People's Procuratorate requesting it to lodge a protest. In the meantime, the plaintiff sued under the PRC judgment in Hong Kong. The Defendant applied to stay the action because the protest procedure had been invoked. At the time, the Ordinance was not in force in Hong Kong. The issue was whether at common law, the PRC judgment was final and conclusive. Cheung J (as he then was), held it was not and stayed the application. He made the following observation about the protest by the procuratorates[13]:

"Under the legal system in PRC, another state organ, the Procuratorate exercises a supervisory function over civil adjudication by the courts: Article 14 of *the Civil Procedure Law of 1991* ("the *Civil Procedure Law*"). Under Article 185, the Procuratorate may lodge a protest to the court in respect of a judicial decision. The circumstances in which the protest may be lodged are set out in art.185, namely,

(i) the main evidence to substantiate the original judgment or ruling was insufficient;

(ii) the law which was applied in the original judgment or ruling was incorrect;

(iii) the People's Court was in violation of the statutory procedure which have affected the correctness of the judgment or ruling;

(iv) the judicial members in trying the case committed embezzlement, accepted bribes, practised favouritism or make a judgment that perverted the law.

It is for the Supreme People's Procuratorate to lodge the protest but under Article 185, the Fujian People's Procuratorate is entitled to refer the matter to the Supreme People's Procuratorate for it to lodge a protest.

Under art 187, the court, upon receipt of the protest, is required to conduct a re-trial of the action."

After referring to the test of finality *in Nouvion v Freeman & Another* and the above dicta of Lord Herschell and Lord Watson, Cheung J held that the judgment of the intermediate people's court was not final and conclusive. He said[14]:

"Based on the material before me, the supervisory function of the Supreme People's Procuratorate and the protest system are not simply an appeal process. The intermediate court judgment is final in the sense that it is not appealable and it is enforceable in China, but it is not final and conclusive for the purpose of recognition and enforcement by the Hong Kong courts because in the words of Lord Watson, it "is not final and unalterable in the court which pronounced it". It is liable to be altered by the intermediate court on a re-trial if the Supreme People's Procuratorate lodge a protest in accordance with the Civil Procedure Law. If upon protest being made, rare the circumstances may be, a Chinese court has to re-try the case, then, clearly it retains the power to alter its own decision. As Lord Watson said at page 13 of *Nouvion*:

"There is no real difference in principle between the case of a court retaining power to alter a decree by an order in the same suit and the case of its retaining power to defeat the operation of that decree by an order pronounced in another suit relating to the same debt."

Mr Kerr referred to Colt Industries Inc v Sarlie (No.2) [1966] 1 WLR 1287 in which Lord Denning, M.R. at page 1291 held that:

"The appeal itself does not render it not final and conclusive, nor should the possibility of leave to appeal. It seems to me that the proper test is this: is the judgment a final and conclusive judgment of a court of competent jurisdiction in the territory in which it was pronounced. The relevant territory here is the State of New York. Applying this test, there was here a final and conclusive judgment."

In my view, Lord Denning's decision does not in any way contradict the principle in *Nouvion*.

<u>Although no protest has been lodged yet, the procedure had actually been invoked. This demonstrated that the judgment is not final and conclusive. To allow the present action to continue would not be satisfactory because the plaintiff is not suing on the guarantee but on the judgment itself which is not final and conclusive.</u>There is a possibility that the judgment may be varied if the application to the Supreme People's Procuratorate is successful, and the debt for which the present judgment is sought to be used as conclusive evidence may have no existence at all."

(My emphasis underlined.)

48. This is a clear ruling by the High Court that despite the PRC judgment was not appealable, it nevertheless was not final and conclusive because the protest procedure had been invoked and there was a possibility that the judgment may be altered by the court pronouncing it upon re-trial. However, Cheung J is far from saying that the protest procedure by itself renders any PRC judgment not final and conclusive.

49. Indeed, in his later decision in *Lee Yau Wing and Lee Shui Kwan*[15] in which the plaintiff also sued on a PRC judgment, Cheung JA sitting in the Court of Appeal expressly acknowledged that this issue has not been

authoritatively determined by the Court of Appeal, and he cited five Court of Appeal decisions[16] to that effect. He concluded in paragraphs 23 to 27 by saying that whether a PRC judgment may be rendered not final and conclusive solely by reason of the protest regime or by the regime and some factual circumstances has not been authoritatively decided and is an important issue involving important public interest which could not be determined by interlocutory proceedings on paper without hearing oral evidence from PRC law experts. He said, after referring to *Nouvion v Freeman & Another*, that the House of Lords has neither clearly stated that the existence of a regime whereby a Spanish "remate judgment" may be set aside was sufficient to determine whether the judgment was not final and conclusive. He said[17]:

「24. 本席認為本案最具爭議性的議題是內地的判決是否純是因為審判監督制度的存在而令判決不能成為最終及不可推翻的判決，抑或是需要視乎實際情況才可以決定有關的裁決是不是屬於這類的裁決。如果法庭要視乎實際的情況來作出判決，它應如何規範或界定這個情況？舉一個例子，如果就某一宗案件，所有審判監督制度內的渠道已經被運用而內地法院最終維持原審的判決，但同時有證據顯示有關權力機構對某個法庭在某段期間所判決的案件重新調查及命令重審，而當事人的案件亦是該法庭在該段期間作出判決的，當事人雖然未能在兩年的期限之內要求有關權力機構重新處理這些案件，但本港法庭在這情況下是否仍因當事人未能符合王教授所指有關制度新運作的規定而裁定內地裁決是一項最終及不可推翻的裁決？若果本港法庭需要考慮案件的實際情況，本港法庭應以甚麼標準來界定內地近期司法解釋文件提出涉及就兩年期限的「正當理由」？

25. 在 *Nouvion v Freeman* (1890) LR 15 App Cas 1 一案，法庭沒有清楚說明到底是不是只要存在着一個可以推翻 'remate 判決' 的制度，法庭就已具備穩固的基礎去裁定這類判決不是最終及不可被推翻的判決。

26. 本港法庭需要考慮實際情況才作出決定的觀點無疑是有它的優點，但這樣做會出現該裁決可能和內地可使用審判監督權力的機關的實質決定有所不同，畢竟本港法庭只能就當時雙方提供的證據來作出法庭認為正確的判決。這正突顯了本港法庭採用這方式處理案件的難處，也突顯了一個原則性的議題即是本港法庭應否單方面認為在內地判決敗訴的一方再沒有可能依賴有關的審判監督制度去推翻有關的判決，就因而裁定這判決是一項最終及不可推翻的判決？鑒於內地審判監督

制度的存在及內地法制沒有一項條文規定內地判決若在外地執行會在甚麼時間或情況下才被視為最終及不可推翻的判決，香港法庭應否作出一個價值判決來裁定一宗案件在內地已經是沒有「正當理由」來啟動「審判監督」制度。在現階段，本席不需要深入探討這些問題或者作出確定性的裁決，因為本上訴只是一項有關簡易判決的上訴。

27. 本案涉及的議題明顯是一項<u>具有公眾重要性的議題</u>。雖然王教授對本席提供了珍貴的意見，但這也只是訴訟一方所提供的專家的書面意見。袁大律師作為法庭之友對案件持中立態度，他是以專業知識協助法庭，雖然他不是內地法律專家，但本席認為他對王教授的意見所作出的回應並不是泛泛之言，<u>王教授是應該出庭作證、接受盤問及全面解釋他的意見。</u>」

(My emphasis underlined.)

In the end, the Court of Appeal, by a majority, held that the issue whether the PRC judgment was final and conclusive could not be determined in interlocutory proceeding and ordered the case to proceed to trial.

50. In *Wu Wei*（伍威）對 *Liu Yi Ping*（劉一萍）[18], the defendant sought to rely on a PRC judgment to support her application to stay the execution of a Hong Kong judgment against her. Tang VP affirmed the Court of Appeal's decision in *Lee Yau Wing and Lee Shui Kwan* that whether a foreign judgment is final and conclusive is an issue of important public interest involving complicated legal questions which could not be decided in interlocutory proceedings without hearing evidence from experts on PRC law.

51. Despite the conclusions reached in *Chiyu Banking Corp Ltd v Chan Tin Kwun*, *Lee Yau Wing and Lee Shui Kwan and Wu Wei*（伍威）對 *Liu Yi Ping*（劉一萍）, the question whether a PRC judgment is final and conclusive, or more precisely whether a PRC judgment is rendered not final and conclusive by reason of the regime of protest by the procuratorate remains open.

52. It should be noted that the decision in *Chiyu Banking Corp Ltd v Chan Tin Kwun* which was endorsed by the other two Court of Appeal decisions was made twenty years ago. *Lee Yau Wing and Lee Shui Kwan and Wu Wei*（伍威）對 *Liu Yi Ping*（劉一萍）were determined nine and seven years ago respectively. PRC law has undergone tremendous changes in the past twenty years. Notably, the Code now operative was promulgated on

31 August 2012 and took effect on 1 January 2013. While the provisions of the Code referred to in *Chiyu Banking Corp Ltd* are similar to the ones I quoted above, the article numbers have changed significantly. The PRC legal expert opinion adduced before Cheung J was that there were five grounds upon which a protest may be lodged under article 185 and that under article 187, the people's court upon receipt of protest from the procuratorate is required to conduct a re-trial. The five grounds in article 185 have been expanded to thirteen grounds under article 200. More importantly, article 211 of the present Code which is equivalent to article 187 under the former Code provides:

「211. 人民檢察院提出抗訴的案件，接受抗訴的人民法院應當自收到抗訴書之日起三十日內<u>作出再審的裁定</u>；有本法第二百條第一項至第五項規定情形之一的，可以交下一級人民法院再審，但經該下一級人民法院再審的除外。」

(Translation:

"211. With respect to a case against which a people's procuratorate lodges a protest, the people's court that has accepted the protest shall <u>make a decision on whether or not to re-try the case</u> within 30 days after receipt of the protest. Under any of the circumstances prescribed in Items (1) to (5) of Article 200 of this Law, the people's court may transfer the case to a lower court for re-trial, unless the case has already been retried by the said lower court.")

(My emphasis underlined.)

53. Though not so argued by the two experts, it is apparent that the protest regime and the adjudication supervision regime have undergone substantive changes since 1 January 2013. Many more articles have been inserted between article 200 and article 211 whereas formerly there was only one intervening article between article 185 and 187. It appears from article 211 of the current Code that under the present protest regime re-trial by the court protested is not a matter of course upon receipt of a protest. First, the people's court which accepts the protest is usually one level higher than the court the decision of which is protested against. It has 30 days to decide whether to entertain the protest by ordering a re-trial or to dismiss the protest. It may or may not order a re-trial. If it dismisses the protest, that is the end of the protest. Second, if it orders a re-trial, it may

conduct the re-trial itself or order it to be tried by a lower level court or the court protested. It may conduct the re-trial itself, except where the protest was made in circumstances under paragraphs (1) to (5) of article 200, ie matters relating to insufficiency of evidence. In that light, the protest regime is more like an appellate regime. The protest by the procuratorate is just another avenue of appeal, except that it is initiated by a non-party. But the result is no different from an appeal by a party. The protest is to be adjudicated by the higher level people's court. The remedies, if successful, are no different from those available under the appellate system in the PRC. Those remedies are also similar to the remedies under our system. The appellate court may set aside the judgment of the original court, re-hear the case itself and reach its own decision or remit it to the court appealed or protested against to continue hearing with further directions or for re-trial *de novo*. There is no doubt that judgments of our courts under our system are final and conclusive. Thus, equally, it can be argued that PRC judgments under a system containing a protest regime as set out in article 211 is final and conclusive. My understanding of Lord Watson's dictum in*Nouvion v Freeman & Another* is that a judgment is final and conclusive if it is unalterable <u>voluntarily</u> (my emphasis) by the court pronouncing it. The court becomes *functus officio* and has no jurisdiction to reopen or amend its decision on its own volition. Hence, it is final and conclusive as far as the court pronouncing it is concerned. Under our law, the fact that the pronouncing court's jurisdiction is revived by an appellate court does not render its original decision not final and conclusive. Applying the same rationale, there is no reason why, if jurisdiction is revived by a protest by the procuratorate resulting in the same remedies available under the appellate system in that foreign jurisdiction, the original decision should be treated as not final and conclusive.

54. In my view, the current Code has significant impact on the question whether a PRC judgment is not final and conclusive by reason only of the protest regime. Article 187 which was referred to Cheung J in *Chiyu Banking Corp Ltd* might or might not be identical to article 211 under the current Code. If it was, Cheung J had been seriously misled to the belief that a re-trial follows a protest as a matter of course, such that the decision was not final and unalterable by the court pronouncing it. If it was not, the law might have changed significantly and suggests that the three decisions I referred to above may no longer be relevant. Those three decisions

were decided many years before the current Code and are distinquishable from the present case by reason of the apparently substantial changes in the Code. In any event, the Court of Appeal has never held that PRC judgments are not final conclusive by reason only of the protest regime. It has expressly left that issue open. For the purpose of the present application, I am not required to answer that question. The issue in these proceedings is whether the Plaintiff seeking relief in aid of a foreign judgment has proved an arguable case or a serious issue to be tried that it will likely obtain a judgment in the foreign court and that such judgment will likely be final and conclusive for the purpose of the Ordinance. In view of the above analysis of the Code, I would be slow to hold that PRC judgments are rendered not final and conclusive by reason of the protest regime. I consider I am bound the Court of Appeal decisions that in view of its complicated nature and public importance, that question could not be determined in interlocutory proceedings without hearing evidence from expert witnesses. However, I am well satisfied for the purpose of the present interlocutory application that the Plaintiff has discharged its burden of showing an arguable case that such judgment, if obtained, is final and conclusive for the purpose of the Ordinance.

Good arguable case – Plaintiff's locus to sue under PRC law

55. Lianghe and Chenghua had taken steps to dispute the jurisdiction of the PRC courts. However, no substantive defence has been proffered. The Defendant has openly admitted in his affirmation that Chenghua has breached its repayment obligation since 2015 and further admitted that Chenghua is in such dire financial situation that it has failed to pay any of its employees' salaries since April or May 2015. He has to date failed to proffer any substantive defence. There is overwhelming evidence that Lianghe and Chenghua have breached their obligation as borrowers and the Defendant has breached his obligation as guarantor in respect of the two loan agreements. The only argument taken by Mr Wong is that the Plaintiff has lost its locus to sue after the debts were assigned to Rizhao Steel, both as a matter of PRC law and Hong Kong law.

56. On the fact, the Plaintiff assigned the Subject Debts along with other non-performing assets to Shandong Assets Management under the Batch Assignment on 29 June 2015, which then assigned the Subject Debts to Rizhao Steel under the Subject Debts Assignment on 2 July 2015. It is the

opinion of the Defendant's expert that the First Authorisation dated 24 June 2015 authorising the Rizhao Branch to collect the Subject Debts on behalf of Rizhao Steel which pre-dated the Subject Debts Assignment has no legal effect because the Subject Debts were still owed to the Plaintiff at the material time.

57. This opinion is neither here nor there as it confuses the question of who owned the Subject Debts and who has locus to sue. According to the Plaintiff, the Batch Assignment, Subject Debts Assignment and Authorisation formed one global arrangement under which the Bank's non-performing assets were assigned together with the condition that the Plaintiff's Rizhao Branch would continue to render services or assistance to the assignee in recovering the Subject Debts. For compliance reasons under PRC law, the Plaintiff assigned the non-performing assets to an asset management holding company first, which then sub-assigned the Subject Debts to Rizhao Steel. The intention of the parties as reflected in the preamble of the Subject Debts Assignment was to sign the First Authorisation after the execution of the Subject Debts Assignment. However, as it took time to go through the internal administrative procedures, the execution of the documents took place in the reverse order. The anomaly was rectified under the Second Authorisation signed on 6 September 2015.

58. The Plaintiff's expert relies on article 51 of the 《中華人民共和國合同法》 （Contract Law of the People's Republic of China） in support of his opinion that the validity of the Authorisation is nevertheless saved by the Second Authorisation and hence the Rizhao Branch has authority to take legal action to recover the Subject Debts on behalf of Rizhao Steel. Article 51 of Contract Law of the PRC provides:

「無處分權的人處分他人財產，經權利人追認或者無處分權的人訂立合同後取得處分權的，該合同有效。」

（Translation:

"Where a person without the right of disposal disposes of another's property, upon ratification by the obligee or if the person without the right of disposal obtains the right of disposal after making the contract, the contract shall be effective."）

On the face, this article supports the opinion of the Plaintiff's expert, whereas the opinion of the Defendant's expert is unsupported by any authority. I accept the opinion of the Plaintiff's expert.

59. Next, the Defendant's expert argues that the Second Authorisation is also ineffective because as a state owned bank, the Plaintiff is in no position to become Rizhao Steel's debt collecting agent. Again, he cited no authority to support his opinion.

60. The Plaintiff's expert exhibits the particulars of the Rizhao Branch registered with the Commerce and Industry Bureau showing that it is authorised to carry out all businesses permitted to be carried out in accordance with laws and regulations within the scope of the licence issued by 中國銀行業監督管理委員會 (China Banking Regulatory Commission). His opinion is that the scope of businesses permitted by the licence does not prohibit the Rizhao Branch from collecting debt on behalf of Rizhao Steel. The Defendant's expert offered nothing to contradict this opinion. I prefer the Plaintiff's expert's opinion.

61. Next, the Defendant's expert opines that as notice of assignment of the Subject Debts had been given to the Defendant through Green's 1st Affidavit filed in this proceeding, the assignment is binding on Chenghua and Lianghe as debtors and the Plaintiff has lost the right to continue the proceedings in the PRC. There is no dispute that before commencement of proceedings in the PRC, no notice of assignment had been given to Lianghe and Chenghua. The Plaintiff's solicitor's affirmation was filed in performance of the Plaintiff's duty of full and frank disclosure after commencement of proceedings in the PRC. The Plaintiff's expert is therefore of the opinion that Green's 1st Affidavit is not notice of assignment. The assignment is binding only as between the Plaintiff as assignor and Rizhao Steel as assignee and has no relevance as between Lianghe and Chenghua on the one part, and the Plaintiff and Rizhao Steel on the other. Both opinions are not supported by any authorities. I prefer the Plaintiff's expert's opinion as more logical and reject the Defendant's expert's opinion as rather strained. In any event, even if the affirmation constituted adequate notice, the Plaintiff has locus to sue under the Second Authorisation.

Good arguable case – Plaintiff's locus to sue under Hong Kong law

62. Mr Wong refers to *Bowstead & Reynolds*[19], and *Malayan Banking Berhad*

v China Insurance Co Ltd[20] and submits that as a matter of Hong Kong law, an agent must sue in the name of his principal. This is to protect a defendant being vexed twice by different parties in respect of the same subject matter. He submits that even though the Plaintiff might have standing to sue under PRC law as Rizhao Steel's agent, it cannot obtain the *Mareva* relief sought in these proceedings under Hong Kong law without joining Rizhao Steel as a plaintiff in these proceedings.

63. In reply, Ms Lok submits that this argument wholly subverts the ancillary nature of the section 21M proceedings. The Plaintiff is not asserting a substantive cause of action in the Hong Kong courts. This court is only asked to assist the PRC actions and under that forum where the substantive dispute is tried, it is not necessary to join Rizhao Steel. I agree.

Risk of dissipation

64. The Defendant had 588,186,432 shares in NURH on 1 December 2014. On his own admission on three occasions between 31 March and 25 June 2015 he had disposed of 55,770,000 shares with a market value of $32 million, representing a reduction of the Defendant's shareholding from 18.69% to 9.496%. The Plaintiff relies on these disposals as evidence of risk of dissipation of the Defendant's assets. There was another disposal of 15,000,000 shares on 1 December 2014 which has not been explained by the Defendant, other than by Mr Wong that the transactions took place before commencement of the PRC proceedings.

65. The Defendant's answer is that the reduction was insignificant in absolute terms, being about 56 million shares out of more than 588 million, ie 9.52% only. He also explained that the sales were for the purpose of settling the interest payable for the margin facilities. Mr Wong submits that there is nothing sinister or untoward in such sales. He also argues that it is difficult to see why the Defendant's shareholding as of 1 December 2014 should be taken as the reference point in assessing the risk of dissipation when the PRC proceedings only commenced much later in 2015.

66. I have examined the Defendant's share trading account maintained with Get Nice Securities Limited for the months of March to June 2015. It was a margin trading account with a debit balance of $30 million and 588,186,432 NURH shares on 1 December 2014. Between March to June 2015, there were sales of NURH shares as price surged from $0.26 to $0.9

which turned the debit balance to a credit balance of $193,869.65. There were also deposits of about $59.58 million, resulting in a credit balance of about $59.59 million and 532,416,432 NURH shares in the account. The activities in the account, though in the nature of disposal, are consistent with a trader maintaining his margin account, selling his pledged shares as the price surged to take profit. By themselves, these activities were neutral and inconsistent with dissipation of assets for the purpose of preventing the Plaintiff from enforcing any judgment to be obtained against the Defendant.

67. However, these activities have to be viewed against the factual matrix. The Defendant was, until 19 May 2015, the chairman and executive director of NURH. As at 1 December 2014, he held 588,186,432 of its shares, representing 19.66% of its issued share capital. Just five months prior, Chenghua, of which he was the legal representative and person in control, failed to repay the loans advanced by the Haiqu Sub-branch. On 28 December 2014, on behalf of Chenghua, he entered into the Chenghua Agreement to refinance Chenghua's indebtedness. Under clause 10.2(11) of that agreement, Chenghua promised that its person in control, ie the Defendant, would not dispose of his shares in NURH at will and if he intended to dispose of any of his shares he would first obtain prior approval from the Haiqu Sub-branch and transfer all proceeds of sale to the Haiqu Sub-branch. He also signed the Chenghua Guarantee on the same day. The disposals should be viewed against the above background. In the light of the circumstances, the Defendant's shareholding on 1 December 2014 must have been at least one of the material considerations for which the Haiqu Sub-branch entered into the Chenghua Agreement and the Chenghua Guarantee. Hence, his shareholding on that date is the appropriate starting point to consider the risk of dissipation.

68. The Defendant never informed the Bank of the above disposals and the proceeds of sale were only applied to reduce his own margin liability instead of being applied to repay Chenghua's debts in accordance with the undertaking in clause 10.2(11). Not only did he blatantly fail to honour his personal guarantee under the Chenghua Agreement, he now resorts to argue that he was not a party to that agreement. Despite the fact that the Defendant is indeed not a party to the Chenghua Agreement and despite the principle of separate corporate personality, the Chenghua Agreement,

the Chenghua Guarantee, and his shareholding in NURH formed one composite against which the Defendant's conduct or commercial morality has to be measured. He was the legal representative and person in charge of Chenghua which was in debt. He negotiated on behalf of Chenghua with the Haiqu Sub-branch for refinancing and offered his personal assets as an assurance, if not a formal security, for Chenghua's indebtedness. On top of all that, he entered into a proper formal Chenghua Guarantee to repay Chenghua's debts. How can he now refuse to honour that guarantee and turn around to say that the undertaking in clause 10.2(11) is not binding on him? That undertaking is at least binding on his moral. Though his shares in NURH are not security for Chenghua's indebtedness, it must have been on the strength of his personal undertaking as the legal representative and person in charge of Chenghua that he will not reduce his shareholding in NURH and his assurance that any proceeds of sales of his shares in NURH will be applied to reduce Chenghua's indebtedness that the Haiqu Sub-branch entered into the Chenghua Agreement with Chenghua and accepted his guarantee under the Chenghua Guarantee as sufficient security for Chenghua's indebtedness.

69. Thus, despite the fact that the transactions in his margin account appear to be regular, that the proceeds of sales of the NURH shares were only applied to reduce his margin indebtedness and that he put in additional funds into the account, his failure to honour the undertaking under clause 10.2(11) of the Chenghua Agreement which he caused Chenghua to give, his expressly denouncing any obligation under that clause and his failure to honour the Chenghua Guarantee suggest that he is a person of low commercial morality. When his attitude is viewed in the round, the inference is that he has no intention to honour the Chenghua Guarantee and would do whatever he could to protect his assets so as to prevent the Plaintiff from successfully executing any judgment which may be obtained against him. He could easily withdraw funds from the margin account resulting in a debit cash balance. He could therefore reduce the net asset value in the account to such minimum level as could be supported by the value of the shares in the account, leaving the Plaintiff with little net asset to levy execution on. The value of the shares and cash in the account as at 30 June 2015 was $360 million, which was less than the amount restrained under the injunction. I am satisfied that the Plaintiff has demonstrated a real risk of dissipation. There is no update of the net asset value in the

account, but from available information from the Stock Exchange of Hong Kong the price of the NURH shares has reduced by two thirds as of the date of this decision. All funds in this account should be restrained.

Balance of convenience

70. The Defendant has so far failed to advance any substantive defence to the Plaintiff's claims. He only argues that there are other guarantors under the two loan agreements and that the Plaintiff has applied for and obtained a number of pre-litigation property preservation orders from the PRC courts against him and other parties. In relation to the debts under the Lianghe Agreement, orders freezing bank deposits of RMB 49.5 million and RMB 80 million and real estate to the value of RMB 10 million have been obtained against the Defendant and others. In relation to the debts under the Chenghua Agreement, an application for pre-litigation property preservation was made. There is no update on the progress of that application. In addition, the Defendant argues that the Plaintiff has claimed as against Lianghe and Chenghua account payables in the amount of RMB 248 million and certain stock rights. Notwithstanding these preservation orders, the Plaintiff has been unable to identify any significant assets held by the Defendant and others in the PRC. The other guarantors have failed to honour their obligations. The limited security provided under the loan agreements is insufficient. The Plaintiff has to resort to litigation and to look to the Defendant's assets outside the PRC. There is nothing in the Defendant's argument which could tilt the balance in his favour.

71. On the other hand, as the Defendant has advanced no substantive defence to the claims and as there are no assets available to satisfy judgment, the balance must tilt in favour of maintaining the injunction than discharging it.

Non-disclosure

72. Lastly, the Defendant complains of material non-disclosure in three respects.

73. First, Mr Wong criticizes the Plaintiff for having failed to inform the *ex parte* judge (i) that the Plaintiff has the burden of showing that the PRC proceedings are capable of giving rise to a judgment which may be enforced in Hong Kong; (ii) how this can be shown in the present case; and (iii) what potential arguments the Defendant may raise on this point. He

submits that on the basis of the skeleton argument presented to the court before the *ex parte* judge there was a complete failure on the part of the Plaintiff to address these fundamental issues.

74. The Plaintiff was represented by another counsel at the *ex parte* stage. In his skeleton submission, he referred the court to sections 21M and 21L of the High Court Ordinance. He referred to all the requirements which have to be satisfied in an application for *Mareva* injunction in aid of foreign proceedings. He has referred specifically to the requirement that the foreign proceedings must be capable of giving rise to a judgment which may be enforced in Hong Kong. But he has not gone into the depth as suggested by Mr Wong. It is, of course, desirable that counsel should have addressed the *ex parte* judge on those mattes. It appeared that counsel has taken that issue for granted. That was an unfortunate omission.

75. However, it has no impact in the present case. Enforcement of PRC judgment is not uncommon in Hong Kong in view of Hong Kong's close economic and geographical ties with the PRC. I do not think it is an issue which is unfamiliar to any civil judge in the Court of First Instance, of which Chow J is one and a very experienced one. He would have no doubt held the same views as I do that a PRC judgment is on the face final and conclusive and that the applicant is only required to show a serious issue to be tried in this interlocutory application.

76. Second, Mr Wong criticizes the Plaintiff's failure to disclose to the *ex parte* judge the assignment of the Subject Debts and the authority issue raised by such assignment. I have dealt with those issues and am satisfied that they have no impact on the PRC judgment to be obtained. Although it is difficult to argue in theory that the Weihai Sub-branch as part of the Plaintiff did not have the knowledge of its superior Rizhao Branch and Shandong Provincial Branch, I accept that was indeed what happened. The court cannot turn a blind eye to that reality. However, upon realizing the true position and in the discharge of its continuing duty of full and frank disclosure, the Plaintiff promptly filed an affidavit revealing the situation well before the Defendant filed his affirmation in opposition for the *inter partes* hearing. Accepting that there was material non-disclosure, I am satisfied that the failure to disclose in the circumstances was unintentional, has no impact to the case and was excusable.

77. Third, Mr Wong refers to the skeleton submission before the *ex parte* judge in which counsel referred to sales of the Defendant's shares in NURH from 1 December 2014 (mistakenly written as "1 December 2015") which reduced his shareholding from 19.66% to 14.46%. He criticizes the Plaintiff for painting a misleading picture exaggerating the extent of the Defendant's disposals of his shares as the reduction was mainly due to dilution caused by issue of new shares. Dilution was one reason, but there was nevertheless about 10% reduction in real terms. At that stage, the Plaintiff could only assess the Defendant's shareholdings based on his own disclosures to the Stock Exchange of Hong Kong. It might have failed to notice the increase in issued share capital of NURH which led to the exaggeration. But as I analyzed, the disposal, though of a lesser extent, nevertheless supports the existence of a risk of dissipation. Such non-disclosure was neither intentional nor material.

78. In conclusion, the material non-disclosure was trivial, unintentional, has no impact to the decision of the *ex parte* judge and ought fairly be excused.

Conclusion

79. For the above reasons, the balance of convenience is in favour of maintaining the injunction. There was some trivial material non-disclosure. Technically, the injunction should be discharged for material non-disclosure. However, the overriding question is what the interest of justice requires in the circumstances. There is no substantive defence advanced on behalf of the Defendant. All his arguments are technical. The non-disclosure has no impact on the case, was trivial, unintentional and ought fairly be excused. Having regard to proportionality and all the circumstances, I am satisfied that justice requires that the injunction be maintained. It is therefore appropriate to discharge the injunction and to make a re-grant on similar terms.

80. Accordingly, I allow the Defendant's Discharge Summons and discharge the *Mareva* injunction but make no order as to costs; and allow the Plaintiff's Continuation Summons by ordering a new injunction on similar terms with costs to the Plaintiff.

(Anthony To)

Judge of the Court of First Instance

High Court

Ms Frances Lok, instructed by Messrs Stephenson Harwood, for the Plaintiff

Mr Anson Wong SC, instructed by Messrs Li & Partners, for the Defendant

1. HCMP 2464/2012 (4 April 2014) at paras 8 to 23, in particular paras 11-12
2. CACV 244/2014, (Unrep) 12 August 2015 at para 22-26
3. [1996] 2 HKLR 395
4. [2007] 2 HKLRD 750 at 757
5. [1999] 1 Lloyd's Law Report 159, at 170-171
6. [1999] HKCFA 38; [1999] 4 HKC 707
7. [1889] 15 AC 1
8. Supra at 9
9. Supra at 10
10. Supra at 13
11. At paragraph 38/36/1
12. Supra
13. Supra, at 397A to E
14. Supra, at 399G to 400C
15. Supra
16. *Chiyu Banking Corp Ltd v Chan Tin Kwun* [1996] 2 HKLR 395; *Tan Tay Cuan v Ng Chi Hung* (unrep HCA No 5477 of 2000, [2001] HKLRD (Yrbk) 195; 林哲民訴林志滔 (unrep, CACV No 354 of 2001, 18 December 2001; 林哲民訴林志滔 (unrep, HCA No 9585 of 1999, [2003] CHKEC 325; and 林哲民訴張順連 (unrep, CACV No 1046 of 2001, [2002] CHKEC 2367)
17. Supra at 760, para 24
18. (unrep) CACV 32/2009, 27 March 2009
19. (20th ed), para 9-010
20. CACV 424/2002 (unrep) 10 June 2003 at para 35

Gustave Nouvion v. Freeman and Another

(1889) 15 App. Cas. 1

In the Matter of the Estate of William Henderson Deceased

Gustave Nouvion v. Freeman and Another

House of Lords

22 November 1889

(1889) 15 App. Cas. 1

Lord Herschell , Lord Watson , Lord Bramwell , and Lord Ashbourne .

1889 Nov. 22

Foreign Judgment, Action on—Foreign Judgment not enforceable here unless final and conclusive—Res Judicata.

An action cannot be brought in this country upon a foreign judgment for the recovery of a debt, if the judgment does not finally and conclusively (subject to an appeal to a higher Court) settle the existence of the debt so as to become res judicata between the parties.

By Spanish law in certain cases summary or "executive" proceedings can be taken to recover a debt, and the plaintiff if successful obtains a "remate" judgment for the recovery of a sum of money. Such a judgment is final in those proceedings unless reversed or varied on appeal. In such proceedings the defendant can plead certain limited defences but cannot set up any defence affecting the validity of the contract. Either plaintiff or defendant, if unsuccessful in the "executive" proceedings, may in the same Court and in respect of the same subject matter take ordinary or "plenary" proceedings, in which all defences and the whole merits of the matter may be gone into. In the "plenary" proceedings the "remate" judgment cannot be set up as *res judicata* or otherwise. A "remate" judgment can be enforced by the plaintiff on giving security, although either an appeal or "plenary" proceedings may be pending.

A "plenary" judgment renders the "remate" judgment inoperative and requires restoration of any moneys paid under it:—

affirming the decision of the Court of Appeal (37 Ch. D. 244), that since a "remate" judgment does not finally and conclusively establish the existence of a debt no action can be brought upon it in this country.

APPEAL from a decision of the Court of Appeal[1].

The facts are stated in full in the report of the decision of North J.[2]. For the present purpose the following outline will suffice:—

The present action was brought in May 1883 by the appellant against the executors of William Henderson, deceased, and claimed administration of his estate. The statement of claim alleged that the plaintiff had on the 5th of April 1878 recovered judgment against Henderson for a large sum of money for principal, interest and costs, in certain proceedings in the Court of the district of San Roman in the city of Seville in Spain; that those proceedings were brought to recover the balance of the purchase-moneys of mines in Spain, payable by virtue of two deeds of conveyance by the plaintiff to Henderson dated in 1872, and that Henderson brought an appeal against the judgment but afterwards abandoned it.

The statement of defence alleged that the judgment was not final nor such as would sustain the plaintiff's claim; that the cause of action was barred by the Statute of Limitations , 21 Jac. 1 c. 16 ; and that the execution of the deeds by Henderson was obtained by fraud. The defendants also counter-claimed for repayment of the purchase-moneys and for damages caused by the fraudulent representations by means of which Henderson was induced to buy the mines.

An issue was afterwards directed to be tried by a judge without a jury, whether the judgment was an order or judgment upon which the plaintiffs' claim in the action, or some and what part of it, could (apart from the question of fraud) be sustained.

At the trial of the issue before North J. evidence was given as to the nature of the proceedings in Spain and the Spanish law administered in that district.

The effect of the evidence is set out in the judgment of North J.[3]. Briefly it may be thus stated: The judgment of April 1878 was termed a "remate" judgment, and the proceedings were summary or "executive." Such a judgment is final in those proceedings unless reversed or varied on appeal. In such proceedings the defendant could plead such defences as payment or waiver, but could not set up any defence denying the validity of the contract. Either plaintiff or defendant, if unsuccessful in the "executive" proceedings, might in the same Court in respect of the same matter take separate and independent proceedings called "ordinary," "plenary," or "declaratory," in which the "remate" judgment could not be pleaded as res judicata or otherwise made use of. In such "plenary" proceedings all defences and the whole merits of the matter might be gone into. Judgment in the "plenary" proceedings practically rendered the "remate" judgment inoperative and required restoration of any moneys paid under it; but the "remate" judgment might be enforced on giving security so long as either an appeal or "plenary" proceedings were only pending.

The "remate" judgment in the present case directed that execution be carried into effect, that sale by auction of Henderson's property be made and with the proceeds payment made to the plaintiff of the principal, interest and costs. Such a judgment, in the opinion of the Spanish lawyers, made Henderson personally, as well as his estate, responsible for payment.

North J. decided in favour of the plaintiff and found that the judgment or decree of the 5th of April 1878 was a judgment upon which the plaintiff's claim could apart from the question of fraud be sustained[4].

The Court of Appeal (Cotton, Lindley and Lopes L.JJ.) reversed that decision[5].

Nov. 21. *Napier Higgins Q.C. and Finlay Q.C.* (*Yate Lee* with them) for the appellant:—

The Court of Appeal took an erroneous view of the nature of the "remate" judgment, which they held was not final and conclusive. Henderson had contracted to make himself liable to be sued in Spain in an "executive" action, that is in a summary manner. In that action he could not raise the defence of fraud or certain other defences: but there were defences which he could set up, such as payment. The judgment in that action made Henderson the plaintiff's debtor: the plaintiff was a judgment creditor for the amount recovered and costs. That judgment was final and conclusive: it was an end of the proceedings. True, the defendant might have brought a "plenary" or "ordinary" or "declaratory" action, a substantive independent suit, in which he could have raised the only case he professed to have, that of fraud. But he could not by any such proceedings stop or embarrass the "remate" judgment. The only way to stop the "remate" judgment was by appealing against it and compelling the plaintiff to give security for repayment if the "remate" judgment should be reversed. But that would not stop execution. Judgment in a "plenary" action would no doubt neutralise or paralyse the "remate" judgment, but the "remate" judgment would nevertheless remain. The nearest analogy in our law is to be found in the practice before the Judicature Acts, when a judgment in a common law action having been obtained the plaintiff might be restrained by the Court of Chancery from enforcing his judgment. But such a judgment would certainly be "final and conclusive."

The respondents did institute "ordinary" proceedings in Spain, and the Spanish Court appears to have held that those proceedings were not affected by the pendency of the present action in England. That decision was affirmed in Spain on appeal, and since then nothing has been done in the "ordinary" proceedings. The plaintiff having got the "remate" judgment could not, it is contended—though this is perhaps not clear upon the evidence—himself have brought "ordinary" proceedings: and if he could, it would have been unjust and oppressive. At the most the "remate" judgment was conditional or defeasible. But that does not prevent its being final and conclusive. The mere fact that the judgment is conditional is no reason why it should not be enforced here if the defeasance has not happened. And if the plaintiff got judgment in the present action and the defendants succeeded in their "ordinary" proceedings in Spain the judgment in the present action could be stayed here by some proceedings in the nature of the obsolete auditâ querelâ. The pendency of an appeal in the foreign Court, it is well settled, is no bar to an action here on the foreign judgment: Scott v. Pilkington[6]. Then why should the possibility of "plenary" proceedings be a bar? The foreign judgment created a personal obligation, and not merely a remedy against the property. That being so, this case comes within the principle that where a Court of competent jurisdiction adjudges a sum of money to be paid, an obligation to pay it is created, and an action of debt may be brought here upon the judgment: Williams v. Jones[7] per Parke and Alderson BB. The "remate" judgment is not like an interlocutory order, which cannot be enforced here because it is merely interim and is subject to revision by the same Court in the same proceedings: see Patrick v. Shedden[8]. The respondents are not in any way prejudiced by the present action. They can raise here their only defence, viz. fraud, for the issue directed expressly saves that question. Suppose the time for bringing "ordinary" proceedings had expired, clearly the "remate" judgment could be sued on here. Then why can it not, subject to the liability of having "ordinary" proceedings brought? And if the respondents succeeded in their "ordinary" proceedings they could obtain a stay of execution here. All that the plaintiff asks is to be placed in the same position here as in Spain, and to have execution here unless the "remate" judgment is properly set aside. In any event the judgment for costs in the "executive" action can be sued on here, and that will be sufficient to maintain this action: Russell v. Smyth[9].

[They also referred to Copin v. Adamson[10] and the cases cited in the decisions below.]

Rigby Q.C. Kenelm E. Digby and *J. D. Davenport* for the respondents were not heard.

Nov. 22. LORD HERSCHELL:—

My Lords, this appeal arises in an action brought by the appellant, the plaintiff below, for the administration of the estate of a deceased gentleman named Henderson. In order to found his claim to an order for the administration of that estate it became necessary for him to shew that he was a creditor of the deceased. The case presented by him for the purpose of making that out was that he had obtained a judgment of a foreign Court upon which he was entitled to sue in this country, and which in this country established the existence of a debt. Under those circumstances the Court ordered that there should be first tried the issue, "whether the judgment or decree" upon which he relied, one pronounced on the 5th of April 1878, "and the other judgments or decrees whereof particulars have been delivered, or any and which of them, are orders or judgments upon which the claim of the plaintiff in this action or some and what part of it can be sustained."

It appears that Mr. Henderson, the administration of whose estate is in question, had purchased certain properties in the district of Seville of the plaintiff, Mr. Nouvion, and that the deeds by which these properties were conveyed, and which contained an obligation to make certain payments, were registered in the registry of the district of San Roman, and where deeds of that description are so registered, according to the law of Spain, the person who is entitled to payment under them can obtain what is called an "executive" judgment.

It is necessary to state distinctly what the nature of that judgment is; because I think it will be found that the decision of your Lordships must be determined by that consideration. In an action of this nature only a very limited number of defences can be raised by the person sued. He cannot impeach the instruments upon which the action is founded or shew that they were obtained by fraud, or that on any other ground they did not properly form the basis of an obligation on his part. He can only defend himself by such defences as are open to him on the assumption that the deeds were valid, and in the first instance did create the obligation. He may shew that there has been a waiver, or that he has discharged the obligation by payment or otherwise, but substantially I think those are the only defences open to him. It is open to either of the parties to such an instrument to sue in the same Court in another form of action, which is called a declaratory or plenary action, and which is said to be the ordinary course, not as meaning that the other is a course which can only be taken under exceptional circumstances, but that the one conforms to the general and ordinary rules of procedure in an action in the Spanish Courts, and that the other is a special procedure allowed in particular cases. In such a plenary action, to which either of the parties may have recourse, every defence which may be available is open as well as every consideration establishing the ground of action; and such a plenary action may be instituted by either of the parties to the executive action; that is to say, the party against whom the decision has been pronounced in the executive action, be he plaintiff or defendant, is at perfect liberty to sue in a plenary action for the purpose of obtaining a declaration of the rights of the parties; and in such a plenary action the fact that a judgment has been delivered in an executive action cannot be set up as at all affecting the rights of the parties, either in the way of proof or of title to succeed in the plenary action. The same points which have been decided in the executive action can again be raised, in the plenary action, as well as other questions which were not open in the executive action. No effect is given, in the Court in which it was pronounced and in which afterwards the plenary action may be pending, to the judgment in the executive action as being res judicata and as finally concluding the rights of the parties upon any point whatever.

My Lords, in the present case the plaintiff, Mr. Nouvion, who was a party to the agreements which I have mentioned, and which had been duly registered, brought an executive action, and in that executive action a decree was pronounced in these terms: "Let an order of execution be issued against the property and goods of Mr. William Henderson for the principal amount of 697,135 reales, 60 centimos, and also for the amount of the legal interests thereon from the date of default being made by not meeting" certain drafts which are there mentioned.

It appears that owing to the absence of Mr. Henderson from Spain it became necessary, in accordance with the procedure of the Spanish Courts, to send letters requisitorial to this country, that is to say, to Scotland, where Mr. Henderson was resident, and to obtain from the Spanish consul in Scotland a return to those letters, which intimated that Mr. Henderson had not discharged, as he would then have had an opportunity of doing, the liability which was declared by the judgment. Thereupon Mr. Henderson having intervened and having alleged that the debt was not due by reason of a promise of the plaintiff not to sue him, and that point having been decided against him, a decree was made, which I think may properly be termed a final decree in that action, that the distraint be carried into effect, "and in virtue thereof sale by auction be made of the property attached, and out of the proceeds thereof entire and complete payment to the executive plaintiff of the amount of the principal demanded" with interest and costs.

My Lords, the plaintiff relies upon that judgment as being sufficient to entitle him, when he sues upon it in the Courts of this country, to a judgment for the amount of the debt for which it was ordered that execution should issue, and the only question in this case is whether, under the circumstances which I have mentioned, that judgment is sufficient to entitle him in the courts of this country to a judgment for his debt as being a creditor of the deceased person, Mr. Henderson.

Now, my Lords, there can be no doubt that in the courts of this country effect will be given to a foreign judgment. It is unnecessary to inquire upon what principle the Courts proceed in giving effect to such a judgment, and in treating it as sufficient to establish the debt. Reliance was placed upon a dictum by Parke B. and Alderson B. in the case of Williams v. Jones[11], where the law is thus stated: "Where a Court of competent jurisdiction has adjudicated a certain sum to be due from one person to another, a legal obligation arises to pay that sum, on which an action of debt to enforce the judgment may be maintained." But it was conceded, and necessarily conceded, by the learned counsel for the appellant, that a judgment, to come within the terms of the law as properly laid down, must be a judgment which results from an adjudication of a Court of competent jurisdiction, such judgment being final and conclusive. I shall of course have something to say upon the meaning which must be given to those words, but the general proposition in that form is not disputed by the learned counsel for the appellant. They contend that this judgment is final and conclusive, and no doubt in a certain sense that must be conceded. It puts an end to and absolutely concludes that particular action. About that there can be no manner of doubt—in that sense it is final and conclusive. But the same may be said of some interlocutory judgments upon which there can be no question that an action could not be maintained; they do settle and conclude the particular proceeding, the interlocutory proceeding, in which the judgment is pronounced. It is obvious, therefore, that the mere fact that the judgment puts an end to and finally settles the controversy which arose in the particular proceeding, is not of itself sufficient to make it a final and conclusive judgment upon which an action may be maintained in the Courts of this country, when such judgment has been pronounced by a foreign Court.

My Lords, I think that in order to establish that such a judgment has been pronounced it must be shewn that in the Court by which it was pronounced it conclusively, finally, and for ever established the existence of the debt of which it is sought to be made conclusive evidence in this country, so as to make it res judicata between the parties. If it is not conclusive in the same Court which pronounced it, so that notwithstanding such a judgment the existence of the debt may between the same parties be afterwards contested in that Court, and upon proper proceedings being taken and such contest being adjudicated upon, it may be declared that there existed no obligation to pay the debt at all, then I do not think that a judgment which is of that character can be regarded as finally and conclusively evidencing the debt, and so entitling the person who has obtained the judgment to claim a decree from our Courts for the payment of that debt.

The principle upon which I think our enforcement of foreign judgments must proceed is this: that in a Court of competent jurisdiction, where according to its established procedure the whole merits of the case were open, at all events, to the parties, however much they may have failed to take advantage of them, or may have waived any of their rights, a final adjudication has been given that a debt or obligation exists which cannot thereafter in that Court be disputed, and can only be questioned in an appeal to a higher tribunal. In such a case it may well be said that giving credit to the Courts of another country we are prepared to take the fact that such adjudication has been made as establishing the existence of the debt or obligation. But where, as in the present case, the adjudication is consistent with the non-existence of the debt or obligation which it is sought to enforce, and it may thereafter be declared by the tribunal which pronounced it that there is no obligation and no debt, it appears to me that the very foundation upon which the Courts of this country would proceed in enforcing a foreign judgment altogether fails.

It has been suggested that a judgment obtained in an "executive" action may be regarded as analogous to a judgment obtained in a common law action in the time prior to the Judicature Act , the execution of which might be restrained by a Court of Equity, so as to prevent the plaintiff who had succeeded in such an action from obtaining the fruits of his judgment. I do not think that such an analogy is a complete one; but even if it were more complete than I think it to be, it appears to me that it would afford very little assistance to your Lordships unless we could know what had been the course adopted with regard to such judgments in countries in whose system of law the same force and effect are given to foreign judgments as are given in the Courts of this country. Upon that point we have had no information whatsoever.

Then, my Lords, it is said that such a judgment is analogous to a judgment which has been obtained upon which a suit may be instituted in the Courts of this country, even although an appeal may be pending. It appears to me that there is a vital distinction between the two cases. Although an appeal may be pending, a Court of competent jurisdiction has finally and conclusively determined the existence of a debt, and it has none the less done so because the right of appeal has been given whereby a superior Court may overrule that decision. There exists at the time of the suit a judgment which must be assumed to be valid until interfered with by a higher tribunal, and which conclusively establishes the existence of the debt which is sought to be recovered in this country. That appears to me to be in altogether a different position from a "remate" judgment, where the very Court which pronounced the "remate" judgment (not the Court of Appeal) may determine, if proper proceedings are taken, that the debt for which this "remate" judgment is sought to be used as conclusive evidence has no existence at all.

My Lords, the plaintiff in such a suit, an executive suit, is not, by the decision which is now under appeal, deprived of his rights. He may still sue upon the original cause of action. Of course it may happen, as in this particular case, that such a suit is barred by lapse of time, but that is an accident. The right of the plaintiff to sue on his original cause of action is not at all interfered with by the judgment which has been pronounced; and in such an action, if it were brought, all questions upon which the rights of the parties depend, and by the solution of which the obligation to pay must ultimately be determined, would be open to consideration and could be dealt with by the Courts, and finally and conclusively settled. I do not, therefore, see that there is any wrong or any hardship done by holding that a judgment which does not conclusively and for ever as between the parties establish the existence of a debt in that Court cannot be looked upon as sufficient evidence of it in the Courts of this country.

Very ingenious arguments have been urged upon your Lordships by the learned counsel for the appellant, and they have strenuously contended that the proper course would be to permit such a judgment to be sued upon and that justice might be done by staying proceedings as might be done in the case of an English judgment sued upon, which was under appeal.

But no authority has been cited, no case has been referred to, which supports the view put forward on the part of the appellant that an action upon such a judgment as this could be maintained, and I certainly cannot advise your Lordships to make such a precedent, because it appears to me, after giving due weight to all the arguments of the learned counsel for the appellant, that on the whole the result would as a general rule be likely to be mischievous and to work injustice rather than justice between the parties.

For these reasons I move your Lordships that the judgment appealed from be affirmed, and the appeal dismissed with costs.

LORD WATSON:—

My Lords, this case has been very ably argued for the appellant. But the reasons assigned for the judgment of the Court of Appeal are to my mind so satisfactory that I agree with your Lordships in thinking it ought not to be disturbed.

That the Court of Seville had jurisdiction to determine all questions competently raised between these parties, when duly convened before it, in relation either to the constitution or subsistence of the contract upon which the appellant relies—and also that the Courts of England would recognise and give full effect to any final and conclusive judgment of the Spanish Court upon these questions—are propositions neither disputed by the respondents nor controverted in the opinions delivered by the learned judges of the Appeal Court. The only question which the facts of this case present for decision is, Whether the decree of the 5th of April 1878, obtained by the appellant in what is termed an "executive" proceeding, comes within the principle established by decisions comparatively recent, of which Godard v. Gray[12] and Schibsby v. Westenholz[13] are leading examples.

The decree of the 5th of April 1878 appears to me to be deficient in certain particulars which are necessary in order to bring it within that principle. It is not necessarily a decision which exhausts the merits of the controversy between the parties, because in "executive" proceedings the Court can entertain no plea stated by the defendant which does not go to payment, satisfaction, or waiver of the plaintiff's claim. What, in my opinion, constitutes a still graver defect is the fact that the same Court which issued the "executive" decree has jurisdiction, in an "ordinary" or "plenary" action, to entertain and dispose of any and every plea which the original defendant may think fit to urge against his liability, and in that action can re-try those pleas which have already been put forward and repelled in the "executive" suit. If the decision of the Court in the "plenary" differs, in whole or in part, from that pronounced by it in the "executive" suit, the latter is, to the extent of that difference, superseded or nullified.

The English cases to which I have already referred establish a more liberal rule in regard to the enforcement of foreign judgments than is to be found in the older authorities; but no decision has been cited to the effect that an English Court is bound to give effect to a foreign decree which is liable to be abrogated or varied by the same Court which issued it. All the authorities cited appear to me, when fairly read, to assume that the decree which was given effect to had been pronounced causâ cognitâ, and that it was unnecessary to inquire into the merits of the controversy between the litigants, either because these had already been investigated and decided by the foreign tribunal, or because the defendant had due opportunity of submitting for decision all the pleas which he desired to state in defence. In order to its receiving effect here, a foreign decree need not be final in the sense that it cannot be made the subject of appeal to a higher Court; but it must be final and unalterable in the Court which pronounced it; and if appealable the English Court will only enforce it, subject to conditions which will save the interests of those who have the right of appeal. The case of Patrick v. Shedden[14] appears to me to be very much akin to the present. There the executive decree of the Court of Session for costs was final in this sense that it was not appealable, and that it was enforceable in Scotland; but the Court of Queen's Bench refused to recognise it as a final and conclusive judgment, mainly on the ground that it might be at any time recalled or modified by the Court of Session on just cause shewn. In my opinion there is no real difference, in principle, between the case of a Court retaining power to alter a decree by an order in the same suit, and the case of its retaining power to defeat the operation of that decree by an order pronounced in another suit relating to the same debt.

I accordingly concur in the judgment proposed.

LORD BRAMWELL:—

My Lords, I think this judgment should be affirmed. I think the proceeding in the Spanish Court which is relied on was final to this extent, that no further proceedings could be taken on it; and I think, also, that it was a personal judgment, as far as such a judgment could be personal; but I also think I am right in reading it, not as a judgment that a debt is due, but as an order that execution do issue. Then, my Lords, if so, this is what I may call, for want of a better expression, a defeasible judgment—that is to say, the defendants who are subject to the order that execution may issue, may take proceedings which would have the effect of defeating or nullifying or making an end of the judgment or order which has been pronounced that execution may issue. It seems to me that that is not such a judgment as can be (to use the old-fashioned expression which Baron Parke used) the subject of an action of debt—that is to say, now that we have got rid of the forms of action, the subject of an action in a court in this country. Whether what is called the comity of nations had anything to do with the matter, I do not know; nor do I think it material. Baron Parke, in the judgment he pronounced, does not refer to the comity of nations as a reason, but he speaks of foreign judgments, and of colonial judgments, and of judgments of inferior Courts; and he seems to consider that where the judgment of a competent Court has been given it shews that there is a debt, and that that being so, there is a legal obligation on the part of the person against whom it was decreed or adjudged that there was a debt, to pay it. But, my Lords, how is that applicable to a case of this description? How can it be said that there is a legal obligation on the part of a man to pay a debt who has a right to say, "I owe none, and no judgment has established against me that I do?" I cannot see. On this ground, it seems to me that this judgment ought to be affirmed.

There are however, my Lords, one or two other observations I should like to make. It was said that the argument I am now using would equally apply to all cases where there was a possibility of error being brought. Not so. There is no presumption that error may exist in the proceedings; the presumption is the other way: the presumption is that a Court of competent jurisdiction has given a right judgment. But there is no such presumption here; on the contrary, we learn that it is possible, not merely that what was decided in the Court may be nullified, but that there may be questions raised between the parties which could not be decided in the former proceeding. There is an essential difference, therefore, between the case where a Court of competent jurisdiction has entertained all the controversies between the parties which they could and chose to raise, and come to a conclusion, which is to be presumed to be accurate, and this case where there is no ground for saying that all possible controversies between the parties have been decided.

Then, my Lords, another argument that was urged was this; it was said, "Why, if this reason is a good one, there never was a judgment in an English Court upon which an action ought to have been maintainable, because it was always possible that it might be nullified by proceedings in equity." Really I do not think any argument can be founded upon what I may take the liberty now of calling the preposterous condition of things that existed in England before the Judicature Act , where one Court gave a final judgment finding a debt due, or damages due, or what not, and another Court with the same Judge said, "Well, that is all very well; I gave judgment for you yesterday and it was perfectly right in point of law; but if you, the plaintiff, in whose favour I gave it, enforce it, I will put you in prison." I think that some twenty or thirty years hence, when the present generation of lawyers have ceased to exist and there is another one, it will scarcely be believed that such a state of things did exist in a civilized country. I do not say this for the purpose of finding fault with that state of things, which is now, happily, at an end; and which was brought about, I daresay, by persons who had very sincere desires to improve the jurisprudence of the country; but I say it for this purpose, that I do not think you can found any argument upon such a condition of things as then existed.

There was a matter brought forward prominently by my noble and learned friend on my left (Lord Ashbourne) which I think is entitled to consideration; and that was, that if we should give judgment for this plaintiff here he would be better off than he would be if there were a mere affirmance of the judgment with all its consequences in Spain, because in Spain the judgment that he has got is liable to be defeated; but if judgment were given for him here, there would not be that liability to be defeated by proceedings being taken here analogous to the plenary proceedings in Spain. It occurred to me that perhaps that might be met in this way. If a judgment in a foreign court were reversed upon error, and an action upon the judgment had been brought in an English court and judgment given in that action on the judgment, then afterwards, when the original judgment was reversed upon error, I suppose there would, in such a case as that, be some remedy for the defendant who had got rid of the first judgment against him. The remedy of auditâ querelâ is now abolished, but there is a rule which says that the Court may give relief (I should suppose that would mean that they must give relief) where the defendant would have got relief upon auditâ querelâ. But the answer is, it is not the same thing. He would have a judgment against him in the Spanish Court which he would have to get rid of; and then he would have to come to England to get rid of the judgment here by proceedings in the nature of the old-fashioned auditâ querelâ. I think, therefore, he would be worse off if judgment were given against him, as is prayed in this action, than he is at present by the proceedings in Spain. It perhaps is not of any very great consequence; but I think it is worth mentioning for the purpose of shewing that we are not dealing with a judgment like a judgment in proceedings where all the questions can be gone into, which is presumably right, and which has decided all the possible controversies that the parties have thought fit to bring before the Court.

Upon these grounds, my Lords, I think this judgment should be affirmed.

LORD ASHBOURNE:—

My Lords, I also am of opinion that the judgment under appeal is correct and should be affirmed. The reasons which have led me to that conclusion have already been expressed by such of your Lordships as have spoken.

My Lords, it is conceded—there is no controversy—that a foreign judgment will not be upheld in this country and made the foundation of relief here, unless it is final and conclusive. That has been treated as axiomatic in the arguments on both sides, and in the judgment of North, J., and in all the judgments of the learned judges who sat in the Court of Appeal. The sole controversy in law before us and before those tribunals was: Is this a judgment which can be regarded as coming within the definition of a final and conclusive judgment?

I entirely concur that in a sense this may be regarded as a final judgment, but only in a limited and narrow sense. It is a summary judgment, it is an executive judgment, it is a "remate" judgment. In its terms there is nothing to contradict the fact that there has been a final judgment; but then it is a judgment upon a claim which could only be encountered by a certain limited number of pleas of a certain prescribed and definite character. It was not a judgment upon a claim which could be met by pleas upon the merits, going exhaustively into all the topics upon which the defendant was entitled to rely if he had the wide scope open to him which in any plenary suit a litigant would have. Therefore in no sense can this be regarded as an adjudication in a cause where the merits were, or where they could be, tried; and I am not aware of a single precedent where in this country effect has been given to a foreign judgment so obtained. No such case has been suggested in the course of the argument, and none was suggested in the courts below. This is a peculiar judgment. There is no analogy to it that I know of in our law; none has been stated. Cases were mentioned as approximations to an analogy; but no judgment known to our law or to the law of Scotland has been suggested which is at all really analogous to this peculiar form of "remate" judgment, which may be nullified, which may be paralysed, which may be reduced to a state of absolutely worthless paper by a proceeding in which the merits can be gone into. We are really asked to say that this judgment shall be accepted by our laws as final and conclusive, when the laws of Spain itself, which produced the judgment, say that it is one which is so little final and conclusive that it may be absolutely swept away when proceedings come before the Court in which the merits can be gone into.

My Lords, it would be, I venture to think, a very startling result if in this country we should hold this executive, summary, "remate" judgment to be final and conclusive, while in the municipal institutions of the country which has sent out this judgment it would not even be regarded as res judicata. That is a point referred to with force and persuasiveness in the arguments addressed to the Court below, and strongly in the judgment of Lindley L.J., and I adopt everything that he said. It strikes my mind as being to the last degree surprising to listen to a suggestion that when the laws of Spain do not regard this judgment as of such a binding character that it can be relied upon in any proceeding as res judicata, the very minute the intervention of a foreign country is invoked it becomes so sacrosanct that it is to be regarded by us as final and conclusive. It appears to me to be almost a contradiction in terms to make the suggestion.

For these reasons, my Lords, I entirely concur in the decision at which your Lordships have arrived.

Representation

1. Solicitors for appellant: Ewbank & Partington.

2. Solicitors for respondents: Freeman & Bothamley.

Order appealed from affirmed and appeal dismissed with costs. Lords' Journals 22nd November 1889.

---

1.   37 Ch. D. 244 .

2.   35 Ch. D. 704 .

3.   35 Ch. D. 707 .

4.   35 Ch. D. 704 .

5.   37 Ch. D. 244 .

6.   2 B. & S. 11 , 38, 41.

7.   13 M. & W. 628 , 633, 634.

8.   2 E. & B. 14 .

9.   9 M. & W. 810 .

10.   Law Rep. 9 Ex. 345; 1 Ex. D. 17 .

11.   13 M. & W. 628 , 633.

12.   Law Rep. 6 Q. B. 139 .

13.   Law Rep. 6 Q. B. 155 .

14.   2 E. & B. 14 .

附錄二

《關於內地與香港特別行政區法院相互認可和執行當事人協議管轄的民商事案件判決的安排》

最高人民法院關於內地與香港特別行政區
法院相互認可和執行當事人協議管轄的
民商事案件判決的安排

（2006 年 6 月 12 日最高人民法院審判委員會第 1390 次會議通過法釋
[2008]9 號）

根據《中華人民共和國香港特別行政區基本法》第九十五條的規定，
最高人民法院與香港特別行政區政府經協商，現就當事人協議管轄的民商
事案件判決的認可和執行問題作出如下安排：

第一條　內地人民法院和香港特別行政區法院在具有書面管轄協議的
民商事案件中作出的須支付款項的具有執行力的終審判決，當事人可以根
據本安排向內地人民法院或者香港特別行政區法院申請認可和執行。

第二條　本安排所稱「具有執行力的終審判決」：

（一）在內地是指：

1. 最高人民法院的判決；

2. 高級人民法院、中級人民法院以及經授權管轄第一審涉外、涉港澳
臺民商事案件的基層人民法院（名單附後）依法不准上訴或者已經超過法
定期限沒有上訴的第一審判決，第二審判決和依照審判監督程序由上一級
人民法院提審後作出的生效判決。

（二）在香港特別行政區是指終審法院、高等法院上訴法庭及原訟法
庭和區域法院作出的生效判決。

本安排所稱判決，在內地包括判決書、裁定書、調解書、支付令；在
香港特別行政區包括判決書、命令和訴訟費評定證明書。

當事人向香港特別行政區法院申請認可和執行判決後，內地人民法院
對該案件依法再審的，由作出生效判決的上一級人民法院提審。

第三條　本安排所稱「書面管轄協議」，是指當事人為解決與特定法
律關係有關的已經發生或者可能發生的爭議，自本安排生效之日起，以書

面形式明確約定內地人民法院或者香港特別行政區法院具有唯一管轄權的協議。

本條所稱「特定法律關係」，是指當事人之間的民商事合同，不包括僱傭合同以及自然人因個人消費、家庭事宜或者其他非商業目的而作為協議一方的合同。

本條所稱「書面形式」是指合同書、信件和數據電文（包括電報、電傳、傳真、電子數據交換和電子郵件）等可以有形地表現所載內容、可以調取以備日後查用的形式。

書面管轄協議可以由一份或者多份書面形式組成。

除非合同另有規定，合同中的管轄協議條款獨立存在，合同的變更、解除、終止或者無效，不影響管轄協議條款的效力。

第四條　申請認可和執行符合本安排規定的民商事判決，在內地向被申請人住所地、經常居住地或者財產所在地的中級人民法院提出，在香港特別行政區向香港特別行政區高等法院提出。

第五條　被申請人住所地、經常居住地或者財產所在地在內地不同的中級人民法院轄區的，申請人應當選擇向其中一個人民法院提出認可和執行的申請，不得分別向兩個或者兩個以上人民法院提出申請。

被申請人的住所地、經常居住地或者財產所在地，既在內地又在香港特別行政區的，申請人可以同時分別向兩地法院提出申請，兩地法院分別執行判決的總額，不得超過判決確定的數額。已經部份或者全部執行判決的法院應當根據對方法院的要求提供已執行判決的情況。

第六條　申請人向有關法院申請認可和執行判決的，應當提交以下文件：

（一）　請求認可和執行的申請書；

（二）　經作出終審判決的法院蓋章的判決書副本；

（三）作出終審判決的法院出具的證明書，證明該判決屬本安排第二條所指的終審判決，在判決作出地可以執行；

（四）身份證明材料：

1. 申請人為自然人的，應當提交身份證或者經公證的身份證複印件；

2. 申請人為法人或者其他組織的，應當提交經公證的法人或者其他組織註冊登記證書的複印件；

3. 申請人是外國籍法人或者其他組織的，應當提交相應的公證和認證材料。

向內地人民法院提交的文件沒有中文文本的，申請人應當提交證明無誤的中文譯本。

執行地法院對於本條所規定的法院出具的證明書，無需另行要求公證。

第七條　請求認可和執行申請書應當載明下列事項：

（一）當事人為自然人的，其姓名、住所；當事人為法人或者其他組織的，法人或者其他組織的名稱、住所以及法定代表人或者主要負責人的姓名、職務和住所；

（二）申請執行的理由與請求的內容，被申請人的財產所在地以及財產狀況；

（三）判決是否在原審法院地申請執行以及已執行的情況。

第八條　「申請人申請認可和執行內地人民法院或者香港特別行政區法院判決的程序，依據執行地法律的規定。本安排另有規定的除外。

申請人申請認可和執行的期間為二年。

前款規定的期間，內地判決到香港特別行政區申請執行的，從判決規定履行期間的最後一日起計算，判決規定分期履行的，從規定的每次履行期間的最後一日起計算，判決未規定履行期間的，從判決生效之日起計算；香港特別行政區判決到內地申請執行的，從判決可強制執行之日起計算，該日為判決上註明的判決日期，判決對履行期間另有規定的，從規定的履行期間屆滿後開始計算。

第九條　對申請認可和執行的判決，原審判決中的債務人提供證據證明有下列情形之一的，受理申請的法院經審查核實，應當裁定不予認可和執行：

（一）根據當事人協議選擇的原審法院地的法律，管轄協議屬無效。但選擇法院已經判定該管轄協議為有效的除外；

（二）判決已獲完全履行；

（三）根據執行地的法律，執行地法院對該案享有專屬管轄權；

（四）根據原審法院地的法律，未曾出庭的敗訴一方當事人未經合法傳喚或者雖經合法傳喚但未獲依法律規定的答辯時間。但原審法院根據其法律或者有關規定公告送達的，不屬上述情形；

（五）判決是以欺詐方法取得的；

（六）執行地法院就相同訴訟請求作出判決，或者外國、境外地區法院就相同訴訟請求作出判決，或者有關仲裁機構作出仲裁裁決，已經為執行地法院所認可或者執行的。

內地人民法院認為在內地執行香港特別行政區法院判決違反內地社會公共利益，或者香港特別行政區法院認為在香港特別行政區執行內地人民法院判決違反香港特別行政區公共政策的，不予認可和執行。

第十條　對於香港特別行政區法院作出的判決，判決確定的債務人已經提出上訴，或者上訴程序尚未完結的，內地人民法院審查核實後，可以中止認可和執行程序。經上訴，維持全部或者部份原判決的，恢復認可和執行程序；完全改變原判決的，終止認可和執行程序。

內地地方人民法院就已經作出的判決按照審判監督程序作出提審裁定，或者最高人民法院作出提起再審裁定的，香港特別行政區法院審查核實後，可以中止認可和執行程序。再審判決維持全部或者部份原判決的，恢復認可和執行程序；再審判決完全改變原判決的，終止認可和執行程序。

第十一條　根據本安排而獲認可的判決與執行地法院的判決效力相同。

第十二條　當事人對認可和執行與否的裁定不服的，在內地可以向上一級人民法院申請覆議，在香港特別行政區可以根據其法律規定提出上訴。

第十三條　在法院受理當事人申請認可和執行判決期間，當事人依相同事實再行提起訴訟的，法院不予受理。

已獲認可和執行的判決，當事人依相同事實再行提起訴訟的，法院不予受理。

對於根據本安排第九條不予認可和執行的判決，申請人不得再行提起認可和執行的申請，但是可以按照執行地的法律依相同案件事實向執行地法院提起訴訟。

第十四條　法院受理認可和執行判決的申請之前或者之後，可以按照執行地法律關於財產保全或者禁制資產轉移的規定，根據申請人的申請，對被申請人的財產採取保全或強制措施。

第十五條　當事人向有關法院申請執行判決，應當根據執行地有關訴訟收費的法律和規定交納執行費或者法院費用。

第十六條　內地與香港特別行政區法院相互認可和執行的標的範圍，除判決確定的數額外，還包括根據該判決須支付的利息、經法院核定的律師費以及訴訟費，但不包括稅收和罰款。

在香港特別行政區訴訟費是指經法官或者司法常務官在訴訟費評定證明書中核定或者命令支付的訴訟費用。

第十七條　內地與香港特別行政區法院自本安排生效之日（含本日）起作出的判決，適用本安排。

第十八條　本安排在執行過程中遇有問題或者需要修改，由最高人民法院和香港特別行政區政府協商解決。

附錄三

《內地判決（交互強制執行）條例》
（香港法例第 597 章）

第 597 章《內地判決（交互強制執行）條例》02/08/2008

本條例旨在施行由中華人民共和國最高人民法院與香港特別行政區政府訂立、並經不時修訂的《關於內地與香港特別行政區法院相互認可和執行當事人管轄的民商事案件判決的安排》，並為該目的訂定條文，使內地在民事或商業事宜中作出的判決可以在香港強制執行，及利便香港在民事或商業事宜中作出的判決在內地強制執行；以及為相關事宜訂定條文。

[2008 年 8 月 1 日] 2008 年第 195 號法律公告

第 1 部 導言

1. 簡稱及生效日期

(1)　本條例可引稱為《內地判決（交互強制執行）條例》。

(2)　（已失時效而略去）

2. 釋義

在本條例中，除文意另有所指外 ——

「已登記判決」（registered judgment）指已根據第 5(2) 條登記的內地判決；

「內地」（Mainland）指中國的任何部份，但不包括香港、澳門及台灣；

「內地判決」（Mainland judgment）指指定法院在民事或商業事宜中作出的判決書、裁定書、調解書或繳付令；

「判定債務人」（judgment debtor）指在內地判決中被判敗訴的人，在該判決根據內地法律可針對某人執行的情況下，亦包括該人；

「判定債權人」（judgment creditor）指在內地判決中獲判勝訴的人，並包括屬該判決所賦權利藉繼承、轉讓或其他途徑而轉歸的對象的人；

「指明合約」（specified contract）指下述合約以外的合約 ——

(a)　僱傭合約；及

(b)　自然人因個人消費、家庭事宜或其他非商業目的而作為合約一方的合約；

　　　「指定法院」（designated court）指附表 1 指明的內地法院；

「香港判決」（Hong Kong judgment）包括香港法院在民事或商業事宜中作出的任何判決、命令及訟費評定證明書；

「原審法院」（original court）就任何內地判決而言，指作出該判決的指定法院；

「認可基層人民法院」（recognized Basic People's Court）指不時根據第 25(1) 條在憲報公佈的清單中指明的任何基層人民法院；

「選用內地法院協議」（choice of Mainland court agreement）具有第 3(2) 條給予該詞的涵義；

「選用法院」（chosen court）指在選用內地法院協議或選用香港法院協議（視屬何情況而定）中指明的作為裁定該協議所適用的爭議的法院，如協議指明多於一所法院，則指其中任何一所法院。

「選用香港法院協議」（choice of Hong Kong court agreement）具有第 3(1) 條給予該詞的涵義。

3. 「選用香港法院協議」和「選用內地法院協議」的涵義

(1) 在本條例中，在第 (3) 及 (4) 款的規限下，「選用香港法院協議」（choice of Hong Kong court agreement）指由指明合約的各方訂立的協議，該協議指明由香港法院或某香港法院裁定在或可能在與該指明合約有關連的情況下產生的爭議，而其他司法管轄區的法院則無權處理該等爭議。

(2) 在本條例中，在第 (3) 及 (4) 款的規限下，「選用內地法院協議」（choice of Mainland court agreement）指由指明合約的各方訂立的協議，該協議指明由內地法院或某內地法院裁定在或可能在與該指明合約有關連的情況下產生的爭議，而其他司法管轄區的法院則無權處理該等爭議。

(3) 除非某協議是 ——

(a) 以書面訂立或證明；

(b) 以任何電子形式（包括電子數據訊息、電報、電傳、圖文傳真電子數據交換或電子郵件）訂立或證明，而藉該電子形式，該協議能夠以可見形式展示以及資料可查閱，以供日後參閱之用；或

(c) 以 (a) 及 (b) 段描述的形式的任何組合訂立或證明，否則第 (1) 及 (2) 款不適用於該協議。

第 (1) 及 (2) 款適用於不論是以一份或若干份文件訂立或證明的協議。

4. 選用香港法院協議及選用內地法院協議的可分割性

除非各方訂立的指明合約另有規定，否則作為該合約一部份的選用香港法院協議或選用內地法院協議，須為本條例的目的被視為獨立於該合約的其他條款，而該協議的有效性並不受該合約的任何變更、解除、終止或無效所影響。

第 2 部 申請在香港登記內地判決

5. 登記內地判決的申請

(1) 　內地判決的判定債權人可在第 7 條指明的期限內，向原訟法庭提出申請，將該判決在原訟法庭登記。

(2) 　有關內地判決按照本條例登記，該等規定為 ——

(a) 　該判決是在本條例生效當日或之後，由 ——

(i) 　屬指定法院的選用法院作出的；

(ii) 　指定法院對根據內地法律自選用法院移送的案件作出的；

(iii) 　指定法院應任何就下述法院對案件所作判決提出的上訴而作出的 ——

(A) 　選用法院；或

(B) 　根據內地法律獲選用法院移送案件的法院；或

(iv) 　指定法院對經下述法院審訊的案件進行再審而作出的 ——

(A) 　選用法院；或

(B) 　根據內地法律獲選用法院移送案件的法院；

(b) 　有關的選用內地法院協議是在本條例生效當日或之後訂立的；

(c) 　該判決對判決各方而言，是最終及不可推翻的判決；

(d) 　該判決是可以在內地執行的；及

(e) 　該判決飭令繳付一筆款項（該筆款項是既非須就稅款或類似性質的其他收費而繳付，亦非須就罰款或其他罰則而繳付的）。

6. 內地判決的終局性

(1) 　如某內地判決 ——

(a) 　是由最高人民法院作出的；

(b) 是由高級人民法院、中級人民法院或認可基層人民法院作出的第一審判決，而──

(i) 按照內地法律，該判決是不准上訴的；或

(ii) 按照內地法律，該判決的上訴期限經已屆滿，並且沒有上訴提出；

(c) 是由不屬認可基層人民法院的指定法院作出的第二審判決；或

(d) 是由指定法院在因下級法院所作判決而引致的再審中作出的，則為施行第 5(2)(c) 條，該判決對判決各方而言，是最終及不可推翻的判決。

(2) 如原審法院發出證明書，證明某內地判決在內地是最終並且是可以在內地執行的判決，則為施行第 5(2)(d) 條，該判決在相反證明成立前，須當作為是可以在內地執行的判決。

7. 申請登記內地判決的期限

(1) 根據第 5(1) 條提出申請登記內地判決的期限為 2 年。

(2) 第 (1) 款指明的期限──

(a) 在有關的內地判決有指明履行該判決的限期的情況下，須由該限期的最後一日起計算；或

(b) 在任何其他情況下，須由該判決的生效日期起計算。

8. 申請費用

根據第 5(1) 條提出的登記內地判決的申請，須連同根據第 23(1) 條訂立的法院規則訂明的須就該申請而繳付的費用。

9. 內地判決中只有部份條文可予登記的情況

原訟法庭在接獲登記內地判決的申請後，如覺得該判決是就不同事宜而作出的，而該判決的部份（但非全部）條文假使是載於分開的內地判決（屬根據第 5(1) 條提出的登記申請的標的者）內，便會符合第 5(2)(a) 至 (e) 條指明的規定，則該判決在登記時，須僅就該等條文登記，而非就該判決所載的任何其他條文登記。

10. 內地判決已獲部份履行

如證明在申請登記任何內地判決當日，該判決已獲部份履行，則該判決在登記時，須只就在該日屬須繳付的餘款登記。

11. 以非港幣的貨幣為幣值的內地判決

凡根據任何內地判決而須繳付的款項，是以非港幣的貨幣為幣值的，該判

決在登記時，須在猶如它是一項以港幣為幣值的判決一樣的情況下登記，而其款額是按登記日期當日的匯率將該須繳付的款項折算為等值的港幣所得之數。

12. 內地判決的登記會包括利息、費用等

除根據內地判決須繳付的一筆款項外，該判決在登記時，須就下述項目予以登記——

(a) 截至登記時，在內地法律下根據該判決而到期須支付的任何利息，以及經原審法院就該判決妥為核證的任何費用；及

(b) 就該判決進行登記的合理費用及其附帶的合理費用，包括取得經原審法院妥為蓋章的判決文本的費用。

13. 內地判決被規定分期履行的情況

(1) 如某內地判決的履行被規定分期履行，該判決的判定債權人亦可根據第 5(1) 條向原訟法庭提出申請，將該判決的任何部份在原訟法庭登記。

(2) 就屬根據第 5(1) 條提出，將內地判決的任何部份登記的申請而言——

(a) 第 5(2)(a) 至 (e) 條須被視為亦包括根據該判決的該部份飭令繳付的一筆款項已到期須繳付的規定，而為免生疑問，在本條例中凡提述第 5(2)(a) 至 (e) 條指明的規定（包括在第 18(1)(a) 條出現的關乎獲登記的該判決的該部份的提述），須據此解釋；

(b) 除文意另有所指外，在本條例中凡提述內地判決（不論如何描述）須解釋為對該內地判決的該部份的提述；及

(c) 本條例的其他條文在經所有必要的變通後，須據此解釋及適用。

第 3 部　登記的效果

14. 登記的效果

(1) 除第 15 條另有規定外，就執行而言，已登記判決具有猶如該判決是由原訟法庭原先作出並且在登記之日登錄的判決一樣的相同效力及效果。

(2) 在不損害第 (1) 款的一般性的原則下，任何內地判決一經根據第 5(2) 條登記——

(a)　法律程序可就該判決而提起；

(b)　該判決所登記的款項須衍生利息；及

(c)　原訟法庭對於該判決的執行具有相同的管制權，猶如該判決是由原訟法庭原先作出並且在登記之日登錄的判決一樣。

15. 已登記判決在某些情況下不得強制執行

任何人不得在 ——

(a)　第 17(1) 條指明的根據第 4 部提出申請以將已登記判決的登記作廢的限期內，或根據第 17(2) 條延長的該限期內；或

(b)　（如在 (a) 段指明的期間已提出該申請）該申請獲最終的處理之前，提起任何行動，以強制執行該判決。

16. 承認內地判決

(1)　凡在根據第 5(1) 條提出的將某內地判決登記的申請中，而該判決是會符合第 5(2)(a) 至 (e) 條指明的規定的，則不論該判決是否已登記，香港任何法院在基於同一訴因而提起的法律程序中，均須承認該判決對判決各方而言是不可推翻的判決，而在任何該等法律程序中，該判決可被援引作為答辯或反申索。

(2)　在以下情況下，本條不適用於某內地判決 ——

(a)　該判決已登記，而該登記已根據第 18 或 19 條因任何理由（該判決已獲完全履行除外）作廢；或

(b)　該判決並未登記，而有證明顯示假使該判決已登記，該登記亦會在為將該登記作廢的目的而提出的申請而根據第 18 或 19 條因任何理由（該判決已獲完全履行除外）作廢。

(3)　本條並不阻止香港任何法院承認某內地判決就其中所決定的任何法律或事實事宜而言，是不可推翻的，但該判決須是在本條例生效前根據普通法會被承認是不可推翻的。

第 4 部　將已登記判決的登記作廢

17. 將已登記判決的登記作廢的期限

(1)　原訟法庭在根據第 5(2) 條作出登記內地判決的命令時，須指明根據第 18 或 19 條提出申請將已登記判決的登記作廢的限期。

(2)　原訟法庭可延長提出第 (1) 款所指的申請的限期（不論是原來所定或

其後經延長者）。

18. 已登記判決的登記須作廢的情況

(1) 凡任何已登記判決可針對某一方強制執行，如該方為此提出申請，而原訟法庭信納任何下述事項，則該判決的登記須予作廢——

(a) 該判決並不是符合第 5(2)(a) 至 (e) 條指明的規定的內地判決；

(b) 該判決是在違反本條例的情況下登記的；

(c) 根據內地法律，有關的選用內地法院協議屬無效（但如原審法院已裁定該協議屬有效則除外）；

(d) 該判決已獲完全履行；

(e) 按照香港法律，香港法院對有關案件具有專有司法管轄權；

(f) 沒有在原審法院席前出庭就有關法律程序作出答辯的判定債務人——

(i) 沒有按照內地法律被傳召出庭；或

(ii) 雖按照內地法律被傳召出庭，但並沒有按照內地法律獲給予充分的時間，就該等法律程序作出答辯；

(g) 該判決是以欺詐手段取得；

(h) 香港法院已就該判決各方之間的同一訴因作出判決，或香港的任何仲裁機構已就該判決各方之間的同一訴因作出仲裁裁決；

(i) 香港以外地方的法院已就該判決各方之間的同一訴因作出判決，或香港以外地方的任何仲裁機構已就該判決各方之間的同一訴因作出仲裁裁決，而上述判決或裁決已獲香港法院承認或由香港法院強制執行；

(j) 強制執行該判決是違反公共政策的；或

(k) 該判決已在依據根據內地法律進行的上訴或再審中，遭推翻或以其他方式作廢。

(2) 如判定債務人是按照內地法律以藉公告送達方式被傳召到原審法院，則第 (1)(f) 款不適用。

19. 已登記判決的登記可作廢的情況或押後將登記作廢的申請的情況

凡任何已登記判決可針對某一方強制執行，如該方為此提出申請，而原訟法庭信納針對該判決的上訴仍未了結，或具有權限的指定法院已命令再審作出該判決所依據的案件，則原訟法庭可按它認為公正的條款——

(a) 將該登記作廢；或

(b) 將該申請押後至一段期間屆滿為止，該段期間為原訟法庭覺得屬合理地充分，使申請人得以採取必需步驟，以使就該判決而進行的上訴或再審由具有權限的指定法院完成處理的期間。

20. 將已登記判決的登記作廢的效果

(1) 除第 (2) 及 (3) 款另有規定外，凡已登記判決的登記已根據第 18 條作廢，判定債權人不得再次根據第 5(1) 條提出登記該判決的申請。

(2) 凡已登記判決的登記 ——

(a) 根據第 18(1)(a) 條純粹因該判決在申請登記當日不能根據內地法律執行而作廢；或

(b) 根據第 19 條而作廢，

則一旦該判決變為可以在內地執行或在該判決的上訴或再審獲得完成處理時（視屬何情況而定），將該登記作廢不影響再次申請登記該判決。

(3) 如某已登記判決儘管在申請登記當日已部份履行，但仍就根據該判決須繳付的整筆款項而登記，而該登記純粹因此而根據第 18(1)(b) 條作廢，則原訟法庭須應判定債權人提出的申請，命令將該判決就在該日須繳付的餘款而登記，該判決一經如此登記，須為本條例的目的被視為已登記判決。

第 5 部　在內地執行香港判決

21. 發出經核證的香港判決文本及香港判決的證明書的司法管轄權

(1) 凡判定債權人擬在內地執行某香港判決，而根據該判決一筆既非就稅款或類似性質的其他收費，亦非就罰款或其他罰則而須繳付的款項須予繳付，且該判決是在本條例生效當日或之後，由 ——

(a) 終審法院或高等法院作為選用法院作出的；

(b) 終審法院或高等法院對根據香港法律自選用法院移交的案件作出的；或

(c) 終審法院或高等法院應任何就下述法院對案件所作判決提出的上訴而作出的 ——

(i) 選用法院；或

(ii) 根據香港法律獲選用法院移交案件的法院，

則在判定債權人提出申請及繳付根據第 23(1) 條訂立的法院規則所訂明的費用後，高等法院須向判定債權人發出該判決的一份經核證文本。

(2) 凡判定債權人擬在內地執行某香港判決，而根據該判決，一筆既非就稅款或類似性質的其他收費，亦非就罰款或其他罰則而須繳付的款項須予繳付，且該判決是在本條例生效當日或之後，由 ——

(a) 區域法院作為選用法院作出的；或

(b) 區域法院對根據香港法律自選用法院移交的案件作出的，則在判定債權人提出申請及繳付根據第 23(2) 條訂立的法院規則所訂明的費用後，區域法院須向判定債權人發出該判決的一份經核證文本。

(3) 在根據第 (1) 或 (2) 款發出判決的經核證文本時，高等法院或區域法院（視屬何情況而定）亦須發出一份證明書 ——

(a) 證明該判決是能夠在香港強制執行的；及

(b) 載有根據第 23(1) 或 (2) 條（視屬何情況而定）訂立的法院規則所訂明的詳情，以及附有該等規則所訂明的文件。

(4) 如香港判決因有待上訴或任何其他理由而暫緩一段期間執行，則在該段期間屆滿前，不得根據本條就該判決提出申請。

(5) 在本條中，「判定債權人」（judgment creditor）指在香港判決中獲判勝訴的人，並包括屬該判決所賦權利藉繼承、轉讓或其他途徑而轉歸的對象的人。

第 6 部　雜項

22. 對提起法律程序的限制

(1) 凡已有內地判決就某一訴因而作出，該判決的任何一方不得在下列情況下再就同一訴因而提起任何法律程序 ——

(a) 根據第 5(1) 條提出的登記該判決的申請尚在待決期間；或

(b) 該判決已根據第 5(2) 條登記。

(2) 除屬登記判決的法律程序外，香港任何法院不得受理任何旨在追討在某內地判決下須繳付的款項的法律程序，而在根據第 5(1) 條提出的將該判決登記的申請中，該判決是會符合第 5(2)(a) 至 (e) 條指明的規

定的。

23. 法院規則

(1) 根據《高等法院條例》（第 4 章）第 54 條訂立法院規則的權力，包括為下列所有或任何目的而訂立規則的權力 ——

(a) 就申請登記內地判決的人士繳付訟費保證金事宜訂立條文；

(b) 就限制處置或限制轉移判定債務人的資產訂立條文；

(c) 訂明在申請登記內地判決時須證明的事宜，及規管證明該等事宜的方式；

(d) 向內地法院提供已登記判決及香港判決在香港的強制執行情況的資料；

(e) 規定向判定債務人送達內地判決登記通知書；

(f) 訂明方法，以就任何在本條例條文下產生的關於下述事宜的問題作出裁定：某內地判決可否在內地執行，或根據內地法律，在某內地判決下已到期須支付甚麼利息；

(g) 就根據第 21(1) 條發出終審法院及高等法院作出的香港判決的經核證文本及證明書，以及一切有關文件訂立條文；

(h) 訂明根據本條例任何條文須由根據本款訂立的法院規則訂明的任何事宜；及

(i) 概括而言，為更佳地施行本條例的目的而訂立條文。

(2) 根據《區域法院條例》（第 336 章）第 72 條訂立法院規則的權力，包括為下列所有或任何目的而訂立規則的權力 ——

(a) 向內地法院提供已登記判決及香港判決在香港的強制執行情況的資料；

(b) 就根據第 21(2) 條發出區域法院作出的香港判決的經核證文本及證明書，以及一切有關文件訂立條文；及

(c) 訂明根據本條例任何條文須由根據本款訂立的法院規則訂明的任何費用。

23. 修訂附表 1 的權力

行政長官會同行政會議可藉在憲報刊登的命令修訂附表 1。

24. 基層人民法院清單的公佈

(1)　律政司司長須為本條例的施行而不時將基層人民法院清單在憲報公佈。

(2)　根據第 (1) 款公佈的清單並非附屬法例。

25. 關於選用法院成為或不再是認可基層人民法院的特別條文

(1)　如在訂立選用內地法院協議當日，有關選用法院不是認可基層人民法院，則即使該選用法院其後成為認可基層人民法院，就本條例而言，該選用法院不得被視為認可基層人民法院。

(2)　就任何內地判決而言，如在訂立選用內地法院協議當日，有關選用法院是認可基層人民法院，並在該判決作出當日仍屬認可基層人民法院，則即使該選用法院其後不再是認可基層人民法院，就本條例而言，該選用法院須被視為認可基層人民法院。

26.（已失時效而略去）

附表 1

[第 2 及 24 條]

指定法院

1. 最高人民法院

3. 高級人民法院

3. 中級人民法院

4. 認可基層人民法院

附表 2

（已失時效而略去）

後 記

寫作本書的時間，是我人生至今最為艱難的一段歷程。2017 年 6 月底，姐姐在香港參加完女兒幼稚園畢業典禮後，返回澳門後不久即突發重病，進入半昏迷狀態。隨後病情加重，完全昏迷。姐姐在澳門家裏只有她、姐夫和五歲的外甥三人，母親不時赴澳陪伴協助照顧。事發後，母親也只能留在澳門照顧外甥。我原以往返於深港之間為日常，也只好改為深港澳三地之間奔跑。然而，即使奔赴澳門，也只能稍作看望，而且真的是只能「看」。眼見姐姐病情的日益惡化，母親的精神越發憔悴，自己內心既無奈也無力。隨着時間一日一日的過去，治療手段消耗殆盡也未見成效，也明白已凶多而吉少，只能做好最壞的打算，也努力讓母親在心理上有所準備。此時所能做的唯有設法減輕母親的悲傷，也時刻擔憂着事發之時無法在澳門陪伴母親身旁。

在這段時間裏，自己已全然失去處理任何正常工作的心力，唯一能堅持下來繼續做的事情，就是本書的寫作。正是借助對本書內容相關問題的探討，有幸可以在區際衝突法微信羣裏經常與多位業內的專家老師交流，也因此而有機會獲邀請參加去年在澳門大學舉行的中國國際私法學會區際衝突法專題研討會。就在研討會舉行當天，在會議接近尾聲之時，接到了山頂醫院傳來的噩耗。這也許就是冥冥中的安排。正是因為參加了這次會議，才能讓我可以在那個時刻陪伴在母親身邊，也算是老天爺在悲傷中給予的一點關照了。

謹以此書紀念人生中的這一段艱難的旅程。

2018 年春天